REVISIONING 007

REVISIONING 007

James Bond and *Casino Royale*

EDITED BY CHRISTOPH LINDNER

WALLFLOWER PRESS

LONDON & NEW YORK

First published in Great Britain in 2009 by
Wallflower Press
6 Market Place, London W1W 8AF
www.wallflowerpress.co.uk

A catalogue record for this book is available from the British Library.

ISBN 978-1-906660-19-2 (pbk)
ISBN 978-1-906660-20-8 (hbk)

Book design by Elsa Mathern

Printed in India by Imprint Digital

Contents

Contributors

BRIAN BAKER is a Lecturer in English at Lancaster University, UK, and is the author of *Literature and Science: Social Impact and Interaction*, with John H. Cartwright (2005); *Masculinity in Fiction and Film: Representing Men in Popular Genres 1945–2000* (2006); and *Iain Sinclair* (2007). He has also published more widely in journals and book collections in the areas of masculinities, science fiction and London fictions.

DOUGLAS A. CUNNINGHAM is a PhD Candidate in Film Studies at the University of California, Berkeley. He is writing his dissertation on representations of masculinity in the World War Two training and documentary films of the US Army Air Forces First Motion Picture Unit. He has also published in a number of journals, including *The Moving Image, Critical Survey, Tennessee Literary Quarterly* and *Screen*.

RICHARD GABRI is a performance artist and English teacher residing in San Francisco. He has published essays exploring issues surrounding the advent and development of various representational technologies (such as writing, painting, photography and film) and how they affect and alter human subjectivity in *Rethinking Marxism and Interpretations*.

MONIKA GEHLAWAT is an Assistant Professor in the English Department at the University of Southern Mississippi. She has published articles on the relationships between painting, literature and Frankfurt School theory, including 'The

Aesthetics of Whiteness: A Study of Melville's *Moby Dick*, Adorno and Robert Ryman's Monochrome Painting' (2005) in the journal *Soundings*; 'Painterly Ambitions: Hemingway, Cézanne and the Short Story' (2007); and 'Individual Types and Social Praxis m' (2009) in a collected book on Frankfurt School writings.

RENÉ GLAS is a PhD candidate in the Department of Media Studies at the University of Amsterdam. His current research topics are control, agency and ownership in computer games, with the popular 'virtual world' of *World of Warcraft* as his main focus. He is also a freelance film and media critic.

JOYCE GOGGIN is an Associate Professor at the University of Amsterdam where she teaches English and Comparative Literature, Film and New Media. She has published articles on a wide variety of topics including gambling, finance, money, computer games, seventeenth-century Dutch painting, literature, Las Vegas architecture and film. She is currently co-editing a book on comics and graphic novels, while conducting research on gambling across media and Las Vegas as a themed urban environment.

DOUGLAS L. HOWARD is Assistant Academic Chair and an Associate Professor in the English Department at Suffolk County Community College in Selden, NY. His publications include articles in *Literature and Theology* and *The Chronicle of Higher Education*, and essays in *This Thing of Ours: Investigating The Sopranos* (2002); *The Gothic Other: Racial and Social Constructions in the Literary Imagination* (co-editor and contributor) (2004); *Reading The Sopranos* (2006); *Reading Deadwood* (2006); *Milton in Popular Culture* (2006) and *Reading 24* (2007).

AUDREY D. JOHNSON is an Assistant Professor of English at Francis Marion University, South Carolina. Her research primarily focuses on Virginia Woolf and feminist historiography; however, her other interests include women's writing in the nineteenth and twentieth centuries, feminist science fiction and the construction of gender in visual media, including comic books, graphic novels, television and film.

CHRISTOPH LINDNER is Professor and Chair of English Literature at the University of Amsterdam and a Research Affiliate at the University of London Institute in Paris. His recent and forthcoming books include *The James Bond Phenomenon* (2003); *Fictions of Commodity Culture* (2003); *Urban Space and Cityscapes* (2006); and *Globalization, Violence, and the Visual Culture of Cities* (2009). He has published widely on literature, film and urban culture in journals such as *American Studies*, *Connotations*, *Journal of American Culture*, *Modern Philology* and *The Yearbook of English Studies*.

KEREN OMRY is a Lecturer at Tel Aviv University and the University of Haifa, where she teaches popular narratives, with particular focus on science fiction and popular culture. Her work on James Bond is part of a larger project investigating the dialogue between aesthetics and technology. She is currently preparing for publication a book on racialised discourses in contemporary Jewish-American and African-American texts.

WILL SCHEIBEL is a PhD student in Film and Media Studies in the Department of Communication and Culture at Indiana University. His research interests are in theories and aesthetics of 'the Uncanny' applied to issues of narrative, genre and authorship during the Classical Hollywood period. Other interests include film noir, comic books, television sitcoms and nineteenth- and twentieth-century American and British literature and culture.

JASON SPERB is a PhD student in Communication and Culture at Indiana University. In addition to contributing to such journals as *Film Criticism, Quarterly Review of Film and Video* and *Senses of Cinema*, he is the author of *The Kubrick Façade* (2006) and co-editor (with Scott Balcerzak) of *Cinephilia in the Age of Digital Reproduction* (2009). He has previously written on James Bond for *Bright Lights Film Journal*.

ESTELLA TINCKNELL is Reader in Media and Cultural Studies at the University of the West of England. She has published widely in the area of popular culture and film, and is the author of *Mediating the Family: Gender, Culture and Representation* (2005); joint author of *The Practice of Cultural Studies* (2005); and co-editor (with Ian Conrich) of *Film's Musical Moments* (2006). She is currently working on a book about Jane Campion's films and on an edited collection of essays about Ageing Femininities.

For Mojo

Acknowledgements

My thanks to the authors in this book for contributing their original work. Among them, Will Scheibel deserves a special acknowledgement. Much of the initial copy-editing was done by him, and his research and editorial assistance throughout the book's development has been invaluable. I also wish to thank the Lilly Library at Indiana University in Bloomington for a visiting fellowship that made it possible to consult archival materials relating to Ian Fleming and *Casino Royale*. Fellow Bond scholar James Chapman was kind enough to share an advance copy of his chapter on *Casino Royale* from the new edition of his book *Licence to Thrill: A Cultural History of the James Bond Films* (2008), which made it possible for contributors to take on board this important work before going to press. Yoram Allon at Wallflower Press helped to give this project some of its momentum. For help in preparing the index, I am indebted to the eagle eyes of Roy Koers. Finally, I am grateful to the students in my various James Bond courses who, over the years and in various countries, have given me so many insights into the strangely fascinating world of 007.

Christoph Lindner

Selected Bond Chronology, 1953–2008

1953 Ian Fleming, *Casino Royale*

1954 Ian Fleming, *Live and Let Die*

1955 Ian Fleming, *Moonraker*

1956 Ian Fleming, *Diamonds Are Forever*

1957 Ian Fleming, *From Russia, With Love*

1958 Ian Fleming, *Dr No*

1959 Ian Fleming, *Goldfinger*

1960 Ian Fleming, *For Your Eyes Only*

1961 Ian Fleming, *Thunderball*

1962 Ian Fleming, *The Spy Who Loved Me*
Dr No (Dir. Terence Young; Sean Connery as Bond)

1963 Ian Fleming, *On Her Majesty's Secret Service*
From Russia With Love (Dir. Terence Young; Sean Connery as Bond)

1964 Ian Fleming, *You Only Live Twice*
Goldfinger (Dir. Guy Hamilton; Sean Connery as Bond)

1965 Ian Fleming, *The Man With The Golden Gun*
Thunderball (Dir. Terence Young; Sean Connery as Bond)

1966 Ian Fleming, *Octopussy*

1967 *You Only Live Twice* (Dir. Lewis Gilbert; Sean Connery as Bond)
Casino Royale (Dir. Val Guest, Ken Hughes, John Huston, Joseph Mc-Grath, Robert Parrish; David Niven as Bond)

1969 *On Her Majesty's Secret Service* (Dir. Peter Hunt; George Lazenby as Bond)

1971 *Diamonds Are Forever* (Dir. Guy Hamilton; Sean Connery as Bond)

1973 *Live and Let Die* (Dir. Guy Hamilton; Roger Moore as Bond)

1974 *The Man With The Golden Gun* (Dir. Guy Hamilton; Roger Moore as Bond)

1977 *The Spy Who Loved Me* (Dir. Lewis Gilbert; Roger Moore as Bond)

1979 *Moonraker* (Dir. Lewis Gilbert; Roger Moore as Bond)

1981 *For Your Eyes Only* (Dir. John Glen; Roger Moore as Bond)

1983 *Octopussy* (Dir. John Glen; Roger Moore as Bond)

Never Say Never Again (Dir. Irvin Kershner; Sean Connery as Bond)

1985 *A View To A Kill* (Dir. John Glen; Timothy Dalton as Bond)

1987 *The Living Daylights* (Dir. John Glen; Timothy Dalton as Bond)

1989 *Licence to Kill* (Dir. John Glen; Timothy Dalton as Bond)

1995 *GoldenEye* (Dir. Martin Campbell; Pierce Brosnan as Bond)

1997 *Tomorrow Never Dies* (Dir. Roger Spottiswoode; Pierce Brosnan as Bond)

1999 *The World Is Not Enough* (Dir. Michael Apted; Pierce Brosnan as Bond)

2002 *Die Another Day* (Dir. Lee Tamahori; Pierce Brosnan as Bond)

2006 *Casino Royale* (Dir. Martin Campbell; Daniel Craig as Bond)

2008 *Quantum of Solace* (Dir. Marc Forster; Daniel Craig as Bond)

INTRODUCTION: REVISIONING 007

Christoph Lindner

The genesis of this book lies in another book entirely. While planning the second edition of *The James Bond Phenomenon: A Critical Reader* in early 2007, I sent out a call for proposals for original essays on emergent and underexamined aspects of the 007 series. To my surprise I received over one hundred proposals from film and cultural studies scholars around the world, many of whom, it turns out, currently teach James Bond films in university courses across the humanities and social sciences. I eventually commissioned a small number of these to publish in the new edition of *The James Bond Phenomenon*. What particularly struck me during this process was the incredibly high level of interest in the 2006 Bond film *Casino Royale*, directed by Martin Campbell. Nearly every proposal I received was concerned with this single film, suggesting that Bond's twenty-first screen outing (if you count only the 'official' films) struck a powerful chord with academics, in-cluding film historians, literary critics, cultural theorists, sociologists, political sci-entists, human geographers, and even architects, designers and urban planners.

Bond, of course, has long been popular inside the 'ivory tower', but it would seem that *Casino Royale* has reinvigorated scholarly interest in 007, much as it has succeeded in renewing broader public interest in the character. This book is a response to this sudden, dramatic renewal of Bond's significance both inside and outside the academy. More importantly, it marks the first major intervention in critical discussions about Bond in the Daniel Craig era – an era that promises to be one of the most significant in the long history of the franchise. My hope is that, as the world of 007 continues to evolve beyond *Casino Royale* and Craig's first outing as Bond, this book will lead the way for a new wave of Bond criticism.

As a collection of new critical essays focusing on one specific film, this book treats *Casino Royale* both as a significant turning point in the 007 series and as a case study in popular film culture. Drawing on current thinking in cultural analysis and film theory, the essays offer innovative readings of *Casino Royale* and its interrelations with the Bond franchise, the culture industry and recent developments in cinema, society and world politics. Essay topics range from the examination of the film's testicular torture scene and the changing role of the secret agent in a post-9/11 world order, to the analysis of 007's masochism, voyeurism and hyper-mobility.

Linked by a shared concern for the ways in which *Casino Royale* revisions 007, the essays are organised into three interconnected sections. The first, 'Enacting Bond', groups together essays concerned with staging, performing and otherwise enacting James Bond, from Daniel Craig's botched Martini order to the performativity of high-stakes poker. The second section, 'Engendering Bond', contains essays addressing issues of gender and sexuality, paying particular attention to the rewriting of masculinity and post-feminist double-agents. The essays in the final section, 'Embodying Bond', all focus on 007's physical body, and the various new ways in which *Casino Royale* uses that body to comment on issues of aesthetics, violence, mobility and globalisation.

Although each essay offers its own perspective on *Casino Royale*, there are nonetheless certain themes and concerns running through the book. Most notable among these is a recurring preoccupation with the film's manipulation of the established 007 formula and, in particular, the deliberate changes *Casino Royale* makes to Bond's character and identity. Related to this concern, the essays also keep circling back to certain key elements of the film, many of which have similarly been important topics of discussion for fans and popular commentators alike. These elements include the gritty noirish pre-title sequence; Bond's athleticism and hyper-mobility in the Madagascar chase scene; the gratuitous intertextual image of Bond exiting the ocean in his swimming trunks; the flirtatious verbal sparring between Bond and Vesper on the train to Montenegro; the conspicuous absence of Moneypenny and Q; Bond's fallibility and vulnerability; the uncomfortable spectacle of the testicular torture scene; and – of course – the long-anticipated moment at the end of the film when Daniel Craig first says the words 'Bond ... James Bond'. Alongside *Casino Royale*'s broader revisioning of 007, the full significance of these elements – to the film, to the series and to popular culture more generally – is what the following chapters seek to understand.

Enacting Bond

Casino Royale has a long, sinuous and often controversial history both on and off the screen. In the book's opening chapter, Will Scheibel traces this history from Ian Fleming's original 1953 novel through the 1954 made-for-TV adaptation and the 1958 *Daily Express* comic strip, to the 1967 psychedelic screen spoof and the 2006 'official' Eon Productions film. Examining these five versions of *Casino Royale* in their socio-historical contexts, Scheibel shows how the Bond writers and directors have worked hard to create a character that reflects (and ultimately influences) the ideology of specific time periods. The discussion begins by exploring the copyright controversy surrounding Fleming's novel, and considers how the novel articulates British imperialist and sexist attitudes of the early Cold War era. Scheibel then turns his attention to CBS's live teleplay in which the character of Bond is crudely Americanised. This television adaptation is contrasted with the London-based *Daily Express* comic and its conservative, upper-class 'Bond look', which restored the character's Britishness. Scheibel goes on to juxtapose this refined image of Bond with the 1967 screen spoof, before commenting on 007's reboot in the 2006 film, which he reads as a distinctly post-9/11 spy thriller. Throughout, Scheibel considers how issues of masculinity and nationality are constructed and entwined across this range of 007 texts.

Douglas L. Howard's chapter focuses on the many ways in which *Casino Royale* deliberately 'gets it wrong' in its treatment of Bond and the 007 film formula. Starting with Bond's bungled Martini order, Douglas shows how the film not only plays against the character's stereotype, but also reinvigorates and re-energises the series by manipulating our expectations about who and what James Bond is. As Howard shows, *Casino Royale*'s Bond lacks the sophistication, experience and savvy of earlier Bonds, leading to various blunders, mishaps and faux-pas throughout the film. This new, inept Bond is attractive, argues Howard, because his imperfections give him a humanity and sympathy that have been lacking up to this point. Howard's conclusion is that *Casino Royale* goes against the very formula for the spy thriller that the series itself created but, in doing so, significantly increases the appeal and impact of Bond at a critical juncture in the life of the franchise.

In the next chapter, Jason Sperb builds on Umberto Eco's early critical work on Bond by using a narratological approach to explore two central motifs in *Casino Royale*: the 'ellipsis' and 'the big picture'. Both devices, he argues, illuminate the film's larger preoccupation with narrative and thematic ambiguity – a concern that paradoxically serves as the film's structural anchor. Rather than following the standard Bond formula, *Casino Royale* keeps the main villains hidden throughout most of the film and even beyond its temporal frame, suggesting a post-9/11 rhizomatic image of evil, while also maintaining and even internalising the Bond series' long-standing fixation with self-disruption. Sperb's insightful argument is that the franchise has survived for so long precisely because it consistently disrupts its own rhythm, a trend that is radically accentuated in *Casino Royale*, which is itself a film about interruption.

Joyce Goggin and René Glas argue in their essay that *Casino Royale*'s reimagining of the Bond formula on aesthetic, stylistic and narrative levels also engages the logic of late capitalism, which relies on a world where the distinction between speculation and gambling has effectively vanished. For Goggin and Glas, it is therefore fitting that the heist in this film is conducted through the game of Texas hold 'em, and that the film constantly reminds viewers of the parallels between poker and the global economy. In Fleming's original novel, baccarat – a very simple and entirely chance-based game – is played. The film's shift from baccarat to Texas hold 'em is particularly significant, argue Goggin and Glas, because it marks a conscious response to the current financial crisis. Indeed, their analysis reveals that, through the tacit grammar of the card game, the film suggests we are now living in a casino economy that is global, profoundly American and based almost entirely on dissimulation and chance.

Engendering Bond

This section on gender and *Casino Royale* begins with a far-reaching discussion by Douglas A. Cunningham and Richard Gabri on the film's rewriting of masculinity. Their premise is that *Casino Royale* is unique in the Bond oeuvre because it works to significantly overhaul the masculine image of 007 that has dominated the character from the Sean Connery years onwards. Using gender models developed by R. W. Connell, Gail Bederman and Judith Butler, Cunningham and Gabri explore the way in which *Casino Royale* moves Daniel Craig's nascent 007 from a desire to occupy a stereotypical space of hegemonic masculinity towards a more 'open-gendered' space of individual potential and possibility. Key to this reading of the 'new Bond' are analyses of 'the bluff' and 'the tell' – two performative strategies derived from the game of poker that influence Bond's high-stakes gambling, as well as the essence of his imagined masculine self. For Cunningham and Gabri, the film's rewriting of 007's masculinity serves not just to critique the Bond genre and its central character, but also to interrogate the identity politics and desires of the consumer culture that keeps the series in circulation.

Estella Tincknell continues to examine rewritings of gender identity in *Casino Royale* but refocuses attention on Vesper Lynd, the film's central female character, reminding us that Bond's role is not the only one to undergo significant change in the 2006 reboot. For Tincknell, *Casino Royale*'s brutally violent 'back to basics' reinvention of the Bond movie is also interesting for its foregrounding of a female double-agent, whose narrative function, she argues, is markedly different from that of the traditional 'Bond girl'. Calling attention to the intertextual connections between *Casino Royale* and earlier espionage thrillers like Alfred Hitchcock's *North by Northwest* (1959), Tincknell explores the figure of the female double-agent in popular culture and situates her reappearance in *Casino Royale* in the context of a long, complex and contradictory cultural tradition of female duplicity in the spy thriller. In particular, Tincknell considers the pleasures, tensions and anxieties surrounding the film's female double-agent, arguing that these have been intensified by the filmmakers' efforts to render Vesper's character in explicitly 'post-feminist' terms.

Returning to the conflicted figure of 007, Audrey D. Johnson suggests that *Casino Royale* presents Bond as a male masochist. As she demonstrates, the creation of a masochist Bond has the effect of subverting the character's privileged position as a heterosexual white male, while also reframing his relationships to women and to the feminine. As such, this presentation of Bond is one of the most significant aspects of the franchise's relaunch in the way that it subverts the iconic aspects of the Bond image and, in so doing, enacts a more thoroughgoing change to the franchise's gender politics by both feminising Bond's body and by constructing more fully-developed and humanised female characters who are, in some instances, more powerful and knowing than Bond. Johnson concludes that *Casino Royale*'s revisioning of Bond and his relationship to both women and femininity indicates a way forward to question and reconstruct the gender categories of the action film genre to which the Bond series belongs.

Embodying Bond

The three chapters in the book's final section take Bond's body as their focus, offering innovative analyses, respectively, of that body's relationship to space and architecture, mobility and the gaze, and art and technology. In her essay on improvisation, action and architecture, Monika Gehlawat examines the relationship between physical action and liminal space in *Casino Royale*, arguing that the film deviates from standard 007 tropes by emphasising improvisation over technological mastery. In particular, Gehlawat studies the film's action sequences in terms of a spatial dialectic, highlighting the link between movement and context. Deciphering the particularity of the architectural spaces in which the film's action sequences take place – construction sites, bathrooms, stairwells – she compellingly demonstrates how the liminal qualities of these spaces require the human body to perform a kind of 'versatile ingenuity' previously unseen in the 007 films. Here, the focus is not on the brute force of Craig's 007, which has already attracted so much commentary, but instead on Craig's miraculous agility – his resourcefulness and imagination in the ruins, corridors and skeletal spaces of contemporary experience.

Continuing with the theme of movement, Brian Baker argues that *Casino Royale* adheres to what he calls contemporary spectacular cinema's 'mobility of the gaze', a mobility and spectacle different from the consumption-oriented, postcard panoramas (or huge Ken Adam sets) of earlier Bond films. The essay analyses key scenes in *A View To A Kill* (1985) and *Casino Royale* through the lens of recent critical work on mobility and the gaze from the fields of geography, sociology and cinema studies. Baker places particular importance on the way that, unlike his predecessors, Daniel Craig's Bond *runs* and does so vertically as well as horizontally. The resulting aesthetic of mobilisation, with its emphasis on free-running bodies in motion, signals what Baker sees as a rupture in the visual regime of the Bond series, one that enables the film to negotiate contemporary globalised capital's own emphasis on free movement: of information, of resources and of the gaze. The chapter also addresses how *Casino Royale* – with its narrative emphasis on gambling, international finance and terrorism – signals broader cultural anxieties about globalised mobility in the post-9/11 world.

In the book's last essay, Keren Omry offers a thematic complement to a key critical piece on 007 and masculinity: Toby Miller's infamous 'James Bond's Penis' (2003). Omry draws on Walter Benjamin to read James Bond, considering how Benjamin's thinking about technology and authenticity in 'The Work of Art in the Age of Mechanical Reproduction' (1935) can inform our understanding of *Casino Royale*'s dramatic return to the body of Bond, a stress that appears most explicitly (and disturbingly) in the film's testicular torture scene. In particular, Omry highlights the ways in which *Casino Royale* stages a crisis of authenticity and originality that becomes inextricably tied to the new corporeality of Bond and, in particular, to the film's conflation of the technological body and the gendered body.

Revisionist Bond

In his landmark study of the James Bond films, *Licence to Thrill*, James Chapman describes *Casino Royale*'s Bond as a 'revisionist Bond' (2007: 241). Certainly, the way the film repositions Bond at the beginning of his 007 career is a revisionist strategy. So too is the film's total disavowal of previous titles and events in the series. Indeed, with the exception of Judi Dench's M, *Casino Royale* features almost no onscreen links to the earlier Bond films. Even the opening credits break with 007 tradition by omitting the internal cliché of gratuitously screening silhouettes of undulating, naked women – a progressive development that many see as long overdue. Chapman also rightly points out that *Casino Royale*'s revisionist strategy is further necessitated by its relationship with Fleming's source material and, in particular, by the film's fidelity to the original novel (see 2007: 245). As many commentators have noted, the film's inclusion of the testicular torture scene from the novel is a bold but important move in reshaping the identity of Craig's nascent Bond. Even bolder, although more problematic, is the film's inclusion of the novel's most memorable misogynist quip (made by Bond in reference to Vesper Lynd): 'The bitch is dead.' Such instances of fidelity to the novel – and thus also to aspects of Fleming's *outré* 1950s sexism and penchant for writing sado-masochistic scenes of homoerotic torture – positively demand a revised approach to screening Bond.

In its overall outlook, this book similarly understands *Casino Royale* as a revisionist film. Hence the book's title (and the title of this introduction): 'Revisioning 007'. Yet, this book also understands 'revisioning' to mean much more. As the authors demonstrate in their various readings of the film, *Casino Royale* is not just a revising of 007, it is also a reimagining, a reintroduction, a re-evaluation, a reinvention and a renewal. And it is precisely the tension this creates between innovation and convention – between departure and arrival, motion and stasis, beginning and ending – that makes *Casino Royale* such an interesting and unusual addition to the ever-expanding Bond canon.

Together, the chapters in this book explore the many ways – both subtle and flagrant – in which *Casino Royale* revisions (in the fullest meaning of the word) the character and world of James Bond, manipulating if not outright breaking with established elements of the 007 formula. As the series evolves beyond Daniel Craig's first few outings in the role, it will be interesting to see the extent to which the formulaic demands of the series reassert themselves. Will the James Bond films continue to venture further into uncharted territory, pushing the boundaries of the character and his fictional world, or will the franchise succumb to the conformist pressure of its own internal conventions and traditions? I suspect the latter, although I would be delighted to be proved wrong. Whatever the future holds for Bond, however, one thing is certain. 007 still has a future, and *Casino Royale* has played a critical role in securing it.

PART 1
ENACTING BOND

1

THE HISTORY OF *CASINO ROYALE* ON (AND OFF) SCREEN

Will Scheibel

'This is not a romantic adventure story in which the villain is finally rout-ed and the hero is given a medal and marries the girl. Unfortunately these things don't happen in real life.'

– Le Chiffre

As every 007 fan knows, James Bond will return. Perhaps that is because, as Kamal Khan (Louis Jourdan) so appropriately put it in *Octopussy* (1983), Bond has a 'nasty habit of surviving'. This lasting endurance is nowhere more apparent than in the long and fascinating history of *Casino Royale*, in which Mr Kiss Kiss Bang Bang experiences a series of disparate permutations in nearly every popular medium: literature, television, comic strips, film, and even an unproduced stage play by Raymond Benson in 1986. But just how did Bond stop playing Red Indians during the Cold War and enter the post-9/11 climate as a reborn spy with a newly-appointed '00' status and a licence to kill? Like director Martin Campbell's 2006 adaptation of *Casino Royale* – the first 'official' screen version of Ian Fleming's first 007 book – this essay is a story of origins. Starting with the character's conception in the 1953 novel, I will trace the evolution of Bond and *Casino Royale* through the 1954 made-for-TV movie and 1958 *Daily Express* comic strip to the theatrical 1967 screen spoof to Campbell's blockbuster hit.

By analysing these five texts in their socio-historical situations, my project is to show how the 007 writers and directors are seldom concerned with faithfully adapting Fleming's source material. Rather, they are more interested in creating a character to reflect (and ultimately influence) the ideology of specific time periods, gauging cultural concerns and social and political preoccupations. I begin by examining the British imperialism and sexism of the novel impacted by the 'red scare' of the Cold War. Moving towards a repositioned national perspective, I will then look at the novel's adaptation for CBS television, which created an American identity for Bond. This leads to a discussion of the conservative, upper-class 'Bond look' in the comic, which restored the character's Britishness pervading the later feature films, and I will contrast this image with the psychedelic lampoon broadly aimed at the late 1960s youth market. Finally, I will conclude with an overview of the recent Martin Campbell/Daniel Craig production, and consider the questions it raises as a post-9/11 spy thriller and a restart for the series. Throughout, this essay pays close attention to how issues of masculinity and nationality are constructed and entwined across this range of texts via certain generic conventions. However, it is important to first understand the background information and copyright controversy surrounding *Casino Royale*, which helps explain why certain choices were made in the novel, comic and films, and how their sociopolitical subtexts and implications may have been affected as a result.

When he published his debut novel in April 1953, Fleming's goal with this trashy British potboiler was simply to distract himself from his impending marriage (see Bennett & Woollacott 1987: 22). The first imprint of Fleming's *Casino Royale* (4,750 copies published by Jonathan Cape) in Britain sold out, and in the second imprint the following year, it sold over 8,000 copies – modest results for a work of commercial fiction. In America, however, sales were less satisfactory. After rejection from three publishers, Macmillan published the novel and it sold fewer than 4,000 copies. CBS paid Fleming $1,000 for the rights to adapt the novel for live television, and, on 21 October 1954, *Casino Royale* aired as an hour-long episode of *Climax! Mystery Theater*, starring Barry Nelson as Bond. NBC then asked Fleming to write a script, but the project was scrapped and Fleming later reworked various plot elements for his 1958 novel, *Dr No*. Producer Gregory Ratoff purchased the motion picture rights for *Casino Royale* at a trifling $6,000 in 1955, which were eventually sold to producer Charles K. Feldman.

By 1957, though, the future of the franchise brightened considerably. Fleming had already published *Live and Let Die* (1954), *Moonraker* (1955) and *Diamonds are Forever* (1956), and Pan began publishing his novels in mass market paperback to great success, 'triggering the American paperback revolution in Britain' (Lindner 2005: 225). The *Daily Express* serialised both *From Russia, With Love* in 1957 and a strip cartoon version of *Casino Royale* the following year. Instead of killing off 007 in *From Russia, With Love* as initially planned, Fleming went on to pen seven more Bond novels and nine short stories before his death in 1964. He even wrote a handful of episode treatments for a proposed 007 television series on CBS, but the project never materialised and Fleming eventually modified these ideas for his first anthology of short stories, *For Your Eyes Only* (1960).

Dr No, directed by Terence Young and starring Sean Connery as Bond, made an international splash at the box office in 1962, marking the first time audiences saw Fleming's British secret agent in a theatrical feature film. The previous year, John F. Kennedy named *From Russia, With Love* one of his ten favourite books in a *Life* magazine article (17 March 1961), and Hollywood producers Harry Saltzman and Albert R. 'Cubby' Broccoli formed Eon Productions, backed by MGM and UA, and bought options on the novels. Broccoli and Saltzman also formed Danjaq, a second company, to control the films' copyright. *Playboy* began serialising Fleming's novels in the early 1960s, and numerous cross-promotional 007 merchandise fostered the already growing James Bond phenomenon, from soundtrack albums to toys to liquor. But *Casino Royale* remained in adaptation limbo. Feldman still owned the rights, and, according to Todd McCarthy in his biography of director Howard Hawks, 'Feldman and Hawks brought Leigh Brackett out to Los Angeles to discuss an approach to the script, and Hawks fancied the idea of Cary Grant in the role of 007' (1997: 595). Once he saw an advanced print of *Dr No* from England, Hawks bowed out of the project. Feldman even suggested a partnership with Broccoli and Saltzman to adapt *Casino Royale* with Sean Connery, but when Eon rejected his offer, Feldman decided not to risk competition with *You Only Live Twice*, the 'official' 007 film of 1967. Instead, he made an 'unofficial' 007 film for Columbia Pictures, an epic spoof, in fact, with five directors, three writers and an all-star cast, including David Niven as James Bond (who was, ironically, Fleming's first choice to play the character onscreen). Although it is now considered a cult classic – a sort of precursor to the *Austin Powers* movies (1997, 1999, 2002)– the film opened in 1967 to mixed reviews, and, despite its strong box-office performance, turned a disappointing profit as a result of its over-budget costs.

The copyright controversy

Connery continued to play Bond until 1971, but George Lazenby substituted for him in *On Her Majesty's Secret Service* (1969), between *You Only Live Twice* (1967) and *Diamonds Are Forever* (1971). From 1973 to 1985, Roger Moore followed in a more permanent tenure as 007. Timothy Dalton then replaced Moore as the Bond of the 1980s, but only for two films: *The Living Daylights* (1987) and *Licence to Kill* (1989). Heading into the new millennium, Pierce Brosnan took over the reins from 1995 to 2002. During the Brosnan years, a series of legal battles affected the outcome of Campbell's 2006 *Casino Royale*, starring Daniel Craig as 007, a quasi-prequel to reboot the series.

MGM and Sony locked horns when Sony threatened to compete with their own 007 series. Fanning the flames of this company war was producer Kevin McClory, who co-wrote ten script drafts with Fleming from 1959–60. Their film was to be an undersea Bond thriller set in the Bahamas, featuring the now infamous terrorist organisation SPECTRE and criminal mastermind Ernst Stavro Blofeld. Fleming did not pursue this film venture, but saved several of the plot points, characters and situations for his 1961 novel, *Thunderball*. McClory argued that since much of today's well-known Bond elements derived from these original scripts, he should have the right to make a series of 007 films. In 1998, *Variety* reported:

> MGM has disputed McClory's claims of ownership in the Bond character and series, claiming that the last of the rights McClory received from 007 novelist Ian Fleming lapsed in the early 1990s ... McClory won the rights to the scripts in a 1963 court case against Fleming where it was accepted that Fleming's later novel, *Thunderball*, did not credit either McClory or the third script collaborator, Jack Wittingham. (Boehm & Karon 1998)

McClory produced the film adaptation of *Thunderball* in 1965 and even remade the film as *Never Say Never Again* in 1983 for Warner Bros., an 'unofficial' Bond film starring Connery, which, incidentally, also depicted a casino called Casino Royale. Sony, which owns CBS and Columbia Pictures, and consequently owned the *Casino Royale* rights, allied itself with McClory. Complicating matters of ownership further, Sony president John Calley was actually the former head of UA. In 1999, Sony and MGM settled, and, in 2000, McClory's case was dismissed, leaving MGM and Eon sole owners of all Bond films past and future, including *Casino Royale* (1954 and 1967), *Thunderball* and *Never Say Never Again*. Perhaps the ultimate irony is that, in 2004, Sony bought out MGM. 'The James Bond franchise will be negotiated under a separate deal with the Broccoli family, but future Bond films would be handled by Sony releasing under the MGM name', reported *Variety* (Fritz & Learmonth 2004).

Since 1990, Eon Productions has been run by Michael G. Wilson and Broccoli's daughter, Barbara, and still employs England's Pinewood Studios. Since Fleming's death, Kingsley Amis (a.k.a. Robert Markham), John Gardner, Raymond Benson and Sebastian Faulks have contributed official 007 novels, and John Pearson wrote Bond's 'authorised biography' in 1973. To target the adolescent market, Charlie Higson began a series of *Young Bond* books in 2005, reminiscent of the young adult spin-off novel by 'R. D. Mascott', *003 ½: The Adventures of James Bond, Jr.* (1967) and the short-lived animated television series, *James Bond, Jr.* (1991).

The scent of smoke and sweat of a casino

Today, Bond has more than just entered the mainstream; he has become a permanent fixture of American and British commercial mass culture. His quotable catchphrases ('Vodka martini – shaken, not stirred'; 'The name is Bond ... James

Bond') have etched their way into our pop lexicon. Few could have foreseen that 007 would grow almost as central to the world of video gaming as he is to film and literature. Even teenagers far too young to know the name Ian Fleming recognise the series' semantic elements – the suave, tuxedo-clad spy; the elongated gambling table; the Aston Martin; the Walther PPK; the exotic, sexually-charged women; the endless assortment of gadgetry – as Bondian iconography. Simply put, Bond grew from a cult hero to a Western cultural institution, like Sherlock Holmes, Superman or Mickey Mouse. And, for better or worse, Fleming's cosmopolitan playboy remains the personification of sophisticated masculinity for the late twentieth and early twenty-first centuries. British film historian Roy Armes regards the franchise as 'the most potent myth of British cinema in the 1960s' (1978: 254), comparable to the Hammer horror classics and the string of 'Swinging London' movies of the time: 'The James Bond series remains a remarkable production achievement, totally recasting the source material so that the upper-class Englishness of Ian Fleming's original gives way to the more classless virility of the Hollywood action film hero' (Armes 1978: 256–7).

Perhaps this is why it seems so easy to forget that Bond's debut in the pages of *Casino Royale* was not the espionage epic we would expect today, alternating between cheeky humour and relentless action. Rather, it all began in a smoky, sweaty casino – a claustrophobic setting that dominates nearly half the novel. With its hard-boiled approach, *Casino Royale* resembles a style and tone closer to a Raymond Chandler detective thriller than a slick, spectacular adventure in the mode of, say, Alfred Hitchcock's *North by Northwest* (1957), which bears notable similarities to the early Connery vehicles. The Chandler comparison is worth more than a passing acknowledgement, though, as the American mystery writer of *The Big Sleep* (1939) and *Farewell, My Lovely* (1940) actually lauded Fleming's work in 1955, which bolstered his confidence about continuing the Bond series during a time of doubt (see Rosenberg & Stewart 1989: 23).

Fleming's opening chapter, titled 'The Secret Agent', immediately plunges the reader into Bond's down and dirty world, possibly as a nod to *The Secret Agent*, Joseph Conrad's 1907 London novel that wallows in the danger and ugliness of professional spying. 'The scent and smoke and sweat of a casino are nauseating at three in the morning', writes Fleming. 'Then the soul-erosion produced by high gambling – a compost of greed and fear and nervous tension – becomes unbearable and the senses awake and revolt from it' (2002: 1). After the gritty, low-key first chapter, we are not envisioning the opening gun-barrel sequence, stunts and sexy pop music montage made famous by Eon Productions. Quite simply, Fleming's milieu is the antithesis of the glamorous and romantic webs of intrigue that later redefined the spy genre. Fleming referred to his novels as 'fairy tales for grown-ups', and, in an interview with the BBC, said, 'Personally I am sufficiently in love with the myth to write basically incredible stories with a straight face' (quoted in Chancellor 2005: 100). The plots were relatively simple, and, after conceiving the blueprint for the formula in *Casino Royale*, Fleming essentially repeated variations of this basic narrative structure in each subsequent book: 'James Bond was St George, the defender of the British government (and the free world), who fights the dragon, named Goldfinger or Blofeld or Dr No, and – having slain him – then beds the girl' (ibid.).

Oddly enough, the thematic core of the best Bond novels hardly emerges as a black-and-white statement about human nature. One of the most compelling passages in *Casino Royale* occurs as Bond recovers from his gruesome torture and discusses the moral ambiguity of his profession:

> Now in order to tell the difference between good and evil, we have manufactured two images representing the extremes – representing the deepest black and the purest white – and we call them God and the Devil. But in doing so we have cheated a bit. God is a clear image, you can see every hair on His beard. But the Devil. What does he look like? (Fleming 2002: 161)

Rarely does Bond take time for such thoughtful introspection during the breakneck pace of the films. This type of meditation seems more akin to the urban philosophy of Chandler's cynical private eye Philip Marlowe on the mean streets of Los Angeles.

Casino Royale is by no means an example of great literature, nor are any of the 007 sequels. Nevertheless, the writing is undeniably strong in its intense display of violence and its blunt, snappy prose (no doubt carryovers from Fleming's journalistic background), creating an aesthetic rhythm not unlike Fleming's contemporaries in crime fiction, which is that of profane, politically incorrect poetry. Fleming's novels have been called racist (*Live and Let Die*) and homophobic (*Diamonds are Forever*; *Goldfinger* (1959)), but their most frequent and obvious transgressions are in their sympathy for the imperialist and patriarchal politics embodied in the Bond character, whom Judi Dench's M glibly indicts as 'a sexist, misogynist dinosaur, a relic of the Cold War' in the more liberal-minded *Golden-Eye* from 1995 (also directed by Campbell). The genesis of these dated worldviews in the 007 universe was *Casino Royale*, which asks the reader to identify with a basically unlikable character in Bond. This sexist, misogynist voice readily lends itself to scrutiny in the current Craig years, where we now have a reformed version of Bond's old self – an anachronistic hero out-of-touch with progressive, millennial thinking, but also a hero we are invited to judge for ourselves like M.

The plot of Fleming's *Casino Royale* involves Bond's attempt to thwart a Russian SMERSH agent known as 'Le Chiffre', who has embezzled a small fortune from his Soviet bosses and enters a high-stakes baccarat game at a casino in Royale-les-Eaux. If he wins, he can replace the deficit of funds. If he loses, he signs his own death warrant. Bond's job is to beat him at the table. When 007 learns that his 'Number Two' on the mission is a woman, Vesper Lynd, Fleming relays Bond's shocking inner-monologue:

> Women were for recreation. On a job, they got in the way and fogged things up with sex and hurt feelings and all the emotional baggage they carried around. One had to look out for them and take care of them ... he said 'bitch' again more loudly and walked out of the room. (2002: 32)

Eventually, against his 'better judgement', Bond falls in love with Vesper, only to discover at the end of the novel that she was working for the Russians all along as a double-agent. In her suicide note, she confesses that she agreed to give her services to the Russians under the condition that they would let her boyfriend, who was a Pole in the RAF, live. Of course, she fell in love with Bond on the assignment, and killed herself in an act of desperation as the enemy grew suspicious of her loyalty. Upon the reading of her deception in the letter, Bond bitterly declares, in one of Fleming's most memorable and troublesome closing lines, 'The bitch is dead now' (2002: 213).

This ideological narrative of misogyny and imperialism informs the entire book series, which, in turn, underscores the film series, albeit to a less egregious degree. Tony Bennett and Janet Woollacott brilliantly dub 007 'a mobile signifier' for his unique malleability, his signification that changes depending on the historical moment, the medium, the genre, the commodity (see 1987: 42). With respect to *Casino Royale*, an early Cold War-era novel, Fleming inscribed into the narrative Bennett and Woollacott's three main sets of cultural anxieties motivated by both knowledge and action, much like a detective story:

> The first concerns the ways in which the discourses of nation and nationhood are articulated with discourses of class and the manner in which the disequilibrating/equilibrating tendencies of the narrative are worked across these. The second concerns an additional series of narrative tensions, centred principally on the relations between Bond and 'the girl', which are worked across discourses of gender and sexuality alongside those of nation and nationhood. Alongside but not separate from these: the distinctive narrative and ideological economy of the Bond novels consists in the way these two sources of narrative and ideological tension are imbricated on to and worked through in relation to one another. (1987: 98)

Christoph Lindner situates Fleming's work even more explicitly in its postwar, geopolitical context. Like Bennett and Woollacott, he also purports that the Bond novels are descendants of classic detective fiction. However, Lindner argues that the difference is designated by Fleming's obsession with crime on a global scale, not merely in a regional, social or private setting: 'In Fleming's case, the Bond novels mark a shift in a cultural understanding of crime that, following the disillusioning experience of two world wars and the dawn of the atomic age, also came to include crimes against humanity' (2005: 227). Here was a new kind of detective that defended and protected capitalism, democracy and British imperialism.

I would like to fuse the Bennett and Woollacott assessment with Lindner's framework, and suggest that Fleming introduces us to a cold, unsympathetic, even fascist Bond, who represents a compulsively heterosexual desire of a boy to be taken seriously as a man. By equating the potency of masculine sexuality with that of British nationalism, and then marginalising the ethnic or gendered Other, the Bond books become problematic instructional guides for retaining one's manhood in the face of impending castration. Whether this is a political or sexual threat, Bond's Britishness and maleness are inexorably intertwined and always in crisis, and his sexism and ethnocentrism go hand in hand.

Numerous critics have discussed how 007's penis constantly hangs in the danger zone – who could forget the close call with the buzz saw in *Goldfinger* or the centipede heading towards Bond's groin in *Dr No*? *Casino Royale* provides the most terrifying of these phallic tortures, in which Le Chiffre assaults Bond's testicles with a carpet beater for an extended period to elicit information. 'There is nothing worse. It is not only the immediate agony, but also the thought that your manhood is being gradually destroyed and that at the end, if you will not yield, you will no longer be a man', Le Chiffre tells Bond (Fleming 2002: 137). One could view both Bond's near castration at the hands of a foreigner followed by his betrayal at the hands of a woman as Freudian primal scenes, which affirm his fear that one day he 'will no longer be a man'. This fear motivates his hatred for everything not male and not British. Just the man for Her Majesty's Secret Service.

Introducing 'card sense' Jimmy Bond

The televised adaptation of *Casino Royale* in 1954 dovetails off this psychoanalytic proposal, but also problematises it by recasting the British James Bond as American 'card sense' Jimmy Bond. Moreover, instead of capturing Bond's classism, carnal lust and fetish for violence, Barry Nelson plays 'Jimmy' as a glorified boy scout – a bland, asexual Everyman cut from the same mould as Ralph Byrd's Dick Tracy from the Republic Pictures matinee serials of the 1930s and 1940s. Directed by the unknown William H. Brown, the film was a B-rate production, but deserves credit for its tight, economic adaptation of Fleming's source material by writers Antony Ellis and Charles Bennet, the latter having scripted several early Hitchcock films, including *The 39 Steps* (1935) and *Foreign Correspondent* (1940). Nelson spent his career working primarily in television and on Broadway, but did appear in *Shadow of the Thin Man* (1941) and *A Guy Named Joe* (1943) before *Casino Royale*, and went on to take small parts in *Airport* (1970) and Stanley Kubrick's *The Shining* (1980). By far the biggest name attached to the film was the legendary Peter Lorre as Le Chiffre, who perfected the art of inhabiting slimy villains in such classic films as *The Maltese Falcon* (1941), *Casablanca* (1942) and, most notoriously, Fritz Lang's *M* (1931).

Sponsored by Chrysler and hosted by William Lundigan, *Climax! Mystery Theater* was a dramatic anthology series that ran from 1954–58 on Thursdays at 8:30 p.m. EST, usually featuring adaptations of popular thriller and adventure novels. *Casino Royale* was the third episode of the series, which brought to the small screen everything from *The Adventures of Huckleberry Finn* and *The Strange Case of Dr. Jekyll and Mr. Hyde* to *A Farewell to Arms* and *The Long Goodbye*. Though Ellis and Bennet substantially condensed and de-politicised Fleming's story, most of the essential ingredients survived intact. The suspenseful baccarat showdown seems especially suited for the film's stagy constraints and generic conventions, which authentically replicate the oppressive casino from the novel.

007 fans tend to dismiss this three-act teleplay as a curiosity piece at best, lambasting the un-Bondian characteristics and melodramatic gestures. What they fail to consider is that Fleming's novel lacked many of the trademarks immortalised in the Eon films, too. Granted, this production of *Casino Royale* has not aged as well as a lot of the feature films, but with its terse dialogue, straightforward plotting and realistic locale, it stands as a more faithful companion to Fleming's original model. Bond scholar James Chapman insightfully criticises the film's unfair evaluation from the 007 fan culture, and praises the spare narrative, bleak mood and precise camerawork (see 2007: 36–7).

Of course, the clearest difference from Fleming's novel is the Americanisation of Bond, which raises further intersections between nationality and masculinity, and continues to show how one is contingent on the other in the world of 007. This time, Bond's masculinity is defined by his Americanism (more on this shortly). The film still tries to explore Anglo-American relations in spite of the transatlantic exchange. Felix Leiter, Bond's American CIA liaison

'Jimmy' Bond (Barry Nelson, centre) introduces Valerie Mathis (Linda Christian) to Clarence Leiter (Michael Pate) in the *Climax! Mystery Theater* presentation of *Casino Royale* (1954)

in the novel, plays an equally significant role in the film, but as Jimmy's British counterpart, Clarence Leiter (Michael Pate). Chapman writes, 'In line with political reality, it is America which is the leading power and Britain which is the subordinate partner in the "special relationship" … Given that *Casino Royale* was made by an American television company for American audiences, then it is perfectly understandable that the hero should be an American' (2007: 37).

Another important difference is that the teleplay forgoes the twist involving Vesper's hidden agenda. In the film, Linda Christian plays Valerie Mathis, a composite of Vesper and Rene Mathis, Bond's ally from the French Secret Service. From the very beginning, we realise that Valerie is one of Bond's former girlfriends, now working for Le Chiffre, but we never have any doubt as to whether she will switch sides again before the end of the film. Thus, she basically inverts Vesper's function from the book. The decision to alter the 'Bond girl' role was probably due to insufficient screen time needed to develop her beyond the standard female foil, but it does take on an ideological significance that the filmmakers may not have intended. Bond has no personal reason to use and abuse women here. In fact, he seems fairly disinterested in them, never highly aroused or incensed. He comes across as just a likable 'good ol' boy', a flat Roy Rogers-type who looks somewhat uncomfortable in his stuffy tuxedo. Nelson's crew cut-topped 007 from the 'Combined Intelligence Agency' proves to know more about playing cards than about being a spy, or an aristocratic gentleman, for that matter.

Jimmy indicates no penchant for expensive cars, fine cuisine, world travelling and stiff martinis (shaken or otherwise), nor does he impress with Holmsian powers of deduction like Connery or a sly wit like Moore. No, this Bond comes from a tradition of homespun, straight-shooting, plainspoken American heroes in popular culture, with no time for such worldly distractions as wine and women when there is a job to be done. It is worth pointing out that *Casino Royale* aired just before Walt Disney's Davy Crockett craze, which epitomised this US admiration for old-fashioned do-gooders. Ellis and Bennet more than just adapted Bond for the screen; they had to adapt to a more conservative audience, who saw no problem with inviting a less ironic, more innocent Bond into their living rooms. Although this marks a different brand of nationalism and masculinity, Brown's *Casino Royale* still seems as preoccupied with these issues as Fleming's. Once again, the lines become blurred between nation and gender, somehow equating one with the other: to be American is to be a man (specifically, this kind of man), and vice versa. Jimmy Bond is the archetype for conventional 1950s masculinity in America, broadcasting the unspoken message that 'this is how you act like a man'. Surely, it is no coincidence that the sidekick of the show is an effete, slightly befuddled Brit, and that the romantic interest, Valerie, cannot resist falling for the American protagonist.

The subsequent feature films present a humorous role reversal: it is the American (Felix, and his eventual replacement, Jack Wade) who plays second-fiddle to the intellectually, physically and sexually superior Englishman (Bond). Joe Don

Baker's boorish Wade almost acts as comic relief in *GoldenEye* and *Tomorrow Never Dies* (1997), and eight different actors have played Felix in his nine screen appearances since 1954, varying significantly in age (twice he was even played by an African-American). Unlike Bond's recurring colleagues from MI6 – M, Q and Moneypenny – his elusive 'brother from Langley' appears not to be important enough to warrant regular screen time or a regular actor.

One could argue that Jimmy Bond does not confront as many threats to his masculinity as James Bond. True, Jimmy does not receive a testicle thrashing, nor is he betrayed by Valerie. However, the prolonged baccarat sequence is rife with phallic tension. Here are two men – one good (Bond) and one evil (Le Chiffre) – facing off in a game of chance. Each man represents his respective Cold War superpower (the US and the USSR), and, in an overtly homosocial turn, both men are competing for the same woman (Valerie). Losing the game, metaphorically speaking, means not only losing the girl, but also accepting the position as the inferior nation and, as a result, the inferior man. Predictably, the American wins, but Le Chiffre seeks retribution for the emasculating victory in a later scene fraught with an equal dose of castration anxiety, which is the only scene depicting any severe physical violence onscreen. Obviously, the torture in Fleming's novel would be far too graphic for 1950s television to imply, let alone show. Instead, Bond is roughed-up and bound in a bathtub, and we are led to believe that Le Chiffre and his goons are mutilating his bare feet with a pair of pliers and forcing Valerie to look on in horror.

The mutilation takes place offscreen – we only see Bond's face wincing in pain – so perhaps there is more going on that we are not allowed to see. Though Bond is not nude as he is in the novel, perhaps we could go as far as reading his submissive, humiliating position in the bathtub as a compromising position, as well, to the point that the torture becomes a symbolic rape. Noir buffs may recall a similar torture in Robert Aldrich's *Kiss Me Deadly* (1955). The heart of the scene speaks to the sadistic and masochistic competition for Valerie's female gaze: who is the better man, the one inflicting the pain or the one enduring it? Jeremy Black argues that 'Bond, himself, in the films is a visual guarantee of the maleness of the Secret Service, a role he carries forward from the novels without equivocation. His sexuality is central to this, because, in both novels and films, a notion of deviant sexuality fits in with menace' (2001: 107). Black goes on to point to the heterosexual sadism of Le Chiffre, Krest, Slugsby, Horror and Scaramanga, as well as other well-known villains in the series, who range from asexual to homosexual to paedophilic. Bond may not exhibit the aggressively or compulsively heterosexual attributes he has in the novel, but he 'gets the girl' in the end regardless. Even though he admits that killing is a part of his profession, he clearly does not take pleasure in the suffering of others like Le Chiffre, which guarantees the superior 'maleness' Black refers to in Bond, even while that masculinity is under attack.

The *Daily Express* comics

Bond's leap from film to comics made for a logical transition. The two visual mediums share an ongoing interaction, and nearly every popular action hero has jumped from one to the other. Batman premiered in *Detective Comics* in 1939 and became the subject of movie serials by 1943, while The Shadow quickly moved from pulp novels and radio to a 1937 feature film and a 1938 cartoon strip. The Lone Ranger, cowboy star of juvenile fiction and radio shows, rode into movie serials and the comic scene almost simultaneously in 1938. Four years after the *Climax! Mystery Theater* presentation, the *Daily Express* commenced the first 007 daily comic strip with an adaptation of *Casino Royale* by writer Anthony Hern and artist John McLusky, introducing Bond as 'the sardonic secret agent who stormed into popularity as THE postwar fiction hero' (Bennett & Woollacott 1987: 12).

In 1957, the previous year, the paper played an integral part in promoting Fleming's novels with the serialisation of *From Russia, With Love*. Bennett and Woollacott cite this period as the first historical moment of Bond as a popular hero, and also as a political hero for the middle classes, as British sales of the Bond novels rose from 58,000 in 1956 to 72,000 in 1957, 105,000 in 1958 and 237,000 in 1959 (see 1987: 24–5). They assume that the readers of the novels and the *Daily Express* fell into the economic sphere of the lower middle class, and were the most receptive to the ideological voice found in these 'low cultured' texts: 'In frustrating the villain's conspiracy, Bond effects an ideologically loaded imaginary resolution of the real historical contradictions of the period, a resolution in which all the values associated with Bond and, thereby, the West – notably, freedom and individualism – gain ascendancy over those associated with the villain and, thereby communist Russia' (1987: 25). The medium may have changed, but the *Daily Express* preserved Fleming's Cold War rhetoric and still provided readers with an escapist fantasy.

McLusky drew most of the 007 newspaper cartoons based on Fleming's novels, usually collaborating with writer Henry Gammidge. This syndicated series ran in the *Daily Express* from 1958–62 and 1964–77, in the *Sunday Express* in 1977 and in the *Daily Star* from 1981–83. All of Fleming's Bond novels were adapted into comic strip form, along with six of his Bond short stories. Even Kingsley Amis's *Colonel Sun* received a cartoon treatment. By the mid-1960s, Jim Lawrence and Yaroslav Horak replaced Gammidge and McLusky as the regular writer and artist on the series, respectively, and eventually showcased brand new 007 adventures. Various 007 comic books were also released as the films' popularity skyrocketed, but with less remarkable results, including movie tie-ins, foreign-language imprints and original issues from American publishers.

Hern and McLusky's *Casino Royale* is nothing less than solid entertainment for comic connoisseurs and James Bond aficionados, but it is also worth examining critically for at least two important reasons. The first is that it remains a historical relic of a lost and underappreciated art form, and can be viewed as a prime example of 1950s comic strip storytelling (and a commercially successful one, no less). Thanks to Titan Books, over a dozen of these *Express* strips are now available in collected, reprinted form. On a more aesthetic level, the *Casino Royale* comic anticipates the 'look' of the 007 films, especially with regards to the look of Bond himself. While *Climax!* already showed audiences a variation on how Bond might look, Nelson was a little too soft, not to mention an American, and therefore could not convey the qualities of rugged masculinity and urbane Britishness that Fleming had established in the novel. Furthermore, the highly visual approach to the storytelling due to the nature of the medium exposes Fleming's inherently visual writing style, making his books all the more ripe for the big screen.

Chapman astutely comments on how 'the short shot lengths of the Bond films, particularly in the action sequences with their fast close-ups of fists, feet and guns thrust into the frame, are the filmic equivalent of panels of the comic strip' (2007: 48), and how this kinetic energy not only hides the typical gaps in narrative logic, but also requires concise information communicated through image. The Titan editors even note how *Casino Royale* in particular contains some strips with no dialogue balloons at all. Unlike the single-setting confinement of the television programme, the comic allows Bond to move fluidly from place to place. This nicely positions the strip as a segue from Fleming's rather short novel and the one-hour film, to the more 'opened-up' theatrical film of *Dr No* in 1962, foreshadowing the possibilities and potential of future 007 adventures.

But we must return to the visual representation of Bond as a character. McLusky's Bond has the definitive face and physique that we typically imagine when we think of 007: the jet-black, mildly curly hair, neatly parted to one side; the steely eyes underneath a pair of thick, dark eyebrows; the square jaw and slight grin of self-deprecation; the cool composure and muscular frame; young, but not too young, and so on. Over the course of the comic series, Bond's physical features gradually became more defined and chiselled, at times almost as if McLusky had Connery in mind all along. Comic fans might also notice an uncanny resemblance to handsome, billionaire playboy Bruce Wayne (Batman's daytime alter ego), but whereas Bruce always appears more at home in his cape and cowl, Bond gives the impression that he would never wear anything other than his tuxedo or finest suit. On the surface, this may seem like a silly or arbitrary detail, but this quintessential 'Bond look' saturates the entire franchise, tying back to the ways in which masculinity and nationality are constructed.

In *Dressed to Kill: James Bond, the Suited Hero*, Neil Norman writes, 'Bond is a hero of refinement. His attire is as much a symbol of what he represents as a reflection of his own personal style. The well-tailored suit is to Bond the armour of his profession ... The trick of tailoring for James Bond is to give him a look that is essentially, though not aggressively, British. Classic, with a twist of international flair' (1996: 117). Norman argues that as scruffier, anti-establishment movie heroes from America, such as Indiana Jones and John McClane from the *Die Hard* series (1988, 1990, 1995, 2007), started dressing down, the suit came to connote snobbery, violence and villainy. Bond's dapper wardrobe, he posits, not only paid homage to the suited heroes of classical Hollywood, but also continued to uphold wealth and conservative, prewar British values during countercultural times.

Too much for one James Bond!

Bond may have been conceived as a mascot for British traditionalism, but he was not always a member of the status quo. His brush with Vietnam-era counterculture is best exemplified by Charles Feldman's sprawling, slapstick send-up in 1967, released on the heels of other madcap 'groove' comedies like *What's New Pussycat?* (1965), *Our Man Flint* (1966) and *Modesty Blaise* (1966). The film was called *Casino Royale* and credits Fleming, technically making it the first adaptation of the novel given a theatrical release. But with the exception of a handful of familiar scenes, the film owes very little to its so-called source material.

Leading the ensemble cast is David Niven as the retired Sir James Bond, 'the greatest spy in history ... the true, one and only original'. Complete with a nervous stammer, Niven delivers a dry performance as this rich eccentric, who disparagingly calls his successor and namesake a 'sexual acrobat who leaves a trail of beautiful, dead women like blown roses behind him'. Chapman adds that he even drives a Bentley like Fleming's Bond, instead of the Aston Martin for the new wave of 'joke shop spies' (2007: 107). Ursula Andress, who previously co-starred with Connery in *Dr No*, plays Vesper. Duncan Macrae plays Mathis, Geoffrey Bayldon plays Q, Barbara Bouchet plays Miss Moneypenny (the 'real' Moneypenny's daughter, to be exact), John Huston plays M (and also co-directs) and Orson Welles plays Le Chiffre. In a jab at the old teleplay, Woody Allen also appears as 007's neurotic, American nephew, Jimmy Bond, who dispenses amusing one-liners like, 'You can't shoot me ... I have a very low threshold of death. My doctor says I can't have bullets enter my body at any time.'

For all the talent involved, however, the film is only moderately funny, devolving into a bloated, incoherent mess. Inspired by the camp craze, psychedelia and pop art movement of the time, *Casino Royale* tries harder to appeal to the late-1960s mod

Vesper Lynd (Ursula Andress) gets acquainted with card shark Evelyn Tremble (Peter Sellers) on a revolving bed in *Casino Royale* (1967)

crowd with its over-the-top humour and visual excesses than to satirise or expand upon the preceding Bond films. Today, the film is most fondly remembered not for its extravagant gimmicks, but for its charming soundtrack by Burt Bacharach, featuring the Academy Award-nominated song 'The Look of Love'.

There is not much plot to speak of, but Sir James' undertaking apparently involves spoiling a scheme by SMERSH, the predecessor of SPECTRE, to botch the 007 reputation and take over the world. Naturally, this entails beating Le Chiffre at baccarat, but Sir James recruits half a dozen other 'James Bond 007s' to better elude the ring of nefarious Soviet spies and complete the operation. The new team-mates include Joanna Pettet as the seductive daughter of Mata Hari (and Bond!) and Peter Sellers as a wacky card shark. This fragmented narrative gives way to a series of non-sequiturs and loosely connected vignettes, almost prefiguring the surreal, sketch comedy style of *Monty Python's Flying Circus* (1969–74) but easily the farthest cry yet from Fleming's approach to the original character and story. In an interview on the *Casino Royale* DVD, co-director Val Guest relays the following admission from Feldman to him during the film's preliminary stages: 'we can't use the book because they've used sequences in every other Bond film; the only thing that we've got left is the title and the casino … treat this as a psychedelic movie, four directors doing four different segments, treat it as fun.' Guest goes on to describe the chaotic conditions of production, such as multiple script and editing revisions, clashes with Sellers and scheduling conflicts.

All the same, Feldman's off-the-wall opus is worth seeing for film buffs, if for no other reason than to witness such a diverse assortment of famous actors occupying the same screen space. The film is packed with cameos from 'guest stars' in addition to its wide principle cast. Nowhere else can one find veterans of classical Hollywood (John Huston, Orson Welles, William Holden, George Raft, Deborah Kerr, Charles Boyer) alongside rising international sex symbols (Barbara Bouchet, Joanna Pettet, Jacqueline Bisset, Daliah Lavi), popular comedians of the decade (Woody Allen, Peter Sellers), French leading man Jean-Paul Belmondo and bikini-goddess Ursula Andress, who had already established a 007 star-text by 1967. This array of celebrity appearances is anchored by David Niven, the Academy Award-winning old hand of both British and American movies, who starred in such classics as *Wuthering Heights* (1939), *Around the World in 80 Days* (1956) and *The Guns of Navarone* (1961). Feldman's star-studded conceit adds to the level of zaniness in *Casino Royale*, but it is also one more way in which the filmmakers play with textual cross-pollination, blending different genres, styles, time periods, nationalities, political references, storylines, music, and artistic and cultural movements. These elements are mixed and recontextualised into one giant, blank parody of 1960s spy films.

The film was shot at three studios for a total of $12 million, but did financially well at the height of the Bond phenomenon. Although its official 007 box-office rival, *You Only Live Twice*, out-performed with ticket sales, *Casino Royale* won the 'Battle of the Bonds' on the record charts:

> Burt Bacharach's *Casino Royale* soundtrack album, which featured numbers by Herb Alpert and Dusty Springfield, reached number 12 on *Variety*'s album charts and was a radio staple throughout the summer of 1967. On the other hand, the soundtrack for *You Only Live Twice*, featuring Nancy Sinatra's rendition of the title song, never got higher than number 42. (Smith 2003: 129)

Jeff Smith reports how the Sinatra song dropped off *Variety*'s charts after a month, and that the soundtracks for the following two Bond films, *On Her Majesty's Secret Service* and *Diamonds Are Forever*, could not even match the disappointing chart performance of *You Only Live Twice* (see 2003: 129–30). This downward slope seems especially odd in light of the record success of the *Goldfinger* and *Thunderball* soundtrack albums in 1964 and 1965, respectively.

For all of its problems in conception and execution, *Casino Royale* most noticeably succeeded as a reminder of the important role synergy plays in the world of Bond, particularly with the selling of soundtracks. Each 007 film's marketability in other areas, such as music, video games, books, comics and toys, is in many ways as vital to its success as the script, the special effects and the actors. This held especially true in the Roger Moore era as 'Live and Let Die' (1973), by Paul McCartney and Wings, and Carly Simon's 1977 'Nobody Does It Better' (for *The Spy Who Loved Me*) became nearly as identifiable with Bond as John Barry's theme music.

The 1967 poster for *You Only Live Twice* proudly claims 'Sean Connery IS James Bond'. *Casino Royale* adopted the opposite advertising slogan: 'It's too much for one James Bond!' Little did the advertisers anticipate that their campaign for Feldman's movie would actually make a profound statement about the 007 franchise at large, and, in an accidental sort of way, offer a useful interpretation of Bond's venture into comedy. Indeed, by 1967 the 007 universe had become too much for just one James Bond. If Bond's world is meant to be an exaggerated version of our own, quelling real-life fears about current events with the logic of fairy tales for the West, then it is necessary for him to evolve with the times. The underlying formula will probably never vary, nor should it, and I doubt fans could accept a Bond that did not symbolise masculinity and British nationalism in some way. But *Casino Royale* reveals how the ways in which Bond symbolises these ideological constructions need not remain the same as when he first appeared in Fleming's novels. While Feldman's *Casino Royale* may not have worked very well from an artistic standpoint, the public's interest in the film indicates that a hipper, 'funnier' Bond could be something to revisit in the 1970s.

Overlooking the more serious *On Her Majesty's Secret Service*, the subsequent Bond films during the next ten years took the increasingly playful spirit of Connery's classics to an even higher echelon of farce. Sometimes Eon struck gold with Roger Moore's proclivity towards the tongue-in-cheek gags, as in *The Spy Who Loved Me*, but frequently the movies failed painfully, such as *Live and Let Die* and *Moonraker* (1979). The growing attention on the comedy also meant a stronger focus on Bond as an anarchist. As Jeremy Black argues, 'although he both represented and safeguarded the Establishment, Bond also reaffirmed the power of the individual ... Bond was presented as a somewhat anarchic figure, defying rules and conventions, having, for example, to be summoned to the office from assignations' (2001: 99). Bond has certainly been rebellious and defiant towards his supervisors at MI6, but the level of outright anarchism is an area of contention for me. After all, the *Casino Royale* trajectory in question here seems to validate Bond as an emblem of right-wing ideals. But I do see a trend in the Bond films from 1967–85 that questions the rules and conventions of cinema.

First and foremost, the inside humour reaches such an ironic point of self-referentiality and self-parody that what little value the films had as genuine spy thrillers has evaporated into a postmodern critique of the genre. Secondly, the stress on intertextuality, bricolage and pastiche prompts audiences and critics to use phrases like 'James Bond meets *Shaft*' (*Live and Let Die*) or 'James Bond meets *Star Wars*' (*Moonraker*) to describe the instalments in that period. Eon may have avoided another free-for-all potpourri like *Casino Royale*, but they did not totally abandon its irreverent sense of humour or sense of itself, which meant upping the ante on sexual innuendo, megalomaniacal villains, outrageous plots and pure physical jokes.

'You know my name'

When, in 2006, *Casino Royale* was announced as the twenty-first official Bond film to be released, this time starring Daniel Craig, audiences and critics did not know what to expect for the future of the franchise. After the uncomfortable kitschiness of *Die Another Day* (2002), some feared that Eon would never be able to wash its hands completely clean of the silly hijinks inherited from Moore's term as 007. As Simon Winder predicted in his book, *The Man Who Saved Britain: A Personal Journey Into the Disturbing World of James Bond*, which was published just before the release of *Casino Royale*: 'For years fans have dreamt of the book being turned into a faithfully adapted film as it could be a brooding, noirish, rather despairing mood piece. I fear however that the reality will consist of John Cleese as Q campily unveiling some follow-up to *Die Another Day*'s invisible car' (2006: 148). Winder maintains that two inescapable reasons for Bond's survival are the two issues I keep returning to in this essay: his masculinity and his Britishness. He refers to a sense of 'man talk' that always weaves itself into Bond's missions, during which 007 always seems to find time to hang out with another man and discuss cars, politics and women. Bond's most lasting legacy, Winder writes, is his role as 'the patron saint of contemporary male-interest magazines': 'Bond's every action and thought may have helped both crystallise and reassure male distress at the collapse of Britain in the world, but his more lasting legacy is perhaps Bond's laughing reminiscence in *You Only Live Twice* of how his friend Dikko smacked a girl's bottom so hard that she fell over' (2006: 171).

But in the wake of 9/11 and the Iraq War, and a much more politically correct time than Fleming's, would audiences still stand for Bond as a 'sexist, misogynist dinosaur'? Just how should the character represent Fleming's concept of British masculinity for the twenty-first century? Some viewers were perfectly happy with the way things were going and saw no reason to rock the boat – after all, *Die Another Day* made more money than any other Bond film up to that point. On the other hand, Winder was probably relieved that Craig's Bond is the hardest, meanest Bond for the screen yet, and easily the most Flemingesque since Connery. However, he is also the timeliest and most vulnerable. At the protest (and confusion) of certain fans, the filmmakers in no way attempted to hide the breaks in the series' chronology with *Casino Royale*, affirming Bond as an ageless and timeless 'mobile signifier' rather than a rounded, realistic character in an ongoing narrative continuity.

This was a smart, deliberate move on Eon's part, especially if their goal was to restart the franchise from scratch. Bond's mother-figure, Judi Dench as M, is the only series regular to return – there was no reason to replace her after she usurped Bernard Lee as the head of British Intelligence. Craig, who was already gaining a minor reputation as a macho tough onscreen in *Road to Perdition* (2002), *Layer Cake* (2004) and *Munich* (2005), makes his new role his own as a young, inexperienced 007. The supporting cast includes Mads Mikkelsen as Le Chiffre, Eva Green as Vesper Lynd, Jeffrey Wright as Felix Leiter and Giancarlo Giannini as Mathis. Aside from a small camp of detractors voicing pointless complaints over 'a blond Bond', *Casino Royale* is the most commercially and critically successful 007 film to date, garnering almost unanimously positive reviews and over $300 million at the box office.

Though this surprisingly faithful adaptation recounts Bond's first mission as a double-0 agent, the events are clearly set in 2006. Without losing much of Fleming's original material, the film updates the story and actually enriches the suspense, psychological complexity and emotional payoff, much like how Francis Ford Coppola improved upon Mario Puzo's pulpy bestseller, *The Godfather* (1969) in his film adaptation of 1972. The writing trio was made up of Neal Purvis and Robert Wade, who scripted the previous two 007 films, *The World Is Not Enough* (1999) and *Die Another Day*, and the Academy Award-winning Paul Haggis, fresh off his success with *Million Dollar Baby* (2005) and *Crash* (2006). At a running time of 144 minutes, the longest yet for a Bond film, Purvis, Wade and

Haggis make room in Fleming's story for a few extra twists and subplots. Prior to this film, it was only in *On Her Majesty's Secret Service* that Bond had actually fallen in love onscreen, but the star-crossed romance in *Casino Royale* is infinitely more compelling. This is the most effective 'serious Bond' since *For Your Eyes Only* (1981), showing off the awkwardness of the most recent attempts at playing it straight with Timothy Dalton.

The larger ambition of the project, though, seems to be introducing Bond to a new generation of potential fans, revising – but not directly changing – the ideology of the series for post-Cold War Britain and America, and the new millennium. Jim Leach explains how the Brosnan vehicles endeavoured to mollify criticisms against the franchise by appropriating them into the very diegesis of the films, such as M's attack on Bond's sexism, and, in a parallel thread, to explicitly acknowledge current world events:

> Like the earlier films, they use topical allusions to link their narratives to actuality: *GoldenEye* refers to the break-up of the Soviet Union, *Tomorrow Never Dies* appeals to concerns about the spread of terrorism and about the power of the mass media, and the politics of oil provides the framework for *The World Is Not Enough*. (2003: 253)

The same could be said for *Die Another Day*, which incorporates conflict diamonds into its convoluted plot. *GoldenEye*'s trailer nicely encapsulates this point with the tagline: 'It's a new world with new enemies and new threats, but you can still depend on one man.'

Along with an increasing awareness of global affairs, Leach claims that Brosnan's films also stayed on the cutting edge of technology. 'These affairs now take place in a world in which electronic technology both transcends the limits of the human body and makes possible a surveillance system that erodes any notion of privacy', Leach writes, citing fireballs targeted at Bond and officials watching video monitors as two recurring images in the new 007 universe (2003: 255). *Casino Royale* is no exception. Characters are constantly hovering over computer screens looking up information on the Internet or spying on each other's background profiles. Bond's mobile phone seems more attached than usual, and he uses it with other characters' mobiles to follow an elusive clue called 'Ellipsis'. There is even a scene in which Bond breaks into a hotel security surveillance room to obtain information on one of Le Chiffre's associates. After Bond kills an international bomb-maker and blows up a Nambutu embassy early in the film, all of which is recorded and leaked to the press, M says:

> They don't care what we do, they care what we get photographed doing. And how the hell could Bond be so stupid? I give him '00' status and he celebrates

by shooting up an embassy ... In the old days, if an agent did something that embarrassing he'd have the good sense to defect. Christ, I miss the Cold War.

What may seem like just another amusing Bondian quip actually positions the viewer both in the film's technological and geopolitical context. Even more telling is when M reports the following to Bond before he leaves for Casino Royale in Montenegro: 'When they analysed the stock market after 9/11, the CIA discovered a massive shorting of airline stocks. When the stocks hit bottom on 9/12, someone made a fortune.' That somebody is a banker known as Le Chiffre, who has been using terrorist funds to play the stock market.

One cannot help but recall Slavoj Žižek's essay, 'Welcome to the Desert of the Real', in which he advances the controversial argument that America's most disturbing surprise on 9/11 was that the country received what it had always fantasised about in countless Hollywood disaster movies. He also draws a provocative comparison between Osama Bin Laden and Blofeld, Bond's arch nemesis:

When the master-criminal, after capturing Bond, usually takes him on a tour of his illegal factory, is this not the closest Hollywood comes to the socialist-realist proud presentation of the production in a factory? And the function of Bond's intervention, of course, is to explode in firecracks this site of production, allowing us to return to the daily semblance of our existence in a world with the 'disappearing working class'. Is it not that, in the exploding WTC towers, this violence directed at the threatening Outside turned back at us? (Žižek 2002: 387)

Žižek is applying his two favourite philosophical lenses to 007 – Marxism and Lacanian psychoanalysis – to elucidate the cultural politics of the film franchise. Blofeld's illegal factory is a perversion of capitalist production, the economic system of the West Bond is fighting for, and therefore it must be destroyed. Both Bin Laden and Blofeld are larger-than-life threats of 'the Real', what Lacan describes as 'the impossible' and 'the object of anxiety' that disrupts the Symbolic order. Thus, according to Žižek, when the World Trade Center towers exploded in real fireworks, Americans became directly involved in what they had always witnessed from the safety and comfort of their living rooms. Either as the stuff of fantastic Hollywood entertainment or news reports of catastrophes in the 'Outside World' (Sarajevo, Sierra Leone, Rwanda and Congo, and so on), these were once events that 'don't happen *here!*' (see Žižek 2002: 388–9).

Martin Campbell almost seems conscious of this postmodern thinking in his film, which is explicitly set after 9/11. He resists the cliché of a captured Bond touring the spectacular illegal factory as the villain explains his plot to take over the world. Moreover, the firecracks in *Casino Royale* do not take on fetishistic significance as they do in the film fantasy of, say, *Independence Day* (1996). The limited scenes of destruction, most of which occur during the film's tragic climax of Vesper's death, are tainted with a sense of melancholy. Unlike most of the previous 007 films, the violence and torture scenes are not stylised or played for laughs, but appear brutal and unsettling. Bond has moved past the communist 'red scare' and plots of world domination to deal with today's nightmares involving international terrorism, financial crimes and technological surveillance. Just as Fleming's novels tapped into a readership disheartened by World War One and Two, the Suez Crisis and Cold War paranoia, Campbell's wearier, more pessimistic Bond articulates the angst, grief and suspicion on the part of Britain and the US in the global aftermath of the 9/11 attacks.

Instead of Bond attacking the Outside, *Casino Royale* also focuses on a more vulnerable and defensive Bond facing threats from the inside. He is a victim of deception – the woman he falls in love with is not who she appears to be – and he is constantly being watched, chased and seriously injured. But he is also arrogant, reckless and insensitive, and, yes, even sexist at times (the film actually preserves 'the bitch is dead' phrase as one of Bond's closing remarks). As I mentioned earlier, this is a flawed 007, albeit more human and realistic than we have seen in the past, but we are also invited to criticise him. M calls him names like 'a blunt instrument' and a 'thug', while Vesper, easily the strongest Bond woman yet, often sarcastically comments on his ego. In a direct reference to Fleming, she actually says to him, 'Now,

After almost 'losing his shirt', James Bond (Daniel Craig) recovers from a poisoned martini thanks to the aid of Vesper Lynd (Eva Green) in *Casino Royale* (2006)

having just met you I wouldn't go as far as calling you a cold-hearted bastard. But it wouldn't be a stretch to imagine you think of women as disposable pleasures rather than meaningful pursuits.'

For the first time, the camera also eroticises Bond as a masculine sex object in the same way that the 'Bond girls' have always been on display for the scopophilic gaze. Campbell supplies lingering shots of Craig's bare, beefy torso, such as the scene in which he steps onto the beach after a swim in the ocean, a moment that harks back to Ursula Andress rising from the tropical waters wearing her now famous white bikini in *Dr No*. Still, as he is protecting Queen and country, and attempting to prevent the funding of terrorism, we root for him as a British hero. When we look back at other Bonds, the self-assured gentleman spy of Fleming's novels and the comics, or the wisecracking, ironic screen spy of the 1960s and 1970s, it is clear that the filmmakers here have made a deliberate effort to vary from these constructions of British masculinity to propose an insecure masculine archetype for the millennial generation full of self-doubts and self-awareness.

Like Matt Damon's amnesiac secret agent, Jason Bourne, of the American Bourne trilogy (2002, 2004, 2007), Bond's most elusive mystery on his first mission as a 'double-0' is learning who he is exactly. He takes himself very seriously because, after all, this is a new world with new enemies and new threats. Behind his harsh exterior, however, he is constantly questioning his identity, learning how to become Bond much in the same way Craig is learning how to 'become Bond' as an actor. This is a 007 that makes poor judgements and botches plans, usually resulting in visible wounds. M's cutting words after the embassy debacle are well put: 'You violated the only absolutely inviolable rule of international relationships … We're trying to find out how an entire network of terrorist groups is financed and you give us one bomb-maker. Hardly the big picture, wouldn't you say?' We see him gradually warm up to the suits and the martinis, and we are forced to wait until the final scene to hear the words, 'Bond, James Bond' over the rousing theme music. It takes an entire film for Bond to decide whether he is indeed *James Bond*, and for the viewer to rediscover the character. As the cycle of Craig films grows, perhaps this identity crisis will resolve itself along with his rough edges, and yet another variation on iconic British maleness will develop for the future. If nothing else, the legacy of James Bond and *Casino Royale* proves that when it comes to surviving, nobody does it better.

2

'DO I LOOK LIKE I GIVE A DAMN?': WHAT'S RIGHT ABOUT GETTING IT WRONG IN *CASINO ROYALE*

Douglas L. Howard

About halfway into *Casino Royale* (2006), a dejected and demoralised James Bond (Daniel Craig), having just lost all of his multimillion-dollar chip stack to the terrorist-banker Le Chiffre (Mads Mikkelsen), walks up to the bar at the lavish Montenegro hotel to order a vodka martini. As the bartender asks, 'Shaken or stirred?' virtually anyone acquainted with the big screen's suave spy hero and the

world's most famous drink order knows what comes next. But Craig's Bond is in no mood to play along. The cards and the villain have gone against him here. 'Do I look like I give a damn?' he growls at the bartender. And with moments like these in the new film, the writers and the director not only play against the stereotype of the character, but they reinvigorate and re-energise the series by thwarting our expectations about who and what James Bond is.

James Bond (Daniel Craig) trying to look like he doesn't give a damn after ordering a martini in *Casino Royale* (2006)

From the previous twenty or so films, Bond had virtually become a kind of cartoon, with little or no realistic credibility, in spite of the intrigue and the danger that the films' creators tried to introduce into their plots. Regardless of the situation, he always had the right gadget and the right comeback, and he always figured out the villain's best laid plans before the credits rolled. If he was not deducing the details of Goldfinger's Operation Grand Slam over mint juleps, then he was beating Scaramanga at his own game in his assassin's funhouse. But in *Casino Royale*, Bond is not so sophisticated or savvy. (Craig, in fact, looks like he might be more at home on a rugby field than at MI6.) He is gloriously flawed, and the spy world that he navigates is riddled with red herrings and trap doors, doors that he all too often kicks open or falls through. We can suspend our disbelief more willingly and invest in this Bond more completely, however, because his world and his confusion seem closer to our own. *Casino Royale* goes against the very formula for the spy drama that the series itself has created by deliberately getting so many things wrong (including the drink order), but, in doing so, in the end, it offers a more satisfying concoction.

Begin with one part opening sequence and title credits

If we look at the primary ingredients that go into the Bond films, we can see how the filmmakers have deliberately played with the 'recipe' to create something different here to appeal to contemporary tastes. Take the opening sequence of the film. Nearly all of the Bond films have prided themselves on their thrilling, ultra-clever dramatic openings, that unique combination of chaos, mayhem, high-tech gadgetry, beautiful women and stunt insanity that, in the span of ten minutes, microcosmically typifies the Bond mystique. The opening of *Goldfinger* (1964 – perhaps the quintessential Bond film) certainly comes to mind in this regard, as Bond (Sean Connery) stealthily scubas into a Mexican industrial compound to sabotage the operation of Ramirez, a drug lord 'using heroin-flavoured bananas to finance revolutions'. Inasmuch as the pre-title sequences have generally focused on the hero, these ten minutes tell us almost everything we need to know about Bond, his world and his lavish lifestyle. From the fake seagull on his headgear to the grappling-gun that he uses to scale the compound wall to the plastic explosive that he squeezes from his scuba equipment onto several drums of nitro, Bond is ingeniously well armed and well prepared with the most advanced technology. Discarding his wetsuit, he reveals a stylish tuxedo underneath, which he immediately accessorises with a red carnation in the lapel, a sign not only of his sophistication but also of his uncanny, almost mechanical ability to adapt to any situation. As his explosives go off and panic the other patrons at a local nightclub, Bond smokes calmly before moving on to the scantily-clad nightclub dancer. Though her affections are a ruse and though Bond must kill her accomplice by throwing him into a bathtub and knocking an electric fan into the water, this manic evening is not disturbing for him, but rather boils down to his offhand pun 'positively shocking'. For Bond, the betrayal, the attack, the exotic locale, the chaos and mayhem are commonplace and met with an impressive upper-class aplomb that must dramatically contrast with our awe as viewers.

Subsequent films, moreover, perpetuate this image, with Bond skiing away from another female betrayal in Austria, evading Soviet assassins and skydiving with his Union Jack parachute in *The Spy Who Loved Me* (1977); skydiving without a parachute and fighting in free-fall in *Moonraker* (1979); battling an assassin in an explosive-laden Jeep before parachuting onto a bored jetsetting beauty's yacht in *The Living Daylights* (1987); destroying a Soviet installation and then motorcycling, skydiving and piloting a nose-diving plane to safety in *GoldenEye* (1995). Sportsman, sophisticate, sensualist, spy – Bond consistently does it all before the opening credits run.

But in the opening moments of *Casino Royale*, Bond is hardly so clever for his own good, and the filmmakers reject the 'can-you-top-this' gauntlet thrown down by their predecessors and the colourful cinematic history of 007. Technical wizardry does not save the day at the crucial moment. Aerial daring-do does not thwart the villain as Bond appears to be at his mercy. And he does not find comfort in the arms of a woman or deal matter-of-factly with her betrayal before business calls (and there are not even any women in this pre-title sequence). In fact, there is nothing particularly flashy about what we do see here. Instead, in a comparatively minimalistic scene, we bear witness to two gunshots and two kills, the first two kills that give him his 'double-0' status. The first that we see is actually his second, a rather polite, almost clinical kill, as Bond confronts the corrupt MI6 section chief Dryden (Malcolm Sinclair) in the recesses of his high-rise Prague office about selling government secrets. While his attempt to turn the tables on Bond fails, as the agent has already emptied his gun, Dryden is, surprisingly, not so much concerned with his impending doom as he is with the psychological toll of all this on Bond himself. Flashing back, the film shows us the death of Dryden's contact, of the man who did not die 'well', whom Bond kills in a brutal, ugly bathroom brawl – no scenic locales or exotic backgrounds here – knocking him through several stalls and smashing him up against the urinals before choking him, apparently to death, in a running sink.

Where Connery quips about electrocuting his foe in a bathtub and Roger Moore spectacularly shoots his assailant while skiing backwards, Craig's Bond demonstrates no such sophistication or flair. Rather, this view to a kill is about as physical and earthy as it gets. Breathing heavily and standing back from the body, he must digest the horror of what he has just done, just as we must be horrified in watching it. As Dryden insightfully realises, this first kill, Dryden's contact, made him 'feel it', made him feel the enormity of taking a life. Rarely, if ever, has a Bond film dealt with the psychological burden behind the licence to kill or shown us the price that Bond must pay in earning it. In spite of the section chief's sympathy and in spite of the fact that he is, essentially, unarmed, Bond still shoots and kills him, too, a sign of exactly how cold he is becoming. Clearly, this is no joke, despite Bond's quip about the second kill being considerably easier.

As his foe grabs an Uzi, in the conclusion to the flashback, Bond wheels for the *coup de grâce* and fires for his first kill, leading into the gun-barrel sequence and the opening credits. These, too, let us know that we are in for a Bond film of a different sort. John Cork and Bruce Scivally explain that, from the very first film, *Dr No* (1962), 'the opening gun barrel', a creation of production designer Maurice Binder, has been 'a signature device, instantly identifying each film as part of a series and drawing audiences through the vortex of the barrel's rifling, into Bond's dangerous world' (2002: 46). In the Bond tradition, the gun-barrel sequence has always been shot against a plain white backdrop, typically with the actor playing Bond walking calmly from right to left before turning and firing on his assailant, an assailant that we never see. The gun barrels have also occurred before the pre-title sequences themselves. Here, Bond, dressed not in a tuxedo or suit and tie but in the open-collared shirt and jacket from his struggle, does not walk across the screen, and the gun barrel does not run before the pre-title sequence. He only turns and fires on Dryden's contact, with the white bathroom tile in the background, a mundane, perhaps even vulgar backdrop for the heretofore sophisticated British spy.

Even the title credits themselves are 'wrong' in the Bond tradition. Nearly all of the Bond films, including *Dr No* (where colourful female silhouettes dance to the upbeat 'Jamaican Rock'), have made use of women during the title sequences and increasingly stepped up the sexual innuendos through their mixture of guns and female figures. As Charles Taylor notes, these psychedelic visions, again a product of Maurice Binder's imagination, reach their peak in the opening to *The Spy Who Loved Me*, 'a sly joke on the phallic imagery in the Bond films', as Bond's 'huge gun barrel ... serves as balance beam and parallel bars for naked women to cartwheel along or swing from' (2007). Moreover, they speak, in rather overt Freudian terms, to Bond's über-masculinity and to the sexuality that the films are selling, with Bond and his 'gun' becoming the ultimate male fantasy and the object of feminine worship. In *Casino Royale*, however, there are no nude silhouettes or belly dancers or gold female forms onscreen during the title credits – only Eva Green's face appears on the queen playing card momentarily as the gunsight passes over it. Throughout the entire sequence, the focus is on Craig's Bond (or an animated version thereof) firing at villains and engaging enemies in hand-to-hand combat amidst a landscape of playing cards. As his foes fall, they explode gloriously into hearts or diamonds, and dead male figures, mortally wounded with a diamond, heart, spade or club, litter the screen. As Craig glares out at the viewer towards the end of the credits, gun in hand, there can be little doubt that this is no barely-disguised Binder sexual metaphor, no fetishistic female worship of the British super-spy. Rather, Bond is all business here, a killer with a job to do, and, amidst the roulette wheels and casino games, there is more at stake than just money.

Add one part sophistication

This Bond is also not quite as sophisticated as his predecessors, or, at the very least, the film emphasises different aspects of the Bond persona. As Deborah Banner points out, the figure of Bond is based upon 'shifting character traits [that] have given him the power to unite ideologically inconsistent forces' (2002: 123). His political inclinations, from conservative consumer to liberal democrat, and his specific sexual tastes, from self-indulgent hedonist to dedicated monogamist, evolve and transform to suit the changing times. Michael Denning suggests that the question of Bond's class status is a part of this formula: 'is he really an upper-class clubman, trained in the public school ethic, or is he an Americanised "classless" moderniser, bringing "the white heat of technology" to the spy thriller?' (2003: 58). Cork and Scivally explain that, in bringing *Dr No* to the screen, the filmmakers deliberately laboured to portray Bond as 'the ultimate in urbane sophistication. 007's stylistic choices had to be impeccable. In short, Bond had to know more about the finer things in life than the audience, than anyone' (2002: 36). Throughout the films, Bond's cultural awareness is, indeed, extraordinary and his tastes distinctive and refined. He returns to the refrigerator for another bottle of champagne because, as he tells Jill Masterson (Shirley Eaton) in *Goldfinger*, 'there are some things that just aren't done, such as drinking Dom Perignon '53 above the temperature of 38 degrees Fahrenheit', a crime that he compares to 'listening to the Beatles without earmuffs'. He later annoys M (Bernard Lee) during their dinner with Colonel Smithers (Richard Vernon) through his analysis of the colonel's 'disappointing brandy', 'a thirty-year old fine, indifferently blended ... with an overdose of bon bois'. (In *Diamonds Are Forever* (1971), Bond similarly outdoes his boss with his analysis of a sherry; although, as M informs him, 'there are no years for sherry', Bond is still able to give a year for 'the original vintage on which the sherry is based'.) In *From Russia With Love* (1963), Bond kicks himself for not suspecting the muscular Grant (Robert Shaw), who is, in some ways, more like Craig's Bond, sooner since he ordered 'red wine with fish'. After narrowly escaping from a crashing plane in *The Living Daylights*, Timothy Dalton's Bond is encouraged by a sign that says '200 km. to Karachi' because, as he informs the cellist Kara Milovy (Maryam d'Abo), he knows 'a great restaurant in Karachi', and they 'can just make dinner!' And, by the time that Pierce Brosnan signs on for the role in *GoldenEye*, Bond's reputation in the spy world is almost absurdly clichéd. Valentin Zukovsky's men, in fact, share a laugh over the Russian's description of him as 'charming, sophisticated secret agent; shaken, but not stirred?'

There are touches in the films that work against Bond's aristocratic lifestyle and that do perhaps contribute to the 'everyman' quality that Banner identifies. Connery's casting, for example, made the character's social background a little more ambiguous. Cork and Scivally note that 'Connery's working-class exterior made Bond a hero who was harder to label as a snob' (2002: 36). And Moore's Bond immediately bristles in *The Man With The Golden Gun* (1974) when Scaramanga (Christopher Lee) contrasts his million dollar assassin's salary with Bond's job as a British agent: 'You work for peanuts, a hearty well done from Her Majesty the Queen and a pittance of a pension. Apart from that we are the same.' For Bond, who consistently prides himself on being the most cultured man in the room, this slight strikes at his core, and he cannot resist retaliating by questioning Scaramanga's qualifications as 'a gentleman.' Through the material excesses that the films continually glorify, from the title and plot references to diamonds and gold to the first-class hotels and exotic locations, however, Bond's upper-class sophistication (or the well-crafted guise of that sophistication) appears at the forefront of who he is. In constructing Bond as male fantasy, Rebecca Carpenter therefore conceives of him as 'an economic/material success, who earns a comfortable living, occasionally nets big financial prizes thanks to his gambling and sporting talents, and gets to live high on expense accounts – driving fast cars, drinking the best champagne, eating incredible meals, smoking quality cigarettes' (2002: 190).

In *Casino Royale*, conversely, Bond's illusion is revealed. Where the other films turned on the fantasy of what male viewers would be, the new film instead shows Bond as something not unlike what most of them are – someone born from more humble origins who aspires to something more. During their conversation on the train to Montenegro, the perceptive Vesper Lynd sees through Bond's well-educated façade, to the man who wears his suit with 'disdain' because he did not 'come from money' and to the orphan who was forced to endure the contempt of his classmates. She also deduces the origin of the chip on [his] shoulder', the by-product of being given a high-class education through 'someone else's charity'. Throughout the film, Bond struggles to blend in, but he is frequently unable to contain his social anxieties or suppress his class prejudices. Aside from the symbolic meaning of Bond's open collar and the bathroom tile in the pre-title sequence – Bond, in fact, appears more at home in short-sleeved shirts during *Casino Royale* than in designer suits and ties – he demonstrates his sensitivity at the Hotel Club in the Bahamas when a guest mistakes him for a valet, leading him to smash the guest's car into a railing and set off a row of car alarms in the process. Prior to his high-stakes card game with Le Chiffre, Bond's taste in clothes is even criticised by Vesper, who schools him in the study of dinner jackets and picks one out for him on her own because he needs to look 'like a man who belongs at that table'. But like his million dollar bankroll, his top-of-the-line Aston Martin, Bond's place at the table is not one that he has earned on his own. Instead, it is one that has been bought for him, one that serves to perpetuate the insecurity and the truth that he vainly tries to mask. Where the other Bonds could sip their vodka martinis in peace, Craig's class concerns continue to keep him both shaken and stirred.

Add some clever gadgets

Bond film purists must also balk at the lack of gadgets in this film. After all, how could Bond get by without his ultra-cool set of toys, the latest in spy technology? Bond's inventive accessories, courtesy of Q, have come to define him, along with his inherent ability to apply them so appropriately to inflict the most damage on his enemies, discover a central plot point and/or remove a woman's clothing. No matter how much or little time Q spends on explaining these devices to Bond or that Bond spends practising and mastering them, he immediately knows how, where and when to use them, and this aspect of his character again speaks to his uncanny sophistication. Writing about *Goldfinger*, Patrick O'Donnell points out that Bond is 'briefed only once by Q on the [Aston Martin's] elaborate controls [but] in the film's car chase scene [he] instinctively moves from gadget to gadget in foiling his pursuers' (2005: 63). When the new Q (John Cleese) hands 007 the sizable manual on his latest Aston Martin ('The Vanish') in *Die Another Day* (2002), with the suggestion that he will 'be able to shoot through that in a couple of hours', Bond playfully throws it in front of the car's target-seeking guns, blasting it to pieces. Regardless of the changes or upgrades to the model, he is again able to use it to maximum efficiency with little or no studying or any practice behind the wheel, engaging its invisibility-stealth option to investigate Graves' Ice Palace in Iceland or to trick the terrorist Zao (Rick Yune) into driving his car off a ledge, and creatively activating the ejector seat option to right it during their car duel on the ice. Bond, moreover, does not have to be in the driver's seat to get the job done. In *Tomorrow Never Dies* (1997), he skilfully steers his souped-up BMW around the tight corners of a multi-storey parking garage to evade, elude and baffle his pursuers, all from the back seat of his car and the touchpad on his mobile phone. Whether he is using a car, boat, ski, jetpack, gun, suitcase, watch, ring, pen or even a high-speed gondola (in *Moonraker*), he is at once an expert with his equipment and incorporates it into his character, so much so, in fact, that O'Donnell considers Bond as cyborg, 'the merging of the human and machinic in the total subject' (2005: 63).

Given that *Casino Royale* itself is more reminiscent of *Dr No* or *On Her Majesty's Secret Service* (1969), films where MI6's gadgets do not come into play or advance the plot, Bond is not as unsavvy as one might expect about the technology that he does use in the film. He is able to review the previous incoming call on the bomb-maker's mobile phone, and, after breaking into M's (Judi Dench) apartment, he traces it to the Bahamas through her laptop. And, after Bond foils the plot to blow up the airliner in Miami, M has a tracer installed in his forearm, the literal merging of man and machine. But, when his life depends on it, when Le Chiffre's girlfriend poisons his drink and a frantic Bond contacts MI6 for help, he cannot get the defibrillator in his car to work in time, accidentally pulling out one of the leads in the process. (Only Vesper's timely arrival saves his life.) Bond's Aston Martin also does not function here as a mechanical extension of the hero, saving him from danger and outdoing his enemies. In an attempt to avoid Vesper out on the dark highway, he flips the car over multiple times, leaving them both a wreck. (Typically, Bond does not wreck his cars until he has made use of all of their 'optional extras', as Dalton calls them in *The Living Daylights*.) Again, this aspect of the film points to a sophistication, instinctual or otherwise, that Bond does not have and, perhaps, refers to the social recasting of the character. Where O'Donnell considers the development of Bond's 'cyber-aristocratic identity' in the previous films (2005: 66), Bond is clearly not an aristocrat, but more of a pretender in this film, and his inability to fully make use of the technology at his disposal speaks to his failed attempt to assume this identity and to the human beneath the defibrillator and behind the wheel.

Add one part torture

And then there is the matter of Bond's torture in *Casino Royale*, certainly one of the most unsettling scenes in the series' history. Other Bonds have been tortured or threatened by their nemeses, of course. In fact, Connery is tortured in his very first turn as Bond in *Dr No*. After the spy taunts his plans for world domination, the sinister scientist orders his henchman to 'soften him up'. Tied to a chair in *You Only Live Twice* (1967), Bond is grilled by SPECTRE's female underling Number 11, who tries to unnerve him by brandishing 'a dermatone', which plastic surgeons 'use ... to slice off skin'. Kananga (Yaphet Kotto) threatens to maim Moore's Bond in *Live and Let Die* (1973) to determine the extent of his involvement with Solitaire (Jane Seymour), as he tells his claw-armed henchman Tee Hee (Julius W. Harris) to 'snip the little finger of Mr Bond's right hand' if Solitaire fails to answer his questions correctly. Brosnan's Bond is threatened with 'chakra torture', designed to inflict 'the maximum amount of pain whilst keeping the victim alive for as long as possible' in *Tomorrow Never Dies*, and nearly strangled to death in Elektra King's (Sophie Marceau) antique torture chair in *The World Is Not Enough* (1999). And, in *Die Another Day*, he is held captive in North Korea and beaten, drowned and repeatedly stung by scorpions over the course of 14 months, until he is exchanged for the terrorist Zao.

Banner points out that, generally, the 'villains throughout the Bond saga are unambiguously fascinated, even obsessed with 007' (2002: 128), and, as such, Bond's masculinity is often the target of their attacks on him, in some cases literally. They want to destroy what they cannot possess or have. In the famous laser scene from *Goldfinger*, Bond is strapped down to a table as Goldfinger's (Gert Frobe) laser burns perilously close towards his groin, a position of 'emasculated spectatorship', in Banner's words, inasmuch as Bond can do nothing more than 'watch as a stronger force looms' (2002: 130). Similarly, in *Never Say Never Again* (1983; the remake of *Thunderball*) Fatima Blush (Barbara Carrera) attempts to demonstrate her superiority to Bond by emasculating him. Aiming her gun at his groin and symbolically asserting a kind of masculine dominance over the über-male Bond, she menacingly asks him, 'Guess where you get the first one?'

In spite of Bond's obvious torments, however, he is never injured in any lasting way and rarely shows any cuts, bruises or scrapes for all of his onscreen fights, duels, car crashes or interrogations. (In *The World Is Not Enough*, Q reminds 007, 'Never let them see you bleed'.) As the men begin their work in *Dr No*, the camera noticeably turns away to spare the audience the horror of seeing their hero treated so cruelly, and, barely bruised from their beating, he is up and about infiltrating Dr No's lair shortly thereafter. While Number 11 shows Bond the surgical blade, she never uses it on him. Instead, oddly, she frees him so that they can embrace, and Bond winds up using the knife to cut the straps on her dress. Tee Hee never cuts off Bond's fingers, even when Solitaire is wrong. Bond and Wai Lin (Michelle Yeoh) also fight their way out of Elliot Carver's (Jonathan Pryce) clutches before Stamper (Götx Otto) can begin his chakra torture, and, though Elektra cranks up her torture chair, Bond chases her up a flight of stairs and shoots her shortly thereafter, all without a chiropractic adjustment or prescription for painkillers. And though the North Korean military tries to break him in *Die Another Day*, Bond immediately returns to form after a shave and a haircut in one of Hong Kong's finest hotels. He even talks his way out of Goldfinger's plan to kill him, convincing the criminal mastermind that he may know enough to jeopardise Operation Grand Slam, and he outwits Fatima by using the slightly faulty explosive in his pen to destroy her. If Bond is heroic male fantasy, then the villains can do their worst, but they will never really do him any harm.

But Bond is not so lucky in *Casino Royale*. While he is durable, he is not invulnerable. As James Chapman points out, 'Bond ... for the first time, is seriously seen to bleed. He emerges plausibly cut and bruised' from his exhaustive pursuit of the incredibly agile bomb-maker Mollaka (Sébastien Foucan) in Madagascar and through his attempt to thwart the terrorist Carlos (Claudio Santamaria) at the airport in Miami (2007: 251). Where Bond's bloody nose from his sword fight with Gustav Graves (Toby Stephens) does not even carry over to the next scene in *Die Another Day*, here he still bears his cuts

James Bond (Daniel Craig) feeling rattled after killing two men in hand-to-hand combat in *Casino Royale* (2006)

from Miami when M debriefs him back in the Bahamas. Bond is also 'covered in blood (his own as well as the African's)' after his harrowing struggle down the stairs with the African terrorist Steven Obanno (Isaach De Bankolé) at Montenegro, a fight that Chapman considers to be 'the most sordid' of all his fights in the film (2007: 251). Staring into the bathroom mirror afterwards as the blood runs down his face, he is forced to guzzle down liquor to steady himself and to deal with the burden of what he has just done and what he must do. When was the last time we saw Connery's Bond unsteady after a kill or Moore's Bond unsettled by hand-to-hand combat?

Following suit and taking a few pages from Fleming's original, the filmmakers, in the ultimate 'transgression' against the Bond film legacy, do not turn away from Bond's torture in *Casino Royale*, but rather show it in graphic detail. For all of the other threats that are made on Bond this way in the other films, no one ever actually carries them out. Whether out of decorum or politeness or respect, his enemies always seem to adhere to certain rules of engagement and certain standards of civility. Even after their inability to break Bond through 14 months of torture, the North Koreans never go after his private parts. Here, instead, we see Bond bloody, distraught and physically stripped, just as Vesper emotionally 'strips' his armour from him, the invulnerable hero now presented at his most vulnerable, both as a hero and as a man. In an attempt to get the password to his winnings, Le Chiffre unceremoniously abandons 'all [of] these elaborate tortures' that have characterised the previous Bond films and instead opts for 'the simplest thing', repeatedly whipping a heavy knotted rope into Bond's groin. We see Bond scream and strain and sweat in agony as Le Chiffre continues his assault. We also see the concern on his face as he hears Vesper scream from another room and fears for her well-being, a well-being that Le Chiffre alludes to and uses as he tries to break the strong-willed spy.

What is particularly impressive about this scene is that, though it breaks the rules for the Bond film formula and though the scene is so horrific, in the end it shows the depth of his strength and integrity, a depth that we do not get from the previous portrayals of 007. While his tormenter disturbingly promises that 'there will be little left to identify [him] as a man' if he does not 'yield in time'. Bond refuses to bargain with the terrorist-banker, but rather boldly goes on to taunt and goad him as his torture continues. Even when Le Chiffre mentions the more than likely possibility that Bond's government will protect him in exchange for information ('the big picture') and that his resistance may all be for naught, Bond, impressively, still refuses to talk, a fact that leads the frustrated killer, finally, to brandish a knife and kneel down to 'feed [him] what [he seems] not to value'.

We also see Bond recuperate from the beating that he sustains at the hands of Le Chiffre, a recuperation that is generally absent from the Bond tradition. Bond, in fact, almost never needs a doctor or a surgeon or any recovery time at all from his adventures, since he rarely sustains an injury on the job. At the beginning of *Dr No*, M, in justifying the switch from Bond's Baretta to the Walther PPK, notes that Bond's gun jammed on his last mission, and he 'spent six months in hospital in consequence', but the film never shows us this scene or Bond's injury or scar, perhaps because this image of Bond in a weakened convalescing state would again be contrary to the portrayal of the hero as fantasy. And though he suffers a dislocated collarbone after his sky high fall at the beginning of *The World Is Not Enough*, he is immediately able to get back on active duty by discarding his arm sling and having sex with his female doctor. Even when he is sent off to a health clinic by his new boss in *Never Say Never Again* to 'eliminate all free radicals' from

his system, Bond is soon sleeping with a clinic nurse, snacking on smuggled vodka and caviar, and duking it out with an assassin in the weight room (the ideal vacation for a super-spy).

Casino Royale's convalescent James Bond (Daniel Craig)

But, in the film of *Casino Royale*, as in the novel, Bond must be hospitalised after his ordeal with Le Chiffre, and not only do we see him at his most unmanly, passed out in a hospital bed and resting in a lounge chair by Lake Como, but Vesper and Bond also speculate as to the extent of his injuries and the remaining state of his manhood. 'Whatever is left of me, whatever I am', Bond romantically professes to Vesper, 'I'm yours'. Ironically, though, as unmanly as this may seem in comparison to the impervious 007s of yore, the film suggests that Bond's masculinity or his 'mojo', in the words of spoof spy Austin Powers, is more than just a matter of anatomy. As Vesper explains, Bond would still be 'more of a man than anyone [she has] ever known', even if all that he had left was his 'smile' and his 'little finger'. While Le Chiffre and the other villains of the world may be able to inflict pain and punishment on Bond's body, they will never really be able to get at what they desire most, his masculinity, because, according to the film, this aspect of his character and his personality is an intangible beyond the physical.

Stir in several beautiful women

Bond's relationship with Vesper marks a further change in the character from the previous films. For all of the relationships that Bond has had with women over the years, rarely has he ever gotten close enough to any of them to feel anything beyond the bedroom. He barely has the attention span to focus on one woman beyond half the film – in a typical film, Bond's libido usually requires at least two different women in a two-hour span to keep him happy – and, in spite of the adventures that he shares with them and the intensity of their experiences together, his interest never makes it beyond the final credits. Regardless of how attached any one woman is to Bond (or Bond to her), he almost never refers to her in a subsequent film or during his next mission, and they never seem to make any lasting impression upon him. (In a rare exception, he places flowers on his wife's grave at the beginning of *For Your Eyes Only* (1981).) Lee Pfeiffer, who believes that Bond's involvement with women may be 'the most defining aspect of [his] lifestyle' (2006: 30), notes that, 'with the exception of the Lazenby film [*On Her Majesty's Secret Service*], his lovers have been sexual conquests rather than emotional relationships' (ibid.). While critics like Robert Arp and Kevin S. Decker argue that 'Bond's treatment of women is a glaring case of objectification' (2006: 203), Pfeiffer offers the defence of 'Bond apologists', who maintain that these women 'use him as much for their selfish pleasure as he uses them for his' and that they are 'the ultimate symbols of female liberation: highly intelligent, highly capable, and very courageous' (2006: 30). Frequently, Bond does manage to use these relationships to help inherently good, but misguided women, like Jill Masterson and Pussy Galore (Honor Blackman) in *Goldfinger*, Domino Derval (Claudine Auger) in *Thunderball*, Solitaire in *Live and Let Die* and Kara Milovy in *The Living Daylights*, realise the error of their ways in associating themselves with criminal masterminds and madmen. Considering his reputation and his effect on women, SPECTRE assassin Fiona Volpe (Luciana Paluzzi) describes it this way in *Thunderball*: 'James Bond ... only has to make love to a woman, and she starts to hear heavenly choirs singing. She repents and immediately returns to the side of right and virtue.' In some ways, whether they do have this religious conversion and 'repent' or not almost seems to matter less to Bond than the physical conquest itself. Both Volpe and Elektra King are immune to Bond's ennobling charms, but Bond never appears to be emotionally wounded by their betrayals. They never affect him in any deep psychological way or, at least, in any way that we see on film. In both cases, he coldly reduces their relationships to the most basic physical level. As he bluntly tells a supremely confident Elektra, 'You meant nothing to me. One last screw.'

Also, whether Bond's women live or die almost does not seem to matter either in the end, as long as he has someone to kiss when the closing theme starts, and this lack of remorse contributes to what O'Donnell describes as 'the notion of Bond as a sex machine' (2005: 64), again with the emphasis on 'machine'. He appears horrified and angered by Goldfinger's 'golden' punishment of Jill Masterson, who is iconically spray-painted from head to toe in gold paint, but Bond moves on to approaching her sister and sleeping with the ever-resistant Pussy Galore. When Japanese agent Aki (Akiko Wakabayashi), for whom Bond demonstrates such fondness, is poisoned by an assassin aiming for the British spy in *You Only*

Live Twice, Bond is barely affected and quickly turns his attention to his mock wedding with Kissy Suzuki (Mie Hama) and to his desire for a mock honeymoon to go along with it. Bond also admits, in *Tomorrow Never Dies*, that former flame Paris Carver (Teri Hatcher) got 'too close for comfort', but, after she is killed on her media magnate husband's orders, he only momentarily mourns her, too, before he is laughing it up from the back seat of his remote controlled BMW and combining forces with the acrobatic Chinese agent Wai Lin. And as tragic as the death of Bond's wife Tracy (Diana Rigg) is at the end of *On Her Majesty's Secret Service*, he is soon back in action and bedding down smuggler Tiffany Case (Jill St. John) in the next film, *Diamonds Are Forever*, without so much as a tear. Who says that love never lasts?

Bond, however, is both less and more in *Casino Royale*. He hardly puts on the guise of caring for the women that he meets and, as he tells Dimitrios's (Simon Abkarian) wife Solange (Caterina Murino), he is primarily attracted to married women because 'it keeps things simple'. Bond initially tells Vesper that she is not his type because she is single. As long as the women are married, he does not have to worry about the possibility of any long-term commitment. Although Solange quickly realises that Bond's interest in her is only based upon his desire to get to her husband, she is still willing to sleep with him, but, unlike his predecessors, Bond is ready to discard her once he has what he needs. Learning that Dimitrios is on a flight to Miami, he specifically orders champagne and caviar to his room 'for one'. Other Bonds might have tried to find time for her, even for just one night, but, for Craig, duty calls.

Through the intense experience of their mission and the nightmarish intimacy of their torture, though, Bond does give his heart (and whatever else 'is left of' him) to Vesper Lynd. He admits that he loves her and promises to 'quit [MI6] and float around the world' with her, secure in the knowledge that he is leaving 'with what little [soul he has] left'. Rarely has a Bond made such a commitment to a woman before or allowed himself to become so vulnerable. Typically, he wears his emotional 'armour', as Vesper calls it, like the designer suits that he sports with such flair. Perhaps the only exception is Lazenby's Bond, who proposes to the troubled Contessa Tracy di Vicenzo in *On Her Majesty's Secret Service* and similarly decides to leave his job for his wife, since 'an agent shouldn't be concerned with anything but himself'. In the film's tragic ending, as the once suicidal Tracy now looks forward to the future that Bond has given her, she is gunned down by Blofeld (Telly Savalas) and his assistant Irma Bunt (Ilse Steppat), and we see the agent overcome, maintaining that 'she is having a rest' as she lies lifeless in his arms.

In *Casino Royale*, however, Bond's commitment and the wound that he is dealt are that much deeper because of Vesper's betrayal. While Bond believes that everyone has 'a tell' except Vesper, his love for her blinds him to the truth and demonstrates just how invested he is in their relationship. Preparing for their new life together, he never suspects that Vesper has taken his poker winnings and is using the money as part of a bargain that she has made. (Compare this betrayal to Fiona Volpe's in *Thunderball* or Elektra's in *The World Is Not Enough*. In both cases, Bond is not so shocked or disappointed because he suspected them to begin with.) He only finds out when M calls to enquire about the money. And after Vesper's death, where we again see Bond holding the dead body of the woman he loves, his bitterness is readily apparent, as he coldly tells M that 'the job's done and the bitch is dead'. For Bond, the betrayal is first and foremost in his mind, and he would try to deny his feelings and maintain his steely façade for M by reducing the enormity of what has taken place with this one sentence. Even here Bond, so caught up in his anger, misses the point and the extent of Vesper's sacrifice. M has to explain the extent of the tragedy to him, too, and the 'obvious' reason why he survived Le Chiffre's torture: that Vesper made a deal to save him and that she knew that, in doing so, 'she was going to her death'. Where Bond is normally portrayed as being so wise in the ways of women and the world and so quick to size up any situation, romantic or otherwise, *Casino Royale* instead shows us a spy who is quick to follow his heart and who is caught up in a relationship whose complexity largely escapes him.

Add one great spy

This complexity, moreover, extends to the scope of his mission as well. In the other films, Bond is generally the best spy that the British government has to offer. When a US spaceship is stolen at the beginning of *You Only Live Twice*, Bond is sent to investigate. When a US nuclear submarine is stolen at the beginning of *The Spy Who Loved Me*, M immediately tells the Prime Minister that he will put his 'best man on it at once' before calling Bond. As Bond and Christmas Jones (Denise Richards) try to disarm a bomb in the King pipeline in *The World Is Not Enough*, M reassures Elektra, 'He's the best we have, though I'd never tell him'. Margaret Thatcher similarly conceives that Bond's 'courage and resourcefulness are a credit to the nation' at the end of *For Your Eyes Only*. Even the Russians have to admit that Bond is that good. After saving Silicon Valley from rogue KGB operative Max Zorin (Christopher Walken) in *A View To A Kill* (1985), the Soviet government awards him the Order of Lenin, making him 'the first ever non-Soviet citizen to receive this award'. If world peace and the safety of the planet are at stake, Bond always gets the call and with good reason. Who else could get to the bottom of such international intrigue, flush out the villains and get them to reveal all of their evil plans within the scope of two hours? Carly Simon's song at the beginning of *The Spy Who Loved Me* says it all: 'Nobody Does It Better'.

Regardless of how complicated the scheme is, Bond somehow manages to figure it all out, if the villains do not go ahead and do it for him, and this ability, as well as the villain's role in the plot's revelation, is also part of the recipe. At Goldfinger's Kentucky compound, he deduces the meaning of the mad millionaire's association with the Chinese scientist and the dual inspiration behind Operation Grand Slam: '[The Chinese] get what they want, economic chaos in the West. And the value of your gold increases many times.' Trying to understand the connection between Mr Big and Dr Kananga in *Live and Let Die*, Bond gets the dictator to reveal his plans to give away over a billion dollars in heroin and monopolise the drug market, leaving him and the phone company 'the only two going monopolies in this nation for years to come'. And, in *Tomorrow Never Dies*, after Wai Lin is captured by Carver's men, a concealed Bond, having faked his death, listens in as Carver explains the specifics of his plan to start a war between England and China, a war whose resolution will ultimately give the media mogul 'exclusive broadcasting rights in China for the next hundred years'. Like his superiors, Bond's villains, too, must acknowledge that he is the very best and that, in being that good, that accomplished, that sophisticated, he is, in the words of Dr No, 'the one man ... capable of appreciating what [they have] done'.

But, in *Casino Royale*, Bond is hardly England's best, at least not yet. His attempt to catch the incredibly agile, free-jumping bomb-maker in Madagascar is botched, to the point where Bond kills him at the Nambutu embassy and sets off an international incident. Instead of returning to the accolades of the Prime Minister, he is denounced in the media for shooting an unarmed man, forcing an irate M to answer for his actions, condemn his stupidity and wistfully long for the days of the Cold War. In contrast to the obvious affection and respect that his other supervisors, as well as his other enemies, had for him, M regretfully admits that 'it was too early to promote' him. This Bond is not a slick international man of mystery – 'yeah, baby', in the words of Austin Powers – or a super-spy who brings finesse to his licence to kill and can balance a keen sense of world politics with smugglers, terrorists and hired guns. Rather, he is, as M so dismissively calls him, 'a blunt instrument', physical, forceful and violent. Although M later goes on to voice her belief in his character – 'I knew that you would be you', she tells him – Bond's 'bluntness' is still something that must be honed through the experience of the film.

Where this Bond myopically focuses on the value of killing one bomb-maker, he needs to see, as M initially explains, 'the big picture', and Bond's encounters with the other major characters in the film – Vesper, Le Chiffre and Mathis (Giancarlo Giannini) – essentially teach him that lesson and the others that he will need to be successful as a spy, lessons that he must learn through deception, suffering and pain. So concerned with his own relationships and interactions with both Vesper and Le Chiffre, he fails to anticipate that his government will protect Le Chiffre, just as he fails to realise Vesper's sacrifice, because he does not readily see the big picture. He also never suspects that his 'friend Mathis' might be 'Le

Chiffre's friend Mathis' or that Mathis might be betraying him all along. In all three cases, someone else has to explain to Bond what is going on. And, unlike the explanations that Bond typically gets from the megalomaniacs and deranged super-villains of the world, explanations that resolve all of the problems in the films and immediately reveal the villain's objective or his weakness, Bond is still left in the dark at the end.

Casino Royale leaves both Bond and the audience with more questions than it ever really answers. Bond never gets to use his villain's weakness against him – Mr White (Jesper Christensen) kills him. He never finds out exactly what Le Chiffre knows. He never finds out what organisation is behind the banker or his murder or the kidnapping of Vesper's boyfriend. He never even finds out if Mathis is, in fact, guilty of anything; suspicious now of a 'double blind', however, he can no longer believe in the agent's innocence and leaves him for further 'sweating'. Broken-hearted from Vesper's betrayal and death, he learns the painful lesson that he cannot trust anybody, a lesson that M clearly endorses. Yet, through it all, as M notes at the end, 'the trail's gone cold', and the real villains, whoever they might be, are still out there, still beyond him. The world may not be enough for the other Bonds, but, for this one, it is too much, too complex to understand, too confusing to navigate.

Shake well...

And so, in the Bond tradition, this one is all wrong. He is brutish and crude at times. He does not subdue or dispatch his victims with flair or finesse. More often than not, his kills are violent, physical, bloody affairs. He is not the most sophisticated man in the room nor is he the acknowledged master of every situation. He is also not the best agent that MI6 has to offer. He does not walk around with the perfect gadget for every situation or use the equipment at his disposal to its utmost. His hair is the wrong colour. He cannot even get the drink order right. But, having said all of that, he may be the most fully realised Bond in the series' history. Pfeiffer suggests that Bond is generally an 'opaque' character and 'one of the least important elements of his screen adventures. His primary focus is to serve as a catalyst for the actions of the far more interesting characters with whom he interacts' (2006: 24). Here, we get a Bond who is flawed, who makes mistakes, and who, at times, is outwitted. In the process, we get a Bond who is an actual character.

These imperfections, these flaws, these cracks in his armour work because they give him a humanity and a sympathy that he never really had. In the past, the question was not if 007 would succeed; the question was how. We did not go to a Bond film because the ending was in doubt. We went to see how he would get there. We went to watch the perpetuation of an icon or a fantasy or an ideal and to believe it for two hours even when our most sceptical sides told us otherwise. For all that those other films might have done for him, this is the first to make him human, to show him bloody, confused, struggling and unsettled. Bond the 'cyborg', as O'Donnell calls him, gives way to Bond the man.

Critics of the Craig selection and the Bond reboot have gone so far as to set up a website, aptly named *Daniel Craig is Not Bond*, in order to voice their displeasure towards the change in the franchise and the previous tone of the films. The site specifically charges that '*Casino Royale* and its attendant publicity seemed to send out the message to long term Bond fans that "the previous films were all rubbish and you were idiots for enjoying them"' (Anon. 2007). The same criticism, perhaps, could be levelled against any of the spy send-ups, like the *Austin Powers* films (1997, 1999, 2002), *Spy Hard* (1996) or *Johnny English* (2003). *Casino Royale*, however, is not so much a critique of the legacy or the genre as it is a necessary recontextualisation of it. Where Bond was once a Cold War hero or a fantasy spawned from it, the reconfiguration of the political climate requires a reconfigured Bond. Without the Soviet Union or SPECTRE, which gun barrel could he aim for next? Terrorism seems like the most obvious choice, but our sense of Bond's heroism after 9/11 and the 'war on terror' certainly must be different than it was before then. Could we, in good faith, go to a Bond film where he insightfully broke up a terrorist cell and captured its leader single-handedly before the popcorn got cold and the drinks got warm when such success beyond the theatre has been so much harder to come by? Could we believe that any one spy could have all the answers when so many elude the combined might of our intelligence communities? (Even other forays into this genre, like the Jason Bourne films (*The Bourne Identity* (2002), *The Bourne Supremacy* (2004), *The Bourne Ultimatum* (2007)) or the *Mission Impossible* movies (1996, 2000, 2006), perpetuate this vision of the 'super-spy', either one step ahead of their enemies or quickly able to catch up and outwit them in the end.) This Bond does not indict or dismiss his predecessors. But he has become a hero for contemporary times, operating in circumstances closer to our own, where the tells are harder to spot and the truth is harder to come by. Like us, he struggles, humanly, to make sense of the big picture and suffers through the process of trying to understand. And his sacrifices and his losses beyond the gaming tables, like our own, can no longer be so easily forgotten or dismissed with a well-timed quip. Getting Bond wrong in *Casino Royale* is right for right now, right for a film franchise in need of new energy and right for audiences who themselves play the odds in a world where they do give a damn.

3

HARDLY THE BIG PICTURE: THE ELLIPSIS AND NARRATIVES OF INTERRUPTION IN *CASINO ROYALE*

Jason Sperb

'I think something's driving you ... And I think I'll never know what that is.'

The above line is spoken to Vesper Lynd (Eva Green) by the newest James Bond (Daniel Craig) late in *Casino Royale* (2006). Despite its inherent ambiguity and central mystery, the statement itself is actually a rare moment of clarity for Bond in the film. It is the recognition that he knows he does not know anything – a logic which also informs the film's narrative structure. The line seems to fit Vesper's ambiguous behaviour in the film as 'a complicated woman', but it also works to illuminate Bond himself. He is never quite sure what is driving her and thus, by extension, what is driving himself – though it is ultimately something akin to the amorphous 'big picture', a concept (repeated twice in the film) which is both crucial and utterly meaningless to Bond. Eventually, it is the mystery of Vesper which drives him too, even beyond the boundaries of the film's finale ('vesper' is also *literally* a code to decipher in the film – highlighted by Bond's decision to use her name as the password to access crucial bank funds). One of the last lines that Vesper says to Bond in the end is that you 'cannot forget the past'. Vesper cannot outrun her past, and by the end of the film, Bond cannot outrun hers either. Moreover, it is her nebulous background which ultimately motivates him, and leads him to the main villain in *Casino Royale*'s closing moments. This co-presence of ambiguity and drive, moreover, gives an added resonance to Vesper's earlier admonition to Bond that women should be a *'meaningful pursuit'*, rather than 'disposable pleasures'. What narratively structures *Casino Royale* is the presence of a richly meaningful pursuit, but the meanings and the directions are not always so clear. And yet the film manages to sustain itself around this uncertainty.

Moreover, there are other clues to this sense of a carefully-crafted narrative ambiguity in *Casino Royale*, besides Bond's line to Vesper. Earlier, Bond first meets his perceived primary nemesis, Le Chiffre (Mads Mikkelsen), face-to-face. Le Chiffre knows his real name is James Bond, even though he is working under the alias 'Arnold Beech'. In a previous scene, Bond registered at the hotel that hosts the film's centrepiece poker tournament as 'James Bond' to complicate the situation and gauge Le Chiffre's response. When they finally meet and shake hands, Le Chiffre playfully says to him, 'Welcome, Mr "Beech" ... or is that "Bond"? I'm a little confused.' Bond, without missing a beat, says, 'Well, we wouldn't want that, would we?', then turns to the bar and walks away without further conversation. Bond's line and dismissal, of course, are played as a joke for the audience and as an insult to Le Chiffre; however, both the acknowledgement of the confusion, and Bond's acquiescence to it, suggests a larger trend to the film. Although it is arguable that we never quite learn of Vesper's true motivations, or of the evil organisation behind everything (signified only by the mysterious, deliberately blank, 'Mr White' (Jesper Christensen)), *Casino Royale* is not sloppily constructed as a narrative – Bond's treatment of Le Chiffre here echoes the film's larger premise that we as an audience are meant to be confused.

In the following pages, I hope to show how continual uncertainties throughout the film provide us with several moments of narrative disruption; however, it is this sustained interruption which is not a roadblock, but rather a key to *Casino Royale*'s narrative and thematic movement. As an ideal text for Bond fandom, the movie is itself a film focused on the co-presence of disruption and anticipation. To be more specific, we can see this co-existence in *Casino Royale*'s deployment of different motifs such as the 'big picture'. Moreover, working through an implied narratological structure, I centre this argument on the film's other central motif: the *ellipsis*, a text message code in the film which serves a larger metaphorical function when examining the film as both textual object, and as a point within the Bond franchise. There is of course 'Bond ... James Bond'. But the ellipsis is not just a critical frame to view *Casino Royale*; it is in the film itself. Throughout the first hour of the film, we see and hear references to 'ellipsis' without any explanation of what it signifies. Both literally and metaphorically, the ellipsis articulates and sustains the movie's persistent disruptions – there is no closure in the film.

Umberto Eco has previously analysed Ian Fleming's original novel of the same name that formed the (loose) basis for *Casino Royale*. 'In the last pages of *Casino Royale*', writes Eco, 'Fleming, in fact, renounces all psychology as a motive for narrative and decides to transfer characters and situations to the level of an objective and conventional structural strategy' (2003: 36). For Eco, this means that Bond's betrayal by Vesper serves as one central agent in the character's conversion away from his own neurosis and towards the exterior story world of people and events. In other words, Bond ceases to have any internal motivation as a central character, which thus causes the novels (and later films) to construct and then follow the same formula. While it is questionable that this new particular Bond will move away from the unconscious or from feelings (not with a title like *Quantum of Solace* (2008)), there is an interesting narratological shift in this new version of *Casino Royale* that we can begin to see developing from Eco's hypothesis. *Casino Royale* restarts the franchise by creating an elaborate, often unseen, world in which Bond reacts. Whereas earlier Bond films were structured around Bond and his adventures, the continual narrative ambiguity of *Casino Royale* suggests that the surrounding story world structures Bond's behaviour. There is no closure because Bond is only one part of a larger equation – the 'big picture', which dictates actions to Bond more so than the reverse. Only at the very end does Bond obtain some degree of knowledge, and hence power. 'Bond ceased to be a subject of psychiatry', writes Eco, 'and remained at the most a physiological object' (2003: 35). In the newest film, too, we see how Bond becomes a remarkable, physical *presence* to anchor this complicated world.

Thus, in *Casino Royale*, the centre is literally embodied by the excellent work of Daniel Craig – and not only that he is Bond, but that he *becomes* Bond over the course of the two-plus hour narrative, in his state of not quite 'James Bond' in the iconic sense. As with *Layer Cake* (2005), another crime film starring Craig, one sees the confidence build and then sustain itself, seeing his performance unfold in time, thus making his eventual 'introduction' that much more powerful. Moreover, Craig is literally positioned as a 'physiological object'. The thrillingly retro title sequence is the first of its kind not to be centred on an objectification of the female body, Maurice Binder-style. In fact, it is Craig himself who is the object. The sequence's final image is a long, patient, extended huge close-up of Craig's face, filling the screen, staring right back at us – as though taunting any remaining doubters in the audience, or those still in denial, about who is now James Bond. Indeed, Craig maintains an intense physical presence throughout the film. His body is prominently displayed on the beach and in the torture scene. After his first kill, we hear Bond breathing heavily. 'Made you *feel* it, did he?' asks Dryden (Malcolm Sinclair) about the experience of murder. (Bond's heavy breathing is juxtaposed with the next scene after the credit sequence, when Le Chiffre struggles to catch his breath with an inhaler after first viewing Obanno's (Isaach De Bankolé) money.) The power of Craig's affect is established in the opening moments, and serves as the physiological anchor that sustains the ambiguous narrative world in which Bond now exists.

Beyond that brutally effective intro sequence, the film has no real beginning or ending. Some critics initially complained that the film is half-an-hour too long. But those same people do not note that the film's plot does not even really begin until an hour in (with the introduction of Vesper and the poker tournament). This is perhaps because they are distracted by the film's first two spectacular action sequences, revolving around two very different chases. But either criticism of the structure misses the point that, ultimately, there is no narrative resolution in the end. Even Mr White's wounding or Vesper's death at the end deliberately raise more questions than they answer, especially the closer one looks. M's (Judi Dench) rhetorical question to Bond about Vesper's true motivation for keeping him alive, for example, does not necessarily contain the answer she thinks. Is Bond's life spared because of Vesper's love, as M believes, or really is it that Bond is kept alive simply because he was the only one who knew the password for accessing the bank funds? As Vesper presciently says to Bond, 'I would [type in the password] if I knew' what the password was.

Moreover, the early extended chase scenes and the film's open-ended narrative reinforce the same point in *Casino Royale* – Bond never figuratively or literally quite gets to where he wants. The trail of clues and half-clues never ends for him, even when the film does. The villains are not quite the people we assume they are. Le Chiffre's perceived ineffectiveness as a villain would miss *Casino Royale*'s explicit and heightened awareness of his own narrative irrelevance. His premature death itself solidifies his own narrative marginality. Le Chiffre may be the most perfect recent Bond villain because he is the first Bond villain to be explicitly positioned in such a way as to highlight how the villain does not really matter in most Bond films. Meanwhile, Bond's final kill is that of a nameless villain wearing half a pair of sunglasses, with one eye exposed – a grotesque image intensified when Bond shoots a nail gun through his covered eye (along with the electrocution in the same sequence, *Casino Royale* also nicely reminds us here that, as serious as this new Bond is at times, he still has not lost his touch for finding silly ways to kill people). Le Chiffre's unexpected end, and those half pair of glasses, *reminds us that this is a film about incompletion*. And yet such interruption also has its roots in the larger history of the Bond films themselves.

'If M was so sure I was bent, she'd have sent a double-0...'

The earliest indication in *Casino Royale* that this is a new James Bond is not so much the presence of a new actor, a process of replacement to which we have become accustomed. Rather, it is Dryden's statement that Bond is not a 'double-0' agent – in fact, it is not only an acknowledgement, but a taunt. He refuses to take Bond seriously because he is not a full member of MI6, which perhaps invites the audience to do likewise. Yet, Bond's cold-blooded assassination of Dryden, followed quickly by a variation on the iconic gun-barrel shot, severs any doubt. He is now '007', but he is also a bona fide threat as James Bond. His quick clean gunshot cuts off Dryden's premonition that 'the second is...'. This interruption is itself anticipated earlier when Dryden is also interrupted saying that it takes two kills to become a double-0 agent. Dryden himself is the 'second' kill, but what else is second? Bond's assassination marks him as '007', while also introducing Craig as the 'second' coming of Bond (in so far as the film restarts the franchise), and marking *Casino Royale* as the start of a 'second' Bond continuity. Hence, the notion of restarting the franchise is very much formally and thematically present in this opening scene. Bond's assassination of Dryden disrupts the latter's speech, but also lays the groundwork for a new beginning. *Casino Royale* violently disrupts the franchise, but creates the conditions for not only new Bond films, but also a new Bond world.

Yet this is only partially novel to the Bond films. As James Chapman has noted, 'as genre films, the Bond movies have to find the right balance between repetition and variation, between continuity and change, so that they can simultaneously provide the sort of entertainment pattern which audiences expect, while at the same time providing new thrills, new set pieces, new variations on old situations' (2003: 94). The Bond franchise may be the single most successful franchise in the history of cinema because of its unabashed willingness to reinvent itself consistently across five different decades, even at times when it does not seem necessary. Hence, we see clearly that to a degree *Casino Royale* is part of the process whereby the Bond films have survived for so long because they consistently disrupt their own rhythm. Those who claim reductively that the Bond films feature an identical formula miss the sometimes stark shifts in tone. Every once in a while, a Bond film will be deliberately different in attitude from the ones that preceded it, even if the predecessor was itself successful. It was only most recently that we see the decision to start over with Craig in *Casino Royale* despite the fact that *Die Another Day* (2002) had been the most profitable Pierce Brosnan Bond film yet, and the filmmakers could have continued down that road if they wanted.

But again, this disruption is rooted in the franchise as a whole. On the heels of five hugely successful Sean Connery films in the 1960s – from *Dr No* (1962) to *You Only Live Twice* (1967) – the Bond producers not only cast a new Bond, George Lazenby (granted, they did not have a choice), but also created a Bond film, *On Her Majesty's Secret Service* (1969), that was unnecessarily but deliberately unlike its predecessors. The result was a film that was more epic, more romantic, but also ultimately more cynical than the Connery films. While the producers could have plugged Lazenby into another *You Only Live Twice*-type of formula, they consciously tried to do something different. Now, flash forward to the early 1980s – although the Roger Moore-in-Space opus, *Moonraker* (1979), had done well financially, the Bond producers realised that the Bond films had become increasingly silly – both with plot elements and with the tongue-in-cheek dialogue. The next film then, *For Your Eyes Only* (1981), was a mixed-bag attempt to be a more serious and 'realistic' spy thriller, while also toning down the humour. The connection between *On Her Majesty's Secret Service* and *For Your Eyes Only* as unique disruptions in the franchise is made explicit in the latter's opening sequence, when Bond not only goes to visit the grave of his dead wife, Tracy (killed in the finale of *On Her Majesty's Secret Service*), but then later re-battles his chief nemesis, Ernst Salvo Blofeld (Donald Pleasence), in the same sequence. Thus, it is probably not a coincidence that Bond's wife is also indirectly referenced ('he was married once, but it was a long time ago') in *Licence to Kill* (1989), the third film to shift the Bond franchise in a darker direction, in no small part as a response to the films which preceded them. *Licence to Kill* fulfilled the promise of a darker Bond, Timothy Dalton, first hinted at in *The Living Daylights* (1987), which itself was an attempt to revise and reframe the tone and content of the franchise in the wake of Roger Moore's more comical Bond.

'On Nov. 17th, Discover How James … Became Bond'

Of course, the promise of a darker Bond put forth in the Dalton version went no further than *Licence to Kill*. It was exactly eleven years prior to *Casino Royale* (17 November) that Pierce Brosnan resurrected the Bond franchise in *GoldenEye* (1995). Both films were directed by Martin Campbell, although they are ultimately quite different. Whereas *Casino Royale* attempts to create an alternate Bond universe, *GoldenEye* attempted to reaffirm all the aspects of the formula that had made the franchise so successful (one might argue that Campbell was deconstructing himself, having known how to pick apart and reassemble something he already knew how to build). The success of *GoldenEye* to appeal to the best of Bond was embodied in no less a figure than Brosnan himself. Pierce Brosnan was very good at being a very generic James Bond. I do not intend that as an insult. He seemed to know that the best Bond in the post-Dalton 1990s was a very hyperreal Bond – that is to say, he negotiated what other Bond actors had brought to the franchise quite well, and in effect became more Bond than Bond (just as George Lazenby had been asked to do, to a lesser extent, while trying to transcend Connery's wake).

Brosnan was tough like Connery, but not *too tough* like Connery. He was tongue-in-cheek like Moore, but not *too tongue-in-cheek* like Moore. He was brooding like Dalton, but not *too brooding* like Dalton. And his films negotiated the generic expectations of the franchise just well enough to stay interesting, if not earth-shattering, and ultimately rebuilding Bond as a uniquely ahistorical character. He was no longer 'a relic of the Cold War', and in fact ceased to be that relic the moment M uttered that now famous line in *GoldenEye*. And ultimately the films, for better and for worse, reflected that, as Brosnan's Bond occasionally embodied all of these qualities. For example, *Casino Royale* was not the first time screenwriters Neal Purvis and Robert Wade attempted a darker and more serious Bond (the tonally awkward *The World Is Not Enough* (1999)). Like Campbell, their previous attempts at experimenting with the boundaries of Bond as a character and as a formula perhaps equipped them to achieve success with both in *Casino Royale*.

To a degree, it is clear then that there is a certain inherent trait to the franchise activated by *Casino Royale*'s explicit narrative and genre disruption and reconstruction. Hence, restarting the franchise, going back to the beginning, seems to be a natural progression for the character. There was a point in the late 1980s and early 1990s when Bond ceased to be a historical figure, and thus evolved into myth. Craig was able to step into the character of James Bond, to recreate an entirely new Bond from the ground up, in part because Brosnan had cemented the genericness of the character (Bond was no longer only a product of the 1960s and 1970s, nor was he any longer just an imitation of 'Connery's Bond' and, to a lesser extent, of 'Moore's Bond').

Additionally, as an intellectual property, *Casino Royale* is the perfect site for a Bond film which both disrupts and restarts the franchise. Of course, it was the original Ian Fleming James Bond novel (published in 1953). But more interesting is the mythology that has developed around the history of the story itself. *Casino Royale* and not *Dr No*, as Bond fans know, was the first Bond novel adapted for the screen, as a 1954 CBS teleplay, starring Barry Nelson as an American James Bond and Peter Lorre as Le Chiffre. Because Ian Fleming sold the rights to that novel separately, it quickly took on a life of its own. In 1967, as Connery's Bond became a global phenomenon, a separate group took the rights to *Casino Royale* and turned it into an incoherent, slapdash and altogether painfully bad spoof of the franchise, starring David Niven, Peter Sellers, Woody Allen and Orson Welles. According to Chapman, producer Charles Feldman 'had apparently wanted to make a "straight" film version of the novel, but having been unable to secure the services of Sean Connery ... he decided to make *Casino Royale* the spy spoof to end all spy spoofs' (2007: 106).

Meanwhile, *Casino Royale* had had the reputation of being the only full-length Ian Fleming novel since the release of *For Your Eyes Only*, not to have been adapted as a part of the franchise – a legacy that started coming to an end in 1999 when the rights were finally reacquired by the Broccoli family that long produced the films. Back then, it was speculated naturally that Brosnan, on the heels of three very successful Bond films, would of course star in it. Only when it became clear that the producers would respect the 'origins' aspect of the novel did it become apparent that Brosnan would not be offered the role. There was also the famous anecdote from the 1990s where filmmaker Quentin Tarantino reportedly expressed interest in directing a version of *Casino Royale*, possibly even as a period piece, prior to the rights settlement. Hence, it was appropriate that *Casino Royale* start the 'second' coming of Bond, as the story had been there all along haunting the franchise as a spectre of possible alternate narrative trajectories. Throughout the last half-century, there have been so many unfulfilled real and imagined ideas of *Casino Royale* to suggest the other characters or franchises that 'James Bond' could have become – Ian Fleming's *Casino Royale*? ... CBS's *Casino Royale*? ... Charles Feldman's (*two* versions of) *Casino Royale*? ... Quentin Tarantino's *Casino Royale*? ... Pierce Brosnan's *Casino Royale*?...

'Does "Ellipsis" mean anything to you?'

It is clear enough that the release of *Casino Royale* in 2006 both stopped and re-started the James Bond franchise. The history of *Casino Royale*'s production is itself one of incompletion. But what else could be said about *Casino Royale* and its various forms of interruption? The Bond franchise and earlier reiterations of *Casino Royale* point towards issues of continuity and disruption which play out narratively in the film itself. An 'ellipsis' – the compressing of time, the jump from one isolated moment to another – both disrupts and restores time. The ellipsis, meanwhile, is not just a critical frame for analysing *Casino Royale*. It is, of course, lit-erally in the film itself. Throughout the first hour of the film, we keep seeing (on mobile phones) and hearing repeated references to 'Ellipsis' without any explanation of what it signifies, though we assume it symboli-cally stands in for the unseen villain. And it does – not literally, but figuratively. Actu-ally, 'ellipsis' proves to be the limited-time password to get into the security areas of Miami International Airport.

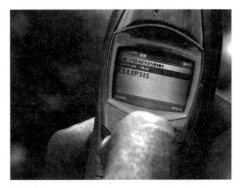

'Ellipsis': the mobile phone, recovered by Bond (Daniel Craig) after the embassy incident in *Casino Royale* (2006)

On this note, it is easy to see how both Vesper and the ellipsis are linked as mu-tual clues to unlocking at least fragments of the 'big picture' of *Casino Royale* – both words are linked by virtue of their plot function as passwords. Both 'vesper' (with the bank) and 'ellipsis' (at the airport) literally unlock new developments in the narrative. Such a parallel reinforces how the omnipresence of the ellipsis, co-existent with its initially nebulous significance, generates a critical space for greater interrogation of its importance. It points towards Bond's real adversary, who even at the end we have yet really to see. Still more, however, can be said about 'ellipsis'.

While seducing Dimitrios's (Simon Abkarian) wife, Solange (Caterina Muri-no), Bond asks her a 'personal question ... Does "Ellipsis" mean anything to you?' By this point in the film, Bond has seen the word on the bomb-maker Mollaka's (Sébastien Foucan) mobile phone, but does not know anything about its significance, other than it points him towards the sender – Dimitrios himself. The connection back to the mobile phone, meanwhile, is made unambiguous when Bond's unanswered question is immediately followed up by Solange's phone ringing, with Dimitrios on the other end. 'Should I ask him about [ellipsis]?', she asks, referring to her husband, before answering. It is telling that our first verbal introduction to the concept of 'ellipsis' centres on an explicit interrogation of the word's *meaning*. It is also curious that Bond prefaces it as a 'personal' question, because the topic does not automatically suggest anything particularly intimate (of course, the timing of the question – in the middle of a particularly steamy moment – is partly played for a joke). Still, the emphasis on the 'personal' aspect of what ellipsis might 'mean' foregrounds the potential depth of the subject – and points towards a larger thematic relevance.

Indeed, does ellipsis mean anything else? There is of course 'Bond ... James Bond'. The famous line does not work without the pause – the implied, unspoken ellipsis that is at the heart of Bond's identity. And there is the ellipsis, too, of the waiting for Bond to say it in every film (something *Casino Royale* plays with to great effect). Even the trademark 'gun-barrel' moment, which opens every Bond film, is delayed here. We think we missed it the first time, but it turns out to close the pre-title sequence, rather than open it. And by incorporating it into the narrative proper – a touch that could never be repeated in another Bond film (not with Craig, anyway) – it becomes all the more overwhelming. And it is the first hint that the usual Bond payoffs will not be delivered in the usual formulaic ways – itself another form of anticipation. But the 'ellipsis', too, is ultimately something like Alfred Hitchcock's 'MacGuffin' (think of the secret formula in *The 39 Steps* (1935) or the wine bottle in *Notorious* (1946)) – the mysterious and central plot device that anchors the suspense, but does not ultimately signify anything other than something to hold the narrative together. Like the MacGuffin, 'ellipsis' is loaded with possible hermeneutic readings, but does not inherently signify one definitive meaning. Yet that emptiness itself is narratively what anchors the film. The absence of linear, explicit narrative logic is both the plot and a theme in *Casino Royale*, one which opens up the film to larger unseen issues.

'Hardly the big picture, wouldn't you say?'

Part of the brilliance of *Casino Royale* is not only that it restarts Bond. It restarts an *entire cohesive world* in which Bond exists. In this sense, *Casino Royale* is markedly different from even the aforementioned earlier Bond films which shifted towards a darker tone. It is not only about reiterating the same formula again through a different tonal lens. There is a bigger picture being developed for Bond in this film, one even he himself barely begins to envision by *Casino Royale*'s conclusion. Moreover, throughout the film, we hear literally about the 'big picture', even though we never see it. In the film, M scolds Bond for killing Mollaka – a 'nobody' – in cold blood. 'We wanted to question him', she says, 'not kill him ... You were supposed to display some judgement'. This scene with M is really the first where we get a sense of the larger narrative universe in which Bond is now immersed in *Casino Royale*. 'We're trying to find out how an entire network of terrorist groups is financed and you give us one bomb-maker. Hardly the big picture, wouldn't you say?', M says to Bond. During this scene, Bond is sitting down, playing solitaire, as M walks around him, her physical positioning heightening her authority and wisdom over his subservience and rash inexperience. Right as she says, 'the big picture', the film cuts to a slight low-angle shot with Bond in the foreground and M looking down at him.

The framing here is not incidental, as it parallels framing in the other scene in *Casino Royale* in which there is a reference to the 'big picture'. Much later in the film, Bond is captured and tortured by Le Chiffre. After being mocked by Bond, Le Chiffre insists that he could kill him and still seek sanctuary with the British and American governments, 'because they need what I know' about the mysterious organisation. Le Chiffre's arrogant assertion also unintentionally anticipates the reasoning for his eventual murder. He is killed because he knows too much and cannot be trusted any longer. Meanwhile, as this point, Bond has begun to understand the complex network of evil that Le Chiffre represents. Bond knows what Le Chiffre is referring to when he says the British government needs what he knows (without quite knowing what that is). 'The big picture', Bond mumbles to himself as a response, recalling M's admonition, beginning to understand Le Chiffre's (lack of) importance. While having his own testicles beaten, Bond's evocation of the big picture is also a relative reminder not to give up the password, and not to lose sight of what is at stake – the financing of terrorism.

As I noted, the framing and spatial positioning of Bond in a low-angle shot is not incidental here. He is strapped naked to a chair, while Le Chiffre towers over him. Whenever Le Chiffre does sit down in this scene, it is to try to reach a compromise with Bond, to concede some power to him, but when that fails he stands back up and continues the torture. Thus, much of this scene is shot with low angles that emphasise a weakened Bond in the foreground, and a dominant Le Chiffre in the background (visually paralleling the scene in M's home). The only shot in this sequence which features Bond looking through a high-angle shot down at a crouching Le Chiffre is appropriately the moment when Bond reaffirms that he is not going to tell him the password no matter what. In other words, it is the only moment when Bond has the upper-hand. Bond's nudity is only one – albeit the most prominent – aspect of his extreme vulnerability in this scene (a sequence which also reinforces the importance of passwords). Hence, in both references to the 'big picture', Bond is framed in a low-angle position of weakness to someone who has literal and symbolic power over him. Throughout *Casino Royale*, low-angle and high-angle images, often point-of-view shots, are used to illustrate a character's level of power over narrative events in the film, and their awareness of the big picture, even though it is not always immediately apparent.

'We'll never know who was behind this'

This is particularly important for the character of Mr White, who is only revealed to be the film's primary villain in the extended third act. Not surprisingly, White's murder of Le Chiffre is framed through Bond's point of view from an extreme low angle (curiously, several images of dead people throughout the film are framed in this same type of low-angle, extreme close-up shot). The torture scene is perhaps the most narratively significant in *Casino Royale*. The film's ambiguity becomes heightened here in a scene which features a premature halt to the earlier plot and a discussion centred on the 'big picture' and passwords (a nod to the earlier 'ellipsis'). Just as importantly, Le Chiffre's insignificance and White's authority are both revealed then to Bond and to the audience. Indeed, Le Chiffre is not the primary villain in *Casino Royale*, and his ultimate irrelevance itself points towards a central narrative ambiguity – '*nothing sinister*', Le Chiffre says to an acquaintance early in the film, in an ironic phrase that also foreshadows his eventual narrative inconsequentiality. The moment of his assassination, meanwhile, also confirms the way in which *Casino Royale* privileges Mr White's dominant spatial position – how he looks down at others, implicitly using formal techniques to quietly assert his point of view and control over events.

After the film's credits, we first meet Mr White. That we meet him before Le Chiffre is a subtle reminder that he and the organisation he represents are really the ones in power. In the first camp scene, Mr White is framed in a high angle point-of-view over Colonel Obanno, indicating early his symbolic power over him and many of the characters throughout *Casino Royale*. When Le Chiffre arrives, he drops to the background. But he never stops watching. That scene's conclusion likewise is again framed from Mr White's point of view, as he watches Le Chiffre's caravan leave Obanno's camp. White's looking is particularly heightened by the subsequent reverse-shot which lingers on his face for a delayed moment.

This panoptic shot is mirrored by a shot much later in the film, as a point-of-view image again captures Mr White watching in the foreground. This time, White is surveying Bond as he kneels besides Vesper's corpse, after the building collapses in Venice, reasserting Mr White's continuing narrative power over diegetic events. Mr White is a literal surveillance mechanism in *Casino Royale*. Writing about the Brosnan Bond films, Jim Leach observed that events 'now take place in a world in which electronic technology both transcends the limits of the human body and makes possible a surveillance system that erodes any notion of privacy' (2003: 255). That surveillance remains a key theme, meanwhile, throughout *Casino Royale* is particularly heightened by the narrative function of surveillance cameras in other moments of the film – the death by shooting of Mollaka, the televisual framing there foreshadowed by an earlier image of a camera in the embassy; and then, later, Bond's use of surveillance cameras to find Alex Dimitrios, itself a moment in the film also privileged by another mobile phone reference to 'ellipsis'. Appropriately, Bond learns quickly from his mistake with the videotaped murder in Madagascar, because in the subsequent scene he uses the security cameras to his advantage, finding the footage of Dimitrios.

Moreover, Leach's belief that in later Bond films 'electronic technology both transcends the limits of the human body and makes possible a surveillance system' (2003: 255) becomes quite explicit in *Casino Royale*. Mr White embodies those cameras throughout the film, as a 'neutral' watcher of events as they unfold. He remains, it seems, the only one with complete awareness of the 'big picture' – at least until the end. But Bond's aspirations to overtake that role of the watcher – to be in narrative control – are also anticipated in the film's early moments. After White watches Le Chiffre leave Obanno's camp, the film immediately cuts to Madagascar, for Bond's first post-007 introduction, where he too is positioned above, at a distance, as an all-seer, overlooking the events of a snake/mongoose fight, while mostly keeping his eye on Mollaka and a fellow British agent. The action sequence which follows is itself a result of Bond's inability to control the situation from afar. Indeed, when Carter (Joseph Millson) draws his weapon and gives chase, we see the situation unfold explicitly from behind Bond's head, his implied point of view, looking out over the emergent chaos of people fleeing the scene. Then, unlike White, Bond is unable to control the situation from a distance. By the end of the film, however, when Bond finally catches up to Mr White, he will be in a position of control. He will literally be the one watching White from a distance.

The importance of control goes hand-in-hand with issues of trust. To trust, or to know not to trust, is for various characters in the film, to be in control. Trust is another motif throughout *Casino Royale*. But it is inverted. The villains keep insisting on trusting each other, and to not be trusted in their network means to be marked for death. 'How do I trust this man I have never met with my money?' asks Obanno. Recognising the gravity of the question, Mr White answers by refusing to guarantee his trust, only the introduction. His response is not incidental or casually considered. By the end of the film, we realise trust is privileged above all to the unseen organisation White represents. Later, Le Chiffre asks Dimitrios if he can trust him, to which he responds that he does not care about such issues. Dimitrios only values his reputation. Then, shortly before White kills Le Chiffre, the would-be assassin says point blank that money is not as important as knowing who to trust – the implicit statement that Le Chiffre must be eliminated because he cannot be trusted. Such a moment bookends the opening with Obanno and highlights how crucial trust ultimately is for White and the concealed organisation he represents.

On the other end, M insists in the beginning that Bond needs to know who he can trust. In their early scene together in M's flat, she dismisses Bond bluntly, reminding him, 'I need to know I can trust you, and that you know who to trust. And since I don't know that, I need you out of my sight.' Much of the film then becomes framed through Bond's slow discovery of the importance of trust (the issue of M and trust is also a carry-over from the end of *Die Another Day*). In the end, finally, Bond admits he trusts no one: after being betrayed by Vesper, M asks him if he trusts anyone. 'No,' he answers bluntly. 'Then,' M quickly responds, 'you've learnt your lesson.' Like the villains, but inverted, Bond has learned the importance of *not* trusting anyone. The villains prioritise trust and connection; the 'good' guys disdain it – 'the bitch is dead'. The inversion of issues of trust points back out to the film's larger narrative ambiguity. M and Bond's final conversation, focused on trust, also ends with her belief that 'we'll never know who was behind this. The trail has gone cold.'

Narratively, the trail *has* gone cold. Bond and MI6 have yet to discover the film's true villain, Mr White. Yet going 'cold' in this moment really speaks to Bond's emotional state in the wake of Vesper's betrayal and death. Literally on the narrative trail, Bond too has 'gone cold', but ironically it is this coldness which is necessary to finding White. While the unseen organisation controls events through a priority of trust, Bond moves out further and further to uncovering the mystery by virtue of refusing to trust anyone. Yet Bond thinks to double-check Vesper's mobile phone, which then leads to another scene, another clue. 'Being dead,' Mathis (Giancarlo Giannini) tells Bond prophetically at an earlier point in the film, 'doesn't mean one can't still be helpful.' Vesper tells Bond that his presence makes her 'feel reborn', and indeed Bond's final actions in *Casino Royale* foregrounds her lingering influence. Both these moments and the sequel will see Vesper symbolically 'reborn'. Thus, one final time, the traces of 'Vesper' as both character and name manage to unlock a mystery for him, as a message on her phone finally calls his attention to Mr White.

There are at least three climaxes to *Casino Royale*: the defeat of Le Chiffre, the defeat of the unidentified villains in Venice and the defeat of Mr White. Moreover, the film's multiple potential ending points – Le Chiffre's death, Vesper and Bond's consummation, Vesper's death, Mr White's capture – also force us to consider the irresolvability of the film's actual plot (which carries us beyond the end of the film). The extended love affair between Bond and Vesper, as they take off to Venice, also undermines the traditional ending of the Bond film, by showing us what happens *after* Bond's (eventual and inevitable) sexual conquest of the main female lead, which is usually how a Bond film literally climaxes, the final image being of his seduction. But in *Casino Royale*, such a moment is only the beginning. Hence, the lack of closure here too continues the anticipation, as nothing is ever fixed, stable or reliable in the ephemerality which defines the world of *Casino Royale*, and *thus* the ending of the film is literally the beginning of the next.

'Christ, I miss the Cold War'

Early in the film, M is reintroduced to us as again played by Judi Dench. While immensely talented in the part, it is awkward and even jarring to see her again in the film that otherwise claims to sever any sense of continuity with the Brosnan films. One of Dench's first lines here (as a response to Bond's carelessness with Mollaka) is to wish that Bond would defect to the Russians. Hence, she says, 'I miss the Cold War.' The line is an ironic variation on Dench's introduction in *GoldenEye*, where M seems all-too-willing to dismiss the Cold War and its 'relic', Bond himself. Now, she longs for it. While subtly hinting at *Casino Royale*'s post-9/11 status (the first Bond film conceived after the event), part of the joke also is that Bond cannot defect. He has nowhere to go, even if he wanted to. The clear boundaries between the West and the Soviet Bloc are gone. Like *Casino Royale*'s notion of 'the big picture', evil is now more ubiquitous, yet also harder to identify. The 'war on terror', another 'big picture', serves the paradoxical function of an unambiguous means for framing ambiguity. Moreover, it is the perfect post-9/11 manifestation of villainy. The 'big picture' of evil still matters, but specific nation-states are irrelevant. Evil here is a rhizome, elusive, shifting, fleeting. And the unseen organisation behind events in *Casino Royale* is explicitly marked as evil.

Of course, SPECTRE, the evil organisation led by Blofeld that Bond battled throughout the 1960s, served this role of an elusive, shifting antagonist before; and it may well suggest why (even beyond the source material) many Bond fans suspect SPECTRE will return at some point during Craig's tenure. SPECTRE worked as a third party, the group that deflected any direct antagonism with the communists for Bond. Indeed, it was often greedy individualists (Dr No, Goldfinger, Largo, Blofeld and so forth) that Bond battled, not the Soviet Empire, as though the franchise was more interested in de-escalating Cold War tensions, rather than in intensifying them. SPECTRE, meanwhile, was the unseen anchor throughout the 1960s Bond films. In this regard, *Casino Royale* is actually an effective throwback to the classic Bond formula. White's organisation is very much a 'spectre' haunting the narrative. Connery's Bond could battle smaller enemies here and there, but what ultimately drives him is the eventual confrontation with the head of the larger organisation itself, Blofeld. In the 1970s, 1980s and 1990s, on the other hand, Bond lacked a larger enemy, a larger purpose. Hence, it became possible for Bond to fall into a cycle of formulaic, generic films that have no connection to one another, other than occasionally some of the same characters. Perhaps, the end of the Cold War and 9/11 has forced Bond producers to rethink the nature and structure of the enemy in such a way that paradoxically draws him back to part of what made the initial cinematic decade of Bond so successful.

Meanwhile, *Casino Royale* does not shy away from direct references to 9/11 and to terrorism (unlike *Die Another Day* – no doubt in part due to careful cultural considerations about North Korea). Early in the film, the stakes of Bond's mission are made hardly subtle or trivial. A major airplane producer, Sky Fleet, and thus the global economy, is the object of an attack. Moreover, the issue is then made direct. 'When they analysed the stock market after 9/11' M tells him, 'the CIA discovered a massive shorting of airline stocks. When the stocks hit bottom on 9/12, someone made a fortune'. *Casino Royale* literally implies that the organisation which Bond is trying to find at least knew of and attempted to profit from 9/11. Later, in case we have forgotten, Vesper reminds Bond that 'I suppose you've given some thought to the notion that if you lose [the poker match with Le Chiffre], our government will have directly financed terrorism'. Of course, despite the need to proceed delicately, these references are also obligatory for the Bond franchise, as Leach has previously noted: 'references to actual events and institutions help to make the fantasy more convincing' (2003: 253).

Still, the explicit emphasis on 9/11 both foregrounds and substantiates the 'big picture' as the thematic and narrative framing of *Casino Royale*. The 'big picture' is what drives Bond, even though it is not strictly speaking ever in *Casino Royale* itself. Even at the end, it sits just beyond the narrative. Is this then a more subtle narrative response to 9/11? Leach argues that 'while Bond's enduring popularity depends upon the appeal of the imaginary solutions to real problems, the terrorist attacks of 11 September, and the subsequent critical and political responses, expose the complexity of the relations between the real and the imaginary in the contemporary cultural environment' (2003: 257). *Casino Royale* acknowledges 9/11 and the complexities which that event re-foregrounded, but seems to also stop short of an imaginary solution. Bond finds Mr White, but so much remains unexplored, let alone defeated. The larger dots have only begun to connect, but what those dots represent remain completely unknown, as with SPECTRE in the early Bond films. And, of course, as with those earlier Connery movies, what still anchors the franchise is the presence of a powerful, even dominant, James Bond.

'You know my name'

After Mr White is shot in the leg by Bond (proving he has taken M's earlier advice that it is important to question a suspect, 'not to kill them'), the film cuts to an ambiguous long-shot of White dragging himself across the gravel driveway. The shot may well be Bond's implied point of view, which reinforces the thematic possibility that Bond, now the watcher, has replaced Mr White in the omniscient position of power. As White makes his way to the edge of the bottom of the stairs, his weakness is reinforced by the high-angle shot looking down on him. Standing upright, Bond's feet move swiftly past him and up the stairs, literally signifying his usurping of White's power. The camera then tilts up to solidify formally and thematically Bond's newfound dominance. The film cuts to a high-angle shot of White looking up, matched then by the iconic medium-close-up of Bond. Unlike in the earlier moments of the film, when Bond had been physically overwhelmed by elements of the 'big picture', he is now the one empowered by the low-angle shot.

It is not a coincidence here, then, that Daniel Craig finally makes his 'introduction' by uttering the famous line we anticipate throughout the entire movie: 'The name's Bond … James Bond.' As with the film's post-credit opening with Obanno and Le Chiffre, Mr White's presence 'guarantees' an 'introduction', albeit not the one White intended. Craig has not only earned the introduction by excelling in his performance throughout the film; Bond as a character has earned it, too. He has begun

'Bond … James Bond': 007 (Daniel Craig) makes his famous introduction in an iconic low-angle shot at the end of *Casino Royale* (2006)

to figure out the larger mysteries that the film has presented him with, thus literally anticipating the sequel. Of course, because it is a James Bond film, we expect a sequel anyway. But the end of *Casino Royale*, and the abrupt but all-too-fitting cut after the iconic line, literally shows us how and when the next film will begin.

It is not a coincidence either that the film plays with this anticipation of Bond's name. 'If the theatrics are supposed to scare me', Dryden says to him in the film's opening scene, 'you've got the wrong man, Bond.' This is the first reference – pre-double-0 status – to Bond's name. The 'James' is missing; it is only 'Bond', not 'Bond … James Bond.' Moreover, the emphasis on the 'wrong man' plays to the initial uncertainty of the new actor, and of the fact that Bond has yet to become 'Bond … James Bond.' Later, M says twice to Bond that people know that 'you were you.' On the beach, M says simply, 'Well, I *knew* you were you.' Later, this is reinforced when M reminds Bond that Vesper too '*knew* you were you.' The idea of knowing 'you were you' is both ambiguous and redundant. We do not yet know that Bond is 'Bond … James Bond', because we have not yet heard him say it, even while we do know of course that this *is* James Bond.

Hence, the song 'You Know My Name' – if not necessarily the best Bond song ever – is at least one of the best song titles in the history of the franchise. Here again rests the redundancy and ambiguity of Bond both being and not being 'James Bond.' 'You [already] know my name' prolongs the ellipsis. That the film closes with Bond's introduction to the main villain of this film (if not the next) reveals and completes the film's incompletion, and disrupts the entire franchise by offering us that perfect ellipsis which is nearly as memorable as Connery's first introduction in *Dr No*. Indeed, it may be the most powerful moment in the history of the franchise – framed definitively from the low angle. The bigger 'big picture' of *Casino Royale* is of course ultimately the durability and continuing presence of Bond himself, stronger and more dominant than ever.

'Bond … James Bond'.

4

IT JUST KEEPS GETTING BIGGER: JAMES BOND AND THE POLITICAL ECONOMY OF HUGE

Joyce Goggin and René Glas

A bigger, blunter Bond

Having just relieved Le Chiffre (Mads Mikkelsen) and international terrorism of over $100,000,000 at poker in an elegant Montenegro casino, Bond (Daniel Craig) suddenly becomes aware that he is 'famished'. He retires with 'Bond girl' Vesper Lynd (Eva Green) to the casino's dining room, where he sips a martini while eating toast and beluga caviar with a visibly ravenous appetite. In the ensuing badinage, Vesper tells Bond that she actually enjoys laughing at *him* more than at his clever rejoinders. Bond responds by opening his mouth to laugh, and disconcertingly reveals a mouthful of the semi-masticated Russian delicacy.

Such glimpses of vulgarity and vulnerability occur throughout *Casino Royale* (2006), disrupting the cool, cultivated, Cold War Bond image embodied by Sean Connery and Roger Moore. Craig's Bond is often the brunt of jokes like Vesper's, rather that the originator; he lacks the polish, wit and subtlety of all the Bonds that came before him; and his manners seem more stereotypically American than European. In short, he is 'a blunt instrument' as M (Judi Dench) calls him. Yet while this new hero laughs with his mouth full, he remains implicitly linked to Bond culture by a signifying chain that conjoins Vesper martinis, brassy theme music and a vintage 1964 Aston Martin, giving one the unsettling feeling that, in spite of all the recognisable franchise trademarks, something has definitely changed.

More importantly, one senses that the changes made to the new Mr Kiss Kiss Bang Bang are not trivial, nor intended simply as a superficial franchise facelift. As Roland Barthes (1982) argued in his essay on Bond and narrative structure, seemingly superficial elements of the series' style such as cigarettes, terry-cloth jumpsuits, martinis and cars function as indices and encode significant cultural, economic and political information through which the 007 movies communicate with viewers. Moreover, indices such as the Bond martini have 'a polysemic value', and function as 'symbolic node[s] grouping several signifieds (modernity, wealth, leisure)', all of which contribute to the ludic structure of suspense and excitement built into the films and novels, 'from the progressive upward integration of [such] functional units' (Barthes 1982: 289, 291). Ultimately these semiotic units or indices combine to form an 'economy of the message', punctuated by risk, in the form of what Barthes calls cardinal moments, or junctures in the story at which the plot takes a turn between options that will have a profound impact on the outcome (see 1982: 266).

The insights offered by Barthes' analysis are, of course, not limited to Ian Fleming's novels nor to the Bond films, since changes in the indices that structure any narrative always result in meaningful shifts in how, and what, that narrative signifies. This said, however, revisions made to the Bondian universe in *Casino Royale* appear to alter how this film constructs 007 more radically than any of the re-vampings that took viewers from Sean Connery to Pierce Brosnan. The re-loaded Bond that screenwriters Neal Purvis, Robert Wade and Paul Haggis have distilled from Fleming's first novel in the series creates an overall impression of basic, brutal and serious, rather than elegant and frivolous. With this in mind, we will attempt in this chapter to articulate how these aspects of the new Bond congregate in and radiate from the signifying potential of one specific indice, namely the poker game that serves as the central plot device of the film, to which we shall return shortly.

The title of this chapter alludes, also, to two seminal articles on Bond, namely Toby Miller's 'James Bond's Penis' (2003) and Christoph Lindner's 'Why Size Matters' (2005). In the first case, Miller argues that Bond's gliding signifier is neither as stable nor as rigid as 'Bond girl' names like Pussy Galore might imply. In fact, Bond's member is often subjected to the threat of violence and, in Fleming's *Casino Royale*, after his manhood is pummelled almost to a pulp, he spends considerable time 'strok[ing] his memories' and worrying about performance, before recovering his sexual potency (Fleming 2002: 163).

Lindner's argument concurs with Miller's exposé of the size and performance anxiety that informs Bond novels and movies, and focuses more generally on why, in the sublime 'criminal vision' of Bond culture, size is everything (2005: 227). He cites, for example, Goldfinger's gargantuan plot to crash the global market economy and reminds us that '*Moonraker*, *Thunderball*, and *Dr No* all contain potentially genocidal atomic conspiracies' (ibid.). While one could cite endless examples of the sublimely huge in Bond, the greater point is that the '007 series as a whole' articulates criminal plots of 'titanic scale' and that, more importantly, these plots are formulated to do nothing less than destroy Western stability (ibid.).

In keeping with the tradition established in *Goldfinger* (1964), the latest production of *Casino Royale* involves villains whose enormous, dastardly plans target the global economy as the precarious lynchpin of Western stability and, once again, total 'super spy' Bond stops the bad guys, however unwittingly. What sets *Casino Royale* apart is Bond's 'weapon' in this struggle, namely $10,000,000 with which he must win an astronomically high-stakes poker game, wherein losing money means financing global terrorism. In what follows we will discuss the card games at the centre of the film, and of Fleming's novel, as a means of describing how *Casino Royale* articulates the global, post-Cold War, political economy, driven by the supposedly constant threat of terrorism that fuels a fast and risky financial market. In the process we will discuss how the 'feel' of this Bond film is different and why this is important, as well as a number of economic and political developments that have taken place in the years between the publication of the novel in 1953 and the release of the 2006 film.

More than a game!

In his classic essay on the semiotics of Bondian good and evil, Umberto Eco (2003) concludes that the Bond films and novels constitute a sort of elaborate game, which cues and invites readers and viewers to interact with them as such. According to Eco, Fleming's novels, and the films adapted from them, are structured around pairs of opposites such as Britishness (Bond) and otherness (Le Chiffre, Goldfinger, and so on), or good (Bond) and evil (the host of ethnically-inflected villains), which battle for control within various play situations, such as a card game in a lavish old-world casino. The oscillating movement of the narrative between these poles creates suspense as viewers follow the trajectory of 007's triumph, and hold their breath while wondering if, for example, Bond's penis will really be severed by Goldfinger's laser.

Picking up where Eco left off, Michael Denning has argued that the Bond thrillers are organised around the Great Game of spying, to which Fleming referred as 'nothing but a complicated game, really' (1967: 118). The ludic, or game-like, articulation of the narrative necessitates the stressing of two kinds of game: 'plot structure [which] itself resembles a game, and second, the attention to the representation of a variety of games in the books' and films (Denning 2003: 60). Moreover, making one's way through the narrative twists and

James Bond (Daniel Craig) stares down Le Chiffre (Mads Mikkelsen) at the poker table in *Casino Royale* (2006)

turns generated by SMERSH and SPECTRE force readers to play a hermeneutic cat-and-mouse game with the text, so that the text itself *is* a kind of game.

What Denning does not discuss, however, is the specificity of card games, and their potential to structure narrative in ways that reflect this specificity. In the latest film adaptation of *Casino Royale*, for example, the card game variously referred to as chemin-de-fer and baccarat is changed to Texas hold 'em poker. Given the emphasis that Michael G. Wilson and Barbara Broccoli have placed on their decision to film the first of Fleming's novels – with all the claims of returning to basics, the original and the source that popular logic justifies – changing the game in which Bond saves the world from baccarat to Texas hold 'em is, as we will argue, no small move.

From baccarat to poker

In *Rouge et Noir*, a chapter whose title is both French and literary, Fleming writes Bond into the 'solid, studied comfort' of Casino Royale, which offers patrons 'the well-padded arms of the chairs, the glass of champagne or whisky at the elbow, [and] the quiet unhurried attention of good servants' (2002: 49). Bond enters with characteristic élan, passing chemin-de-fer games and roulette wheels, observing that, 'many nationalities were represented' and that of them, 'good Americans were fine people and … most of them seemed to come from Texas' (2002: 55). The game that the select members of this glamorous international crowd (and the good Americans) play with Bond is baccarat – a game to which card historian David Parlett refers as 'plush but mindless' (1991: 82). In other words, unlike the Texans whose presence Fleming feels compelled to justify, the plush but mindless game of baccarat is perfectly at home in the high-class, Euro-setting of Casino Royale, volubly signifying old-world charm and leisure.

While Fleming expends many pages on having Bond explain the rules of baccarat to Vesper, and thereby emphasising the game structure of the text, he is silent on the history of the game, a detail that bears closer inspection. Baccarat belongs to a fifteenth century, Western European subspecies of card game, grouped by a number of 'ludemes' (game elements) such as requiring a banker, and includes chemin-de-fer, baccarat-banque, commerce and punto banco. As the names of these games imply, the players that coined them thought there was an explicit connection between these banking games and commerce. Fleming was also apparently aware of this connection and describes Le Chiffre, the baccarat banker in *Casino Royale*, as having 'knowledge of accountancy and mathematics', making him a 'fine gambler' (2002: 17). And these more institutionally acceptable forms of knowledge that make Le Chiffre a good gambler are important, we are told, because a baccarat 'banker should be able to win by … first-class accountancy' (2002: 70).

As we remarked earlier, in the film of *Casino Royale* the now somewhat ob-
scure game of baccarat is replaced with the poker variant Texas hold 'em, and this
decision affects how the film signifies in a variety of ways. The most obvious effect
of changing the games is heightened audience appeal. The televisation of poker
leagues like the World Series of Poker as well as the multi-billion online gambling
industry have made the game hugely popular in the last decade. Likewise Texas
hold 'em and casino culture in general have been subjects of Hollywood hype in
flashy films like *Rounders* (1998) and particularly the *Ocean's Eleven* series (2001,
2004, 2007). And since celebrities playing poker in television tournaments have
become part of a steady media diet, extended close-ups of Craig's piercing blue
eyes nervously searching for Le Chiffre's 'tell' effectively suture in amateur players
longing to master the visual grammar of cool.

As we noted above, baccarat and the other games in the same family are profoundly economic in nature and are led by a banker. The suggestion in the novel
is, in fact, that those playing baccarat are largely 'bankers and businessmen' – just
the sort of people whom one might expect to find in a casino (Fleming 2002: 14).
Fleming's inclusion of a 'Jamaican plantocrat whose father had made his pile in
tobacco and sugar and whose son chose to play it away on the stock market and in
casinos' (2002: 25), further implies that, in a market rapidly becoming global, the
words 'stock market' and 'casino' may comfortably be uttered in the same breath.
Such insights crop up throughout the narrative, and make it clear that Fleming was keenly aware of the rapid erosion of the nineteenth-century distinction
between speculation and gambling, market and casino, that was occurring as he
wrote. By 1953, discourses on the 'prolonged political, cultural, and legal struggle
surrounding the meanings and boundaries of "the financial sphere" and the character and behaviour of the "financial man"', that had been mobilised to police the
artificial separation of gambling and finance, were sounding very hollow indeed
(de Goede 2005: 48). Hence, when Fleming writes that 'the "Bourse" is too slow'
for Le Chiffre (2002: 14), who sees gambling as a viable alternative, he is signalling
a major shift in economic thought that took effect in the West over the course of
the twentieth century.

But poker is a game and a narrative indice of an entirely different order than
baccarat. According to Parlett, poker is 'not so much a card game' because the
cards 'have little part to play beyond sitting around looking pretty. The true instruments of play are coin of the realm' (1991: 104). In other words, poker gives
up the pretence of being about anything else but money and risk. So where baccarat was an appropriate signifier of the postwar, Western economy as it developed
an increased propensity to behave like a casino, Texas hold 'em is an uncannily
fitting signifier of what, in Susan Strange's terms, is currently known as global
'casino capitalism' (see 1986: 1–25). Hence, in the 1953 novelistic world of Bond,
Le Chiffre lost his clients' money gambling, whereas in 2006 Le Chiffre loses their

money playing the stock market. What the film suggests in the tacit grammar of the card game is that we are living in a casino economy that makes Susan Strange's predictions look tame; that this economy is global; that this economy is profoundly American; and that it is based on chance and dissimulation. And indeed, the film *Casino Royale* never lets us forget that the current global market, based on derivatives trading, hedging and other hugely risky gambles, flows directly into the proceeds on the poker table, which will determine our fate in the face of global terrorism.

Moreover, like the scene in which Bond laughs with a mouthful of caviar, the quintessentially American game of Texas hold 'em played in a plush, nineteenth-century European casino presents a striking hybrid of cultures and styles. But there is also a political payoff to injecting an American game into a European, old-world setting. While Fleming was sporting enough to let the good Americans, most of whom were Texans, into Casino Royale, the producers of the movie construct their entire film around a game that hails from Texas, implying that Americans are now dictating house culture even in Europe, and indeed around the globe. Hence, in the casinos of Montenegro everyone plays American poker with Texas rules, and in Mbale, Uganda, where the plot picks up after the opening credits, a child soldier plays a pinball machine, implying that American culture has insinuated itself here as well. And stylistically, while the film exudes old-world charm and recalls the casino culture portrayed in European productions like *Bob le flambeur* (*Bob the Gambler*, 1955), the casino's location fits seamlessly into the global texture of the film with its itinerant movement from England, to Uganda, the Bahamas, Montenegro and finally Venice. Whereas previous Bond films were often located in the 'pleasure periphery', in countries 'dependant on the neo-colonialism of the tourist industry' (Denning 2003: 66), the film's new locations are part of what we would like to call the *financial periphery* of the world economy, namely rogue states used for money laundering, high-stakes gambling and other marginal activities. This kind of global, colonising view of the world projects an eroticised vision of capitalism, and helps to propagate the incredibly sexy notion that using the world as a personal playground and site of spectacle makes you huge.

European style: a casino scene from the French gangster film *Bob le flambeur* (1955)

It has been frequently suggested that the Bond films reflect contemporary politics in ways that are worthy of note (see Black 2001; Lindner 2003a; Chapman 2008). For example, by the time Pierce Brosnan assumed the role of Bond, the

Cold War was effectively over, and it is no coincidence that the Brosnan-as-Bond films focused first on the remnants of the Cold War with *GoldenEye* (1995), then floundered about in the remaining three films looking for an enemy to justify the necessity of his existence. In *Tomorrow Never Dies* (1997) and *The World Is Not Enough* (1999), Bond finds that enemy in the diffused form of media manipulation and oil politics, disrupting the financial economy in the process. Although M remarks in *Casino Royale* that she misses the Cold War, this first Bond film completely created post-9/11 returns to the franchise moorings as the Very Good confronting a supposedly Tangible Evil. By now, the West is able to name its first global enemy since 1989: the Cold War era over, we have entered the War on Terror. What this of course also means is that Bond, whose image was so important to the postwar construction of Britishness scrambling to regain face by becoming hip and groovy, is now a global, hybrid composite with a dominant strain of 'American'.

Here, the issue of poker versus baccarat seems once again to acquire significance, given the clichéd contemporary notion that 'the poker factor of everyday life' mirrors 'historical and political' events (Parlett 1991: 106). Indeed, famous poker ace Herbert O. Yardley went so far as to claim that his mastery of the subtleties of poker prepared him for his life as a secret agent and that counting cards aided him in 'cracking the Japanese Diplomatic Code' (1957: 65). And the notion that card games and politics go hand in hand is reiterated in Fleming, where he tells readers that Bond's world is informed by the logic and 'impartiality of the roulette ball and of the playing cards' (2002: 49), wherein futures are determined on the 'grass-green baize battlefield' of the card table (2002: 82). For Fleming, one of the consequences of a world run on gambler's logic is that 'the villains and heroes get all mixed up ... History mov[es] pretty quickly ... and the heroes and villains keep changing parts' (2002: 159–60).

As one might expect, Texas hold 'em, as a central fictional device, reflects the logic of full-blown, very late capitalism, in a world where no one claims that anything remotely like a Smithian 'invisible hand' morally regulates the market, and where everyone is in bed, so to speak, with everyone else. As Thomas Elsaesser has argued, global politics and economics produce cinematic worlds 'in which motivation, causation and agency block each other, as each layer of possible explanation of the [precise source of conflict] creates a denser web of hypothetical premises and unproven presuppositions' (2007: 159). Or, as M calmly tells Bond at the close of the film, 'we'll never know who was behind this'. In a world where the poker logic derives from a Texan strain that deceptively claims to be rational while the ultimate driver is still chance, it should come as no surprise that the bad guys are difficult to spot, even though terrorism is supposed to be a clearly defined evil, and terrorists readily recognisable.

Pure pop culture for now people

When asked about some of the more vague details of her financial past, Hillary Clinton regularly turns for answers to the current synergy (or lack of difference) between gambling and finance. As she explains in her autobiography, on the advice of broker and 'former poker player' Robert 'Red' Bone she and Bill made a cool $100,000 from an initial investment of just $1,000, without ever really understanding how they got so lucky! (2004: 113). According to Hillary, this tremendous windfall came to the Clintons because the commodities market, and the economy it drives, have 'more in common with Las Vegas than Wall Street' (ibid.). In this section, we want to concur with Clinton's notion that Vegas and Wall Street have a great deal in common and argue, along with Mark C. Taylor, that Wall Street has 'become even more exciting than Vegas because the stakes [are] so much higher and the game so much faster' (2004: 221). What this shift in market geography and action does (not to mention substituting Texas hold 'em for baccarat) is analogous to what Fleming did to detective fiction by taking it outside, leaving the world of 'low-impact social crime' and 'the myopic world of Agatha Christie's drawing room dramas' (Lindner 2003a: 77), and turning it into the world of fast-paced global intrigue.

This change in pace, we would argue, is directly related to the temporality of money in economic modernity, as well as to the nature of gambling itself, both of which are essential features of Fleming's novels, the Bond franchise and the global economy. Money is a medium of exchange that regulates prices between incommensurable things, and as such it is always between poles of being and 'dictates the condition of possibility' for trade (Taylor 2004: 60). Money is therefore also always liminal and in a state of becoming, which is why we speculate on what it *will be* worth. In its modern form, paper money is essentially a promissory note, often flaunting its own ephemerality with messages such as 'In God We Trust', rather than asserting itself as a supposedly 'real' thing like gold. This development has led to 'increasing dematerialisation and complexity', a process that further enables instruments of credit such as mortgages with which people also speculate (Taylor 2004: 2). Money was, therefore, virtual even before e-banking, inviting speculation as to what it will be worth, and always concerned with projecting future value.

Gambling, on the other hand, is always about very intense moments of the 'now' that will become the future when the dice land, hence the casino rule of no clocks that might distract gamblers in the here-and-now as they worry about what will happen next. As Gerda Reith explains, a gambler's time is about becoming, waiting for the turn of a card that will determine wins or losses, a state to which she refers as a 'pathology of becoming' (1999: 140). Gambling, therefore, knows two temporalities: the right *now*, which the gambler experiences as a heightened and lucid sense of the moment, or a 'sharp, exhilarating present that refresh[es] itself over and over again' (ibid.). Gambling's other time is, of course, the future.

The futurity of money and gambling fuels the market as well as the Bond franchise, which has serially offered a 'condensed expression of a new style and image of Englishness around which the clock of the nation was made to run imaginarily ahead of itself, [as] a pointer to a brighter and better future' (Bennett & Woollacott 2003: 23). So when Bond gambles with astronomical sums of money in *Casino Royale*, viewers are treated to a mega dose of the now and the future, but of a very particular variety, with very sexy packaging. This is a post-9/11, pop-culture representation of the current political economy, where the stakes have been raised dramatically, and the players hail from even further afield than the crowd in the novel. As M casually tells Bond, after 9/11 'the CIA discovered a massive shorting of airline stocks. When the stocks hit bottom on 9/12, someone made a fortune'. In M's version of the events of 9/11, politics and the market are indistinguishable from one another, and terrorists may or may not have been employed in the service of insider trading before 9/11. The attacks on the Twin Towers were part of a business deal and someone made a fortune.

In *The Shock Doctrine: The Rise of Disaster Capitalism*, Naomi Klein worries about the government's role in the market and argues that the Bush Administration has made major strides in the direction of fusing government and market interests. As she sees it, when Donald Rumsfeld rose to the office of Defense Secretary and refused 'to divest himself of any holdings that stood to lose or gain from decisions he might make while in office' (2007: 311), the interests of government and the market visibly and undeniably united. These interests fused perhaps irrevocably after Dick Cheney became Vice President without divesting his interests in companies to which the Bush administration has out-sourced the war on Iraq, and through which Cheney and his holdings have made tremendous profits (see ibid.). These 'corporate-politicians', as Klein calls them, 'maintained their interests in the disaster capitalism complex even as they have ushered in a new era of privatised war and disaster response, allowing them to simultaneously profit from the disasters they help unleash' (ibid.).

Klein also believes that the political and economic thinking that made it possible for M to see 9/11 as a financial event got underway in the 1970s. This era marks the beginnings of an expansionist campaign to install free-market government management, centring on radical privatisation and complete faith in something like an 'invisible hand', which supposedly insures a self-regulating market, that acts as its own good conscience. The current incarnation of this model was the brainchild of Chicago University economist Milton Friedman and, rather anachronistically, owes much to Adam Smith's eighteenth-century market theory. However, because Friedman's plans for freeing the market require wage deregulation, the cutting of government funding to social services such as public education, and the privatisation of government resources, his programme generally meets with public resistance and is difficult to implement.

What has helped this model along tremendously is the artificial acceleration of something that Charles Kindleberger and Robert Aliber (2005) identified some time ago, namely that capitalism thrives on catastrophes and crashes. According to Klein, various US interests (ITT, Ford, the CIA) began working on this notion globally by backing military coups in places like Chile, Argentina and Brazil, and setting up puppet governments that would comply with Friedman's shock programme of radical privatisation. From these politico-economic experiments, it was determined that financial growth and re-growth appear to be stimulated by disaster, which is also key in the quest for economic expansion, especially into other people's counties. Yet, as Klein writes, since 9/11, the Friedman policy for economy reform led by the US has entered into 'a new, self-referential phase', not only because 'Bush's solution to economic trouble is for the government to deconstruct itself – hacking off great chunks of the public wealth and feeding them to corporate America' through privatisation, but also because the West has now entered into a brave new area of what Klein calls 'disaster creation and disaster response' (2007: 288–9, 295).

Moreover, 9/11 has seen an explosion in the security industry and risk management, a discipline that used to involve what Anthony Giddens called 'colonising the future' with possible nightmare scenarios in the hope of preventing them (2006: 29). In its current form, risk management, and ostensibly prevention, now involves what Richard Grusin (2004) has dubbed 'premediation', which often takes the form of CGI representations of war scenarios or computer-generated projections of possible terrorist attacks. This maintains a high level of fear in the populace, insuring fantastic revenues for the rapidly growing risk management sector. On the downside, as de Goede and others have pointed out, the visual premediation of disaster has a nasty habit of bringing it about, and gives one the unsettling feeling that government in the West is in the process of aligning itself with SMERSH or SPECTRE, which may lack 'official government resources' but whose 'finances, technology, and task force rival those of any small nation' that might be interested in controlling its populace through the constant, visually spectacular threat of disaster (Lindner 2005: 229).

While moments of Bond have followed the political economy, and the market, from an ideology of criminal detection to the 'ideology of prevention' (ibid.), we would like to return to Bond's member and the question of premediation. Although we began with Bond's uncouth table manners as an example of one of the many changes to his image, we would like to conclude by addressing the scene in which Craig is stripped naked for his nemesis who proceeds to emasculate him with a knotted rope in slow, excruciating increments. As Miller pointed out, this is not the first time the Bond penis has been in peril, yet previously this amounted to near-miss episodes like Goldfinger's laser castration scheme. What we would like to suggest in this regard is twofold: the gesture of having Bond really mutilated this time reflects capitalism's current need to not only *flirt* with disaster but actually to *produce* it, so that in Bond, as in the current market economy, 'the greatest pleasure arises not from excitement but from relief' (Eco 2003: 52) – that is, from rebuilding after catastrophe. What is more, one suspects that Bond's own people (Mathis (Giancarlo Giannini) or M who 'seriously consider[s] feeding' him to Le Chiffre) may actually have caused his own personal, physical disaster only to rebuild him for more episodes in the future, which seems to accord well with what, according to Klein, happens when Friedmanian economics meets postmodernism – one begins eating one's own. Indeed, although the Bond series 'positively delights in the gratuitous destruction of property' (Chapman 2007: 251), this is the first time it has almost destroyed its very own 007.

James Chapman has argued that *Casino Royale* constitutes a sort of levelling of Bond history, starting before the other Bonds hit the screen, thereby wiping the slate clean. This 'revisionist Bond narrative,' writes Chapman, 'places Bond at the start of his career as if events in previous films had not taken place' (2007: 245). The desire to erase the past – perhaps by shredding it, disappearing people who know about it or blowing it up – is another feature of what Klein has called the 'shock doctrine'. This kind of revisionism gives like-minded world leaders the chance to claim the past never happened and implement radical economic reforms that seem invariably to benefit certain interested parties. If, indeed, we have driven ourselves into the end of history as G. W. F. Hegel and Walter Benjamin predicted and Francis Fukuyama has observed, then Daniel Craig incarnates the end-game Bond, as opposed to the 'happening' Bond of the 1960s and 1970s, or the more recent 'millennial' Bond brought to the screen by Brosnan.

Huge, huger, hugest...

We have argued that the Bond novels and films are game-like in structure, and contain many instances of game playing such as card games, as well as the Cold War, spying and the global economy, all of which Fleming understood as 'nothing but a complicated game, really'. As it has often been observed, the Bond franchise is always a reflection of its contemporary political and economic situation in some measure. In its present incarnation it is therefore fitting that the producers of *Casino Royale* chose Texas hold 'em as the centrepiece of their film, even though they have claimed that the choice was made because the game is more aesthetically exciting and popular among the members of their largely working-audiences. As we see it, Texas hold 'em is also an appropriate signifier of the global economy, because it is a no-limit game, widely referred to as a 'thinking man's game', creating the illusion that it is more manageable and predictable than other gambling games. But this is not the case: people like Le Chiffre regularly lose enormous sums playing the game *and* the market, which regularly crashes even without the benefit of government assistance.

Moreover, Fleming saw gamblers as being just another form of chartered accountant, really, and therefore perfectly suited to the game of baccarat. On this count again, Texas hold 'em, which likes to bill itself as more abstract yet more probabilistic than other games of chance, is a particularly fitting indicator of the current global economic and political mood. In *Casino Royale*, Mathis complains that 'the accountants seem to be running MI6 these days', and M objects that Bond sees her as some kind of accountant, a 'bean-counter', while Le Chiffre is described as a 'chess prodigy and a bit of a mathematical genius'. In short, the current financial economy, like Texas hold 'em, is commonly conceptualised as faster, sexier and more refined that its predecessors, infused with a kind of abstract purity.

But we have also sketched an argument about the nature of money, gambling and speculation in relation to time and the future, which now bears closer investigation. If it is fair to say, following Eco and others, that the Bond novels are a kind of game that contains many games including war, then it is also fair to bring Carl von Clausewitz on board and his argument in *On War* concerning the ludic nature of warfare and its relation to card games. After commenting that, of all games, card games are the most akin to war, he goes on to dissect military strategy along the lines of synchrony and diachrony. Clausewitz inserts temporality into his game model of military strategy as the opposition of a synchronic axis or *tactics* (a series of 'acts, each complete *in itself*' considered simultaneously) and *strategy* ('planning and executing these engagements themselves' over time) (Clausewitz 1976: 128; emphasis in original). As Eco has pointed out, the Bond novels have extended synchronic moments where, for example, the rules of baccarat are explained over a number of pages without advancing the plot, as well as diachronic moments that move the story along a fast-paced chronology.

Our point is that games, war, Bond movies and the market also have (or have had) both diachronic and synchronic axes, but that in the current political economy, the diachronic axis has all but disappeared. According to Dick Cheney and many others we are living at the end of history; and we are now presented with a revisionist Bond who bypasses all previous incarnations of Bond. As 'now' people, in the moment, poised at the end of history, we are living in a revisionist world that constantly reinvents itself as needed. It is only natural, then, that the sublime enormity of Bondian-style destruction continues to influence popular culture. Nothing says now or huge like 007.

PART 2

ENGENDERING BOND

5

'ANY THUG CAN KILL': REWRITING THE MASCULINE BOND

Douglas A. Cunningham and Richard Gabri

I sometimes believe that most gamblers are the stepchildren of love, whether of parental or sexual love, and that here at the gaming tables they are looking to fate to provide them with an adoption that ennobles them more than the origins that repudiated them.

– Walter Benjamin, 'In Parallel With My Actual Diary'

Near the middle of *Casino Royale* (2006), the viewer is treated to an unusual image of a man silhouetted at the window of an upscale hotel room, his back to the camera. He is a mystery – but to whom? To us? To himself? Both? We ask a question the man could very well ask of himself. What *kind* of man is he? What kind of man has he been and what kind can/will he become? What factors will make the difference? The image represents an unusual, pensive moment for a James Bond film, to be sure, yet only one of many such moments in *Casino Royal*. Consider, for example, a Bond who, after killing two men in brutal hand-to-hand combat, frantically washes their blood from his cut, bruised body and desperately regards his own face in the mirror. Consider, too, a Bond who, later, tenderly comforts a violence-shocked woman by embracing her and gently sucking from her fingers the

Silhouette of James Bond (Daniel Craig) in a luxurious hotel room in *Casino Royale* (2006)

blood she imagines on her hands. Finally, consider a Bond with 'no armour left', willing to surrender his hard-won 'double-0' status for a life of monogamous attachment and romantic abandon.

How to account for Bond's occupation of this space of gender liminality? Certainly, in the past, Western culture has championed and/or denigrated Bond as an icon of what R. W. Connell terms *hegemonic masculinity*, a 'configuration of gender practice which embodies the currently accepted answer to the problem of the legitimacy of patriarchy, which guarantees (or is taken to guarantee) the dominant position of men and the subordination of women' (2005: 76). The new film does little to change Bond's status as an exemplar of an idealised manhood. He is still, after all, held up as a hyper-masculine role model, quick-fisted and suave, well in command of his body and able to employ it to his physical and amorous advantage. As always with Bond, the tired phrase still rings true: 'Women want him and men want to be him.'

What the film does attempt, however, is a kind of positioning of Bond *outside* of a definitive hegemonic masculinity. There is a finagling with gender and genre here that forces Bond to re-evaluate his dogged pursuit of a traditional hegemonic masculinity (which, the film tells us, he has not yet achieved) in favour of a different masculine status – one that necessarily draws on aspects of the stereotypical hegemonic ideal and yet supplements them with wisdom garnered through discipline and the help of 'open-gender' exemplars (that is to say, mentors who ground their strengths not in rigid gender binaries of male or female, but, rather, in a free-flowing space of gender conflation).

Bond's journey towards the open-gender state takes place over the course of two distinct phases in the film, followed by an ambiguous phase – the epilogue – in which his future maintenance of that open-gender state remains in question. We shall examine each of these phases and their implications for the Bond character and franchise while exploring some of the key concepts behind theories of masculinities and gender.

The masculinities contest

Understanding Bond's open-gender breakthrough in *Casino Royale* necessitates an understanding of the cultural obstacles to his project. Chief among these is the juggernaut of 'masculinity' itself, the definition for which, as Connell points out, must constantly be placed within a larger context of overall gender practices:

> Rather than attempting to define masculinity as an object (a natural character type, a behavioural average, a norm), we need to focus on the processes and relationships through which men and women conduct gendered lives. 'Masculinity', to the extent the term can be briefly defined at all, is simultaneously a

place in gender relations, the practices through which men and women engage that place in gender, and the effects of these practices in bodily experience, personality, and culture ... 'Hegemonic masculinity' is not a fixed character type, always and everywhere the same. It is, rather, the masculinity that occupies the hegemonic position in a given pattern of gender relations, a position always contestable. (2005: 76)

Masculinity, therefore, is not a singular category or ideology. Rather, it is a fluid category subject to varieties of human interactions within differing cultural and embodied contexts. Connell demonstrates the validity of this claim by exploring the ways in which concepts of masculinity have changed over the last 600 years of Western history, noting in particular that the Protestant Reformation, imperial practices, urbanisation and war all played important roles in 'transforming' what had been a collection of primarily rural European societies ruled by scattered monarchies and the Catholic church. This collection was later transformed into secularised states with colonial assets, gentry classes and emerging calls for the emancipation of women (see Connell 2005: 186–91). By the late nineteenth century, Connell writes, suffrage groups and other women's organisations posed major threats to contemporary ideals about masculinity, as did increased mechanisation and industrialisation (see 2005: 195–6). Fascist movements in the first half of the twentieth century took advantage of masculine insecurities, just as technological advancements later in the century would shift traditional ideals about hegemonic masculinity to include technical savvy and 'wage earning capacity' (see Connell 2005: 191–7). As this brief summary indicates, the nature of any given 'ideal' masculinity necessarily changes over time based upon issues of class, race, economics, politics and many other factors.

Historian Gail Bederman agrees. In *Manliness and Civilization*, Bederman states that masculinity is 'a continual, dynamic process', not reducible to time-specific empiricisms (1996: 7). Particularly useful in her argument is the assertion – similar to Connell's, yet differing in some key respects – that multiple ideas about manhood circulate within culture(s) at any given time, none of them necessarily achieving a secure status as 'the' masculine ideal:

At any time in history, many contradictory ideas about manhood are available to explain what men are, how they ought to behave, and what sorts of powers and authorities they may claim, as men. Part of the way gender functions is to hide these contradictions and to camouflage the fact that gender is dynamic and always changing. Instead, gender is constructed as a fact of nature, and manhood is assumed to be an unchanging, transhistorical essence, consisting of fixed, naturally occurring traits. (Ibid.)

While Connell, then, argues that a single masculine ideal always occupies the coveted (and 'contestable') space of hegemonic masculinity, Bederman views the gender order as less structured but more dynamic – the masculinities contest rages constantly without a clear victor. Certainly, particular masculinities predominate over others, but the top position of masculine categorisation – Connell's hegemonic masculinity – is itself in constant flux. No single ideology ever finds a completely secure foothold there. Granted, the masculinities competing for dominance in this hegemonic space tend to share certain broad and traditional traits in common – the primacy of male dominance in society, for example, and ideas about male aggression vs. female passivity. Nevertheless, for Bederman, the hegemonic space remains 'unoccupied' (at least, in a permanent sense) by a monolith definition of ideal masculinity.

Race and class act as two of the primary reasons for the contest that is hegemonic masculinity, for these are the arenas in which masculine ideologies are played out, the same influences that continue to destabilise more traditional conceptions of masculine power. As Connell succinctly states, 'it is now common to say that gender "intersects" – better, interacts – with race and class … To understand gender, then, we must constantly go beyond gender' (2005: 75–6). Connell's use of the word 'interacts' seems especially important when discussing masculinity, for an interaction implies a constant giving and taking, a perpetual re-negotiation of stakes and boundaries, and a necessary 'bleeding-over' of issues sometimes dangerously considered in isolation from one another. To a certain degree, Connell lays bare these bleedings-over by designing a four-tiered structure of masculinity to reflect 'the current Western gender order' (2005: 77). The aforementioned category of hegemonic masculinity sits atop the structure, supported by three sub-categories of masculinity: complicit (composed of men who fail to meet the hegemonic standard but whom, nevertheless, reap the rewards of the same in the form of 'patriarchal dividends'); subordinate (homosexual men); and marginal (working class men and/or men of colour) (2005: 77–80). Despite his assignation of a specific masculinity category to this latter group, however, Connell does little in *Masculinities* to genuinely address their marginalised positions. Rather, most of Connell's case studies focus on white-collar and/or college-educated males, and most if not all of the study subjects are Caucasian.

Bederman, on the other hand, not only explores the ways in which white men (such as educator and masculine 'primitivist', G. Stanley Hall) sought to mould *fin de siècle* masculinities, she also examines in depth how white women (Charlotte Perkins Gilman) and men and women of colour (prizefighter Jack Johnson and writer/activist Ida B. Wells) significantly joined the fray, seeing in the same contest opportunities to advance causes for women, African-Americans and other marginalised peoples (see 1996: 41–4). Another key takeaway from Bederman's book, then, is that wealthy, white males are not the only agents sculpting the various masculinities vying for hegemony. Indeed, as *Casino Royale* demonstrates, the new Bond's masculine maturation depends on female and black male 'interventions' at several crucial narrative and developmental crossroads.

Blunt instrument

The first half of *Casino Royale* introduces us to an upwardly mobile Bond, a Bond of reckless ambition whose disciplined body nevertheless belies his class insecurities. As Mick LaSalle says of Bond in a review of the film for the *San Francisco Chronicle*, 'He's a working-class guy who has made his way into upper-class circles but retains some residual coarseness that will never smooth out' (2006: E1). True, and these class issues commence playing themselves out as early as the pre-title sequence, during which the film toys with the inevitable conflations (read: Connell's 'interactions') of masculine rites of passage with class-like structures of bureaucratic/military status. As the film begins, the audience is denied the usual gun-barrel opener in favour of a leap directly into the narrative. The message to Bond fans here is immediately clear – the mould is being broken, something heretofore assumed as accomplished or achieved has not yet become so. The masculine contest is raging, the prize is in flux.

In this opening scene, then, set in Prague, Bond (Daniel Craig) confronts an MI6 section chief, Dryden (Malcolm Sinclair), whom Bond accuses of selling secrets. The section chief sneers at Bond's audacity, noting that if M (Dryden and Bond's MI6 superior) had been so certain Dryden were traitorous, 'she'd have sent a double-0', which, Dryden points out, Bond is not, for his file shows no kills. Already, the film positions Bond as an upstart, a would-be member of an elite club whose inexperience in matters of masculine dominance and execution (in both senses of the word) relegate him to a lower caste in both the pecking order and, hence, the gender order. Dryden's aristocratic 'look' and condescending manner during this sequence contrast sharply with the intercut and intensely violent flashback scenes that interrupt his face-off with Bond. In these flashbacks, Bond fights brutally with Dryden's espionage contact in a tiled restroom. The framed pictures of gentry in polo attire on the restroom walls similarly contrast with the ruthless battle, in which the two combatants crush urinals and ram each other through the walls of toilet stalls. The irony of the contrast is apparent: again, what *kind* of man is this Bond? A smooth member of the gentry class or a thug who drowns enemies in seedy restroom sinks? Bond seems not to know himself as he looks down at his apparently dead opponent (his first 'kill'), exhausted and, we sense, disturbed. Only after shooting the restroom combatant (who had feigned a drowning death) and Dryden does the film 'award' this Bond with the famed gun-barrel intro and, during the extended credits, the *de facto* confirmation of his double-0 status. Ritual acts of extreme violence, then, serve as Bond's entry into the highest levels of the masculinities contest.

And yet, as the dazzling, computer-generated, animated credits reveal, with their depictions of a Bond silhouette (again) felling opponents with spades, clubs, diamonds and hearts amidst casino carpet patterns and swirling playing card motifs, this Bond remains empty, 'blacked out' and only intermittently a man in his own right. Something lingers that keeps this Bond from becoming whole. We do know Bond's name, of course – but is the name enough for us? For Bond? The animation in the credits associates Bond with the icon of the Jack in a deck of cards. Like the Jack, he is a 'face card' – royalty, if you will – but not yet the King, not yet the man on top. In the iconography of the cards, the masculinities contest finds a very apt metaphor. Poker presents itself as an equaliser in which a skilful bluff or a revealing 'tell' may trump any hand a given player may be dealt. At this point however, even as – at the end of the credits – Daniel Craig's face momentarily fills the screen, his blue eyes challenging the gaze of the camera, the CGI animation blacks out his face yet again. The masculinities contest continues to rage, and this Bond remains incomplete, closed off, still subject to his breathless quest to achieve a hegemonic masculinity that remains dangerously unstable and, in fact, indeterminate.

An extended foot chase, shortly after the credits, only compounds the sense of masculine posturing designed to conceal lack. As Bond relentlessly pursues an amazingly agile bomb-maker through the streets and construction sites of Madagascar, issues of masculinities and their interactions with race make themselves apparent. Played here by Sébastien Foucan, the Afro-French creator of the acrobatic/dance endurance sport known as 'free-running' (in which runners career off rooftops, staircases, walls and ledges in a ballet-like display of perpetual forward motion), Bond's prey seems rabbit-like in his evasive efforts. Bond, however, continues the pursuit, matching the moves of the bomb-maker's black body at every turn with an equal demonstration of the white body's physical prowess. As the two balance atop a giant construction crane, Bond even catches in mid-air a pistol thrown at him by the bomb-maker and immediately tosses it back, striking the bomb-maker in the face. The chase continues and intensifies after the bomb-maker seeks asylum in his embassy. Bond brazenly infiltrates the embassy, pistol whips the ambassador, kills the bomb-maker and several guards, and causes a massive fuel explosion.

At first glance, Bond's efforts in this sequence recall the 'shorings up' of white masculinity described by Bederman in her analyses of the 1910 Jack Johnson vs. Jim Jeffries fight and the immense popularity of Edgar Rice Burroughs' 1912 novel, *Tarzan of the Apes* (see 1996: 1–10, 217–38). Each of these 'texts' – if we may, for convenience's sake, label the Johnson-Jeffries fight as such – pit ideal white bodies against those of blacks. In the reality-based former, the white body is found to be bleeding, bruised and wanting, whereas in the fictive latter, the white body emerges as hyper-masculine and triumphant against multiple black bodies. As Bederman states of Tarzan, 'Above all, he has a superb body. If manhood is a historical process that constructs the male body as a metonym for power and identity, *Tarzan*'s cultural work was to proclaim that "the white man's" potential for power and mastery was as limitless as the masculine perfection of Tarzan's body' (1996: 221). Bederman also takes note of Tarzan's noble birth to the Grey-stoke family of England, claiming, 'He thus represents the cutting edge of civilised racial evolution and possesses the inborn intelligence and manly character of the most highly bred Anglo-Saxons' (ibid.). Per Bederman's analysis, then, the white, hyper-masculine Tarzan serves a reactionary function for the threatened white masculinities of that era, an era which had seen a white man lose the heavy-weight boxing title to a black man for the first time only two years before (see 1996: 217–39).

One could argue that Bond's chase of the bomb-maker here serves much the same purpose as Tarzan's battles against native Africans – a shoring up of the white male body. And yet, this sequence serves quite another function for the Bond character, one quite contrary to its more overt function. Rather than simply validating the white male body (which the sequence does admittedly attempt), its overall objective is to demonstrate white male insecurity, lack, the need to 'prove something' – hence the excessive nature of the chase and its almost ridiculously violent conclusion at the embassy. The entire sequence parodies, in a way, the excesses of the Bond series as a whole, the ways in which the films constantly strive to secure Bond a place in the category of hegemonic masculinity, and the cultural cost these acts exact on the racial other.

Casino Royale, in fact, tells us as much through the character of M (Judi Dench), whose rebukes of Bond's recklessness, arrogance and cold-heartedness embody the film's efforts to rewrite this masculine Bond. 'I want you to take your ego out of the equation', she tells Bond after he has embarrassed the Ministry with his excessive acts of violence in Madagascar. Dench's M plays an extremely important role in this Bond film, more so than in any of the others in which she has appeared since *GoldenEye* (1995). Her assumption of a tough exterior in a male-dominated world does not inhibit her ability to exercise the feminine and maternal sides of her personality, and – for the first time in the series – her example of an open-gendered existence significantly influences the development of Bond's moral and gendered character. 'Arrogance and self-awareness rarely go hand-in-hand', she tells Bond in *Casino Royale*, a lesson Bond will remember after his initial loss to Le Chiffre (Mads Mikkelsen), during the high-stakes poker game. In fact, as the film progresses Bond begins to share in M's liberating and empowering gender possibilities. By curbing his lust for hegemonic masculine power, M seems to suggest, Bond might cease to remain a dinosaur of the Cold

War era (her accusation directed at Pierce Brosnan's Bond in *GoldenEye*) and become instead a vessel for new gender possibility.

No armour left

Bond's class insecurities, which, as we have seen, feed his masculine insecurities, continue into the second part of the film. A telling exchange – without doubt, the most frank and compelling dialogue between a man and a woman in the entire Bond oeuvre – takes place between Bond and his British Treasury contact, Vesper Lynd (Eva Green), in the luxury dining car of a train bound for the nascent country of Montenegro. Obviously inspired by a similarly telling train scene in Alfred Hitchcock's 1959 spy thriller, *North by Northwest*, the dialogue here shares similar goals – first, to demonstrate two attempts at counter-psychoanalysis, and second, to fill the air with sexual tension. In both cases, issues of identity and origin are at stake, and the pretensions of the players in these respective games depend almost exclusively upon effective deployment of such poker tactics as the bluff and the hiding of the 'tell'.

'I'm the money', Lynd declares confidently as she takes a seat assertively across from Bond. Lynd refers to her status as the authorised governmental financier for Bond's buy-in at the Texas hold 'em poker game with terrorist finance broker Le Chiffre at the Casino Royale, but, predictably, Bond chooses to read the statement in a different way. 'Every penny of it', he replies. We assume we are on familiar Bond ground here, his innuendo obviously checking a genre box. Yet, these two statements already reveal a great deal about these two characters. Lynd intends the statement to sound 'insider-ish', as if she has just walked out of a con-artist film like George Roy Hill's *The Sting* (1973) or David Mamet's *House of Games* (1987), with which *Casino Royale* bears an endearing affinity. Bond, however, plays on the statement's other streetwise manifestation, that popularised by the hip-hop and 'gangsta' cultures of the 1980s and 1990s (that is, 'I'm the money', as in 'I'm all that' or 'I'm the bomb'). She, the less-than-stodgy middle-management bureaucrat, takes her initial cues from fictive but knowing undressings of streetwise con culture; he, the would-be-suave avatar of male hegemony, takes his from the language of marginalised masculinities. Each reveals something to the other – a 'tell', of sorts, that will fuel the mutual analyses that follow.

Later in the conversation, after Lynd expresses misgivings about the British government's plan to back Bond in the luxury poker match that will, they hope, break the financial back of an international terrorist network, Bond asserts he can be trusted to win the game. He knowingly claims that, 'in poker, you never play your hand ... you play the man across from you', and he demonstrates by performing a once-over pseudo-psychological assessment of Lynd, noting first that her beauty 'is a problem', for she fears she will not be taken seriously. 'Which one can say of any attractive woman with half a brain', Lynd replies. 'True', Bond is quick to acknowledge, although his remaining comments follow the same trajectory. Does he immediately recognise the shallow and predictable nature of his developing profile of her? After all, are not such comments, which masquerade here as nuggets of profound perception and analysis, in truth merely reactionary appraisals voiced by frustrated white-collar males since the advent of second-wave feminism? Granted, Lynd denies none of Bond's assessments; they could be, after all, perfectly accurate. What is missing from the profile, rather, is imagination, an acquiescence to the odds and probabilities of the human mystery – a flaw of pride that will initially prove his undoing during the poker confrontation with Le Chiffre. Indeed, Bond's hubristic proclamation regarding his ability to extract the essence of others speaks to the still-lingering arrogance that continues to inhibit his self-awareness and, hence, the possibilities of an open-gender state.

Lynd's counter-evaluation, however, rings more true than Bond's, perhaps because it originates from a place outside of Bond's would-be hegemonic masculinity while, at the same time, sardonically critiquing that masculinity. The monologue is worth reproducing here in its entirety, for the whole of it provides an extremely self-reflexive examination not only of Bond himself, but of the Bond series as a canon and the concept of hegemonic masculinity in general:

> By the cut of your suit, you went to Oxford, or wherever. Naturally, you think human beings dress like that. But you wear it with such disdain, my guess is you didn't come from money, and your school friends never let you forget it. Which means that you were at that school by someone else's charity, hence that chip on your shoulder. And since your first thought about me ran to orphan, that's what I'd say you are. [Bond tries to keep a 'poker face'.] Oh, you are! [pause] And that makes perfect sense, since MI6 looks for maladjusted young men who give little thought to sacrificing others in order to protect Queen and country. You know, former SAS types with easy smiles and expensive watches.

Lynd's diatribe speaks volumes. She sees through Bond's class posing, dismissing both his Oxford pedigree and his wardrobe as blatant attempts to overcome his class insecurities. She recognises, too, that his methods for doing so take the form of hyper-masculine posturings – his rise through the military's and the Ministry's elite ranks intended as a buffer to a lack of familial history or a genuine masculine identity. Lynd's critique, in truth, is of a gender order in which a 'licence' to perform sanctioned acts of violence stands in for a failure to achieve a coveted form of masculinity. Her orphan accusation is more than literal, for Bond's is truly an orphaned, maladjusted masculinity – replete with the capabilities of a hegemonic masculinity, yet constantly in service to an even higher hegemonic order, shocked at its capacity for violence yet determined to slough off its psychological implications. When Vesper later asks if killing bothers Bond, he replies, 'I wouldn't be very good at my job if it did.' Vesper sighs. 'I don't believe you', and neither do we. Bond here seems to be attempting to convince himself of his feelings, based upon what he has come to understand as being masculine. Hence the Walter Benjamin comment at the beginning of this essay – the appeal of poker to an orphaned masculinity such as Bond's seems only appropriate. Like his many other 'climbing' tactics, gambling, too, serves as a method of ennobling, of filling a masculinities void that continues to remain empty despite all efforts.

Yet, rather than ennobling Bond in the material sense with a reward of noble birth or an official recognition of his acceptance into the hegemonic patriarchal order, the Texas hold 'em poker game that serves as the backbone of the film's second act, and the torture scene that follows, offer Bond the opportunity to complete the rewriting of his own masculinity, a process already begun by M and Lynd. His humiliating initial loss to Le Chiffre comes about as a result of his arrogant belief in masculine, panoptical knowledge – his faith in his ability to read, to 'know' others, to see them for what they are and from a position he perceives to be that of hegemonic masculinity. But as the poker scenes in *Casino Royale* reveal, hegemonic and essentialist notions of masculinity are merely fictions masquerading as facts.

Judith Butler fully explores this theme in her book *Gender Trouble: Feminism and the Subversion of Identity* where she formulates a theory of identity and gender which is predicated on performativity, repetition and the reiteration of various identifying practices:

> The rules that govern intelligible identity, i.e., that enable and restrict the intelligible assertion of an 'I', rules that are partially structured along matrices of gender hierarchy and compulsory heterosexuality, operate through repetition. Indeed, when the subject is said to be constituted, that means simply that the subject is a consequence of certain rule-governed discourses that govern the intelligible invocation of identity. The subject is not *determined* by the rules through which it is generated because signification is *not a founding act, but rather a regulated process of repetition* that both conceals itself and enforces its rules precisely through the production of substantialising effects. (2006: 198; emphasis in original)

For Butler, gender ('*a corporeal style*, an "act", as it were, which is both intentional and performative, where "*performative*" suggests a dramatic and contingent construction of meaning') and sex are cultural performances that are produced through the repetition of the rules that govern intelligible identity (2006: 190; emphasis in original). In turn, 'There is no gender identity behind the expressions of gender; that identity is performatively constituted by the very "expressions" that are said to be its results' (2006: 34). According to Butler, then, 'agency' is within the 'orbit of compulsion to repeat ... within the possibility of varia that repetition' (2006: 198).

Bond is introduced to this new Butlerian world and the rules govern identifying practices of gender binarism, as well as the contradictions/va inherent in the performance of gender that contest and challenge the 'rigid codes' of that 'binarism', through his encounters with the arch villain, Le Chiffre. After his initial poker 'showdown', Bond confidently tells his cohorts that in losing to Le Chiffre he has discovered a weakness (his opponent's 'tell') that will inevitably help him win the 'showdown'. According to Bond, the 'tell' (an unconscious behaviour that is thought to betray an attempted deception) is 'the twitch [Le Chiffre] has to hide when he bluffs'. Here, the bluff represents one's ability to pretend to have a strong/winning hand (poker's version of the *phallus*, a marker of masculine power and privilege) while masking any sign of fear, doubt or insecurity that would reveal its opposite, the *lack* of a strong hand. Meanwhile the 'tell' represents a self-emasculating principle where the (male) poker player, unable to control and compose his emotions, tips his weak hand through an uncontrollable gesture.

But Bond misreads Le Chiffre's 'twitch', interprets it as an external sign of inward weakness and real lack rather than 'a variation on that repetition', and loses the pot, precisely because he relies on an essentialist model of how signification works. What he does not account for is Le Chiffre's ability to vary the game, to produce/perform the twitch or the 'tell' (to display and exteriorise a seemingly 'essential' disposition) as a strategy to bluff him. What makes Bond's presumption, regarding Le Chiffre's 'tell', especially ironic is that the game of poker denaturalises and theatricalises essentialists' account of identity by using stereotypical labels of masculinity and femininity, such as a strong hand, weak hand, the 'tell' and the fold, to describe a player's *acts* irrespective of his/her sex. Moreover, the strategy of bluffing (originally meaning to blindfold or hoodwink, derived from the Dutch *bluffen*, to boast or brag) allows a player to change his/her role within the game by performing any of the above-mentioned acts in order to gain an advantage over his/her opponent. And yet, despite this deconstructionist bent, poker's vocabulary and the objective of the game still reflect traditional gender hierarchies that exist outside of the game.

In poker, a player *shows* his masculine prowess by courageously risking money (his phallic placeholder) and by using his bluffing skills to control and overcome various emasculating obstacles (for example, other players, chance or lady luck, and most importantly himself) in order to win the pot. Hence, even the player who plays his cards right, must be able to conceal the emasculatory side effects ('the twitch he has to hide when he bluffs') that performing masculinity in poker engenders. The bluff, then, represents the ability to signify the phallus, by pretending to have a winning hand, or (as in Le Chiffre's case) dissimulate it, by pretending to have a weak hand – while controlling the feminising forces triggered by the act of risking and bluffing – in order to evade emasculation or emasculate one's opponent by either making them fold, or by luring them into a losing proposition.

This scenario introduces an interesting wrinkle to the masculinity contests, for if one can make a strong hand seem weak and a weak hand seem strong then not only does the phallus become performative ('where *performative* suggests a dramatic and contingent construction of meaning') but the ability to perform a successful bluff becomes phallic. It allows one to produce the effects of the phallus regardless of the hand they hold. This is because, like the production of gender, the signification that ultimately constitutes or determines the phallus is a '*regulated process of repetition* that ... enforces its rules precisely through the production of substantialising effects'. Which means, there is no phallus behind the *expressions* of the phallus, the phallus 'is performatively constituted by the very "expressions" that are said to be its results'. In turn, for both the player who holds the proverbial ace in the hole, and the one who lacks the trump card, but successfully pretends to have it, the only way the phallus in poker will ultimately manifest itself is by either emasculating one's opponent (by taking his money), or averting emasculation (by not losing one's own money), or by losing one's money and experiencing the phallus as loss. In other words, the phallus, and in particular *this phallus* (since according to Bederman multiple ideas about manhood circulate within cultures at any given time), is an effect that is retroactively produced through a prescribed set of actions that are motivated by the desire to substantialise it.

In this way, *Casino Royale* metaphorically connects the regulated processes of repetition that determine masculinity, and in turn the phallus, in poker, with those that underwrite the Bondian formula to reveal how the ways in which masculinity is performed (that is, acted out as well as used to carry through an action) retroactively reifies the Bondian phallus. For instance, one way that the Bondian formula substantialises the effects of the phallus is through action sequences wherein the protagonist uses his strength, intellect and composure to escape danger/emasculation and to defeat/emasculate his enemies. Consequently, the more Bond places himself at risk, the greater the threat of symbolic castration (at the hands of those who want make him the trophy that instantiates their phallus), the more masculine he appears to become when he overcomes those obstacles.

In *Casino Royale*, this process is parodied in an episode that begins with Bond narrowly defeating one of his foes, Alex Dimitrios (Simon Abkarian), at a high-stakes poker game by winning his Aston Martin. The victory at the poker table, and the ensuing action, succinctly summarise the operations of the Bondian phallus: showing how Bond produces the substantialising effects of the phallus by emasculating his opponent in various ways. After defeating Dimitrios at poker, Bond uses his winnings (Dimitrios's car) to cuckold him by seducing his wife, Solange (Caterina Murino), which leads to him using her to foil his plans, and to finally killing him with his own knife. But Bond's *performance* of his masculine identity is not complete until he can overcome one final hurdle. After successfully foiling Le Chiffre's terror plot, Bond meets M at Dimitrios's residence where he finds Solange tortured to death. While Bond impassively assesses the scene another agent quickly turns away to avoid vomiting. Despite his initial lack of emotion, Bond eventually tips his hand when, during an exchange with M (in which she reminds him of his culpability in the innocent woman's murder), his head twitches to the side and momentarily dissolves the frozen expression on his face. Later, after a brief stroll through the house, where Bond and M discuss his new assignment, they return to the corpse, which is now being placed inside a body bag. As Bond absorbs the scene through his poker face, M uses the opportunity to chide him once more: 'I would ask if you could remain emotionally detached but I don't think that's your problem, is it, Bond?', to which Bond responds by bluffing, 'No'. Hence, unlike most of his predecessors who, in performing the Bondian phallus rarely revealed the effects that their performances had on them, Craig's Bond registers, and then conceals, the psychological effects of these masculinity contests on his troubled psyche.

These inward wars become more manifest when, in between the endless games of posturing, and the repetitive actions of the bluff and the 'tell' at the poker table, Bond is forced to perform his masculinity through several death-defying acts. In the first instance, Bond murders the two Ugandan rebels who have come to collect their investment from Le Chiffre. After this bloody, harrowing ordeal we see a distressed Bond, covered in his opponents' blood, standing before his bathroom mirror – the same mirror he used to survey his suave image earlier in the film – tending to his wounds, while trying to calm his shaken nerves with swigs of whiskey. Here, we are reminded of Chris Cornell's choral commentary in the opening song: 'If you take a life do you know what you'll give?/Odds are, you won't like what it is'. Weighing those odds before a mirror, we sense Bond questioning his own resolve, while trying to convince himself to continue playing this most dangerous game. The scene's lack of music, quick cuts and jarring close-ups give it a sense of sudden urgency, marking it as a pivotal moment in the narrative. In the final shot, Bond, mirroring a move he will use later at the poker table (where he leans forward peering into his opponent's soul, searching for the 'tell' while daring Le Chiffre to call his 'bluff'), leans forward to interrogate himself, to see if he can detect a bluff behind his own steely blue eyes. But before he (or we) have a chance to see what is behind his poker face he returns to the poker table, where he and Le Chiffre (who was emasculated earlier by the Ugandan rebels) try to conceal the recent chinks in their masculine armour by outperforming each other through strategies of the bluff. Le Chiffre states, 'You changed your shirt, Mr Bond. I hope our little game isn't causing you to perspire.' To which Bond replies, 'A little. But I won't consider myself to be in trouble until I start weeping blood.' Bond's caustic retort is not only meant to cut down Le Chiffre but bolster his bruised ego. Listening to the statement with Bond's ears, we can hear him telling himself, 'I'm not nearly as vulnerable as my visibly deformed enemy'.

Bond, however, is not allowed to bluff away the evening's bloody proceedings so easily. When he returns to his hotel room later, he is reminded of his earlier misgivings when he sees Vesper, his accomplice and aid in the murders, sitting in the shower, and trying, *à la* Lady Macbeth, to wash the invisible blood (her guilt) off her fingers. In a rare and moving gesture (especially for a Bond film) he acknowledges his vulnerability and their mutual ordeal by comforting her while simultaneously assuaging his own fears by playing the man to her distressed damsel, effectively reinforcing gender binarism by showing himself that there is little room in these brutal masculinity contests for feminine vulnerability.

Perhaps this explains why Bond, after the incident with the Ugandans, frantically tries to wash away his physical and psychic wounds with water and whiskey. It is as if any thoughts, feelings or emotions that threaten and weaken privileged notions of masculinity (that is, the same feminising forces that hegemonic masculinity uses to differentiate itself from the feminine) trigger an almost autoimmune-like response in the masculine subject who must – like the 'twitch' one has to hide when one bluffs – conceal or cancel out these alienating forces before being undone by them. And like the 'tell' in poker, these 'feminising' forces are themselves triggered and unleashed by masculinity contests that are meant to substantialise the Bondian phallus by continually putting it at risk. Which means, in order for Bond to become (and to remain) 'Bond', he not only has to *showcase* his brand of masculinity, by continuously risking the phallus and coming out on top, but he also has to conceal and repress any trepidation or doubt that might prevent him from performing his masculine identity. In this way, the masculinity games of *Casino Royale* (by having Bond mask his feelings and then elicit his own suspicion for doing so) add a new wrinkle to the spy games of the Bond genre. As Cornell's lyrics state: 'If you come inside things will not be the same/When you return to the night/And if you think you've won/You never saw me change/The game that we have been playing.'

Hence, Bond's gesture of peering into the mirror, to look for the 'tell', shows how strategies of bluffing bleed into more private performances of masculinity and how the ability to hoodwink one's self, to 'to hide your hand' and 'forget how to feel', helps advance hegemonic masculinity's agenda. But Cornell's lyrics, 'if you must pretend/You may meet your end', also suggest that this performance comes at a price, because Bond's poker face (his alienating armour) operates as a kind of death mask that metaphorically enacts the process of killing him through the ritual act of wearing/performing it. For what Bond 'must pretend', is that his feelings of fear, doubt and vulnerability (brought on by daring displays of masculinity) are not warning signs that ought to be heeded but feminine insecurities that need to be defeated and contained, either through repression and denial, which represent a kind of self-mutilation, or through outward acts of displaced aggression and violence, which dehumanise in their own way.

Consequently, bluffing helps transform these inward *acts* of self-destruction into seeming acts of self-preservation by producing the psychic effects of the phallus – for 'the phallic is always a matter of *swagger*, something puffed up and inherently *denying* its primordial vulnerability, an illusion of coherence and omnipotence that *denies* the reality of its own internal division and potential for loss' (Clark 2005; emphasis in original). This phallic stance of posturing and denial encourages the subject to overcome his feelings of doubt and remorse, in order to continue performing his dangerously deformed masculinity.

That Bond's own brand of masculinity is toxic to him is symbolically expressed through a heart-stopping episode, where Bond is poisoned by a drink which is synonymous with his name, the martini. The venomous cocktail sends Bond reeling into the men's room – the symbolic place of his birth (his first kill) – and afterwards to his car where Vesper eventually revives him with a defibrillator. Upon returning from the dead – the film makes various visual and verbal references to birth and rebirth – the wounded hero quips to Le Chiffre, 'that last hand nearly killed me'. Bond's playful jest cleverly conflates the poker game with those other masculinity contests while hinting at the dangers posed by both. Meanwhile, the shot/reverse-shot, operating as a kind of mirror during the protracted poker scenes, reiterates this notion by showing how both men, like the poker-playing corpses at the *Body Worlds* exhibition in Miami, wage a never-ending, soul-deadening battle over an illusory phallus that must constantly be performed in order to be possessed.

In Le Chiffre's case, the cost of pursuing this phallus is mapped on to his face, in the form of a tear duct that weeps blood. And yet, the blood that uncontrollably oozes from his eye does not seem to be caused by what he feels but what he will not allow himself to feel: his body forever mourning for that part of his psyche that has been sacrificed to masculinity. If this lack of emotion makes Le Chiffre more ruthless and dangerous, then all the better for him. But what does Le Chiffre's deformed soul mean for Bond? Is that soul the fate that awaits Bond if he continues to bluff/hoodwink himself into thinking that his muscular performances will eventually fulfill him? Bond himself acknowledges this sentiment when, near the end of the film's second act, he admits to Vesper, 'You do what I do for too long and there won't be any soul to salvage. I'm leaving with what little I have left.' And yet, ironically, the 'little' that Bond has left, is given to him by Le Chiffre who, during the seminal torture scene, strips Bond of his armour by teaching him that if he does 'not yield soon enough, there will be little left to identify [him]', not just as a 'man' but a human.

During the torture scene, the camera's literal and figurative undressing of the Bond character, which occurs throughout the film, and is morbidly thematicised in the exhibition of anatomised bodies, reaches its visual and narrative climax. Having survived chase scenes, love scenes, card games and near-death experiences that stretched the Bond character and the genre (from a spy action film to romantic/screwball comedy, to drama and even self-parody) to its very limits, we now find Bond at his most vulnerable. Sitting naked and hunched over in a dark and dank room, with his hands and feet tied and his genitals dangling in the air, Le Chiffre threatens him with castration. When he tells Bond that his body is such 'a waste', his words do not just refer to Bond's physicality – the word 'waste', together with the seedy underground locale, echo the bathroom stalls where Bond's nascent identity was first performed – but everything that his gladiatorial body symbolises, including those desires, which are tied to performing a particular notion of the phallus and consequently masculinity.

Visibly shaken, and at the mercy of the sadistic Le Chiffre, Bond nevertheless tries to maintain his composure and bluff his way out of danger, in this strip poker-less version of the masculinities contest. While pretending to masochistically enjoy the torture Le Chiffre dolls out, Bond tells him that if he (meaning Bond) is killed, then Le Chiffre will have nowhere to seek refuge from those disgruntled associates who wish to kill him. But Le Chiffre calls Bond's bluff, telling him that the British government will welcome him with open arms and give him sanctuary for the valuable information he can offer them, even if he murders both Bond and Vesper. Upon hearing this, a demoralised Bond begrudgingly nods in agreement, muttering M's words ('the big picture') from a previous scene. In calling Bond's bluff, Le Chiffre not only tries to show that Bond is not his 'own man', but that his stubborn show of resistance (that is, his performance) is being *wasted* on those (Queen and country) who consider him to be as expendable as waste. And yet, in this new permutation of the masculinities contest, what determines victory is not to merely call your opponent's bluff but to get him to stop bluffing and acknowledge his weakness (the 'tell') in order to get him to talk or tell.

Tell, however, is precisely what Bond will not do. Although his hand is exposed (in a most humiliating and painful way) he refuses to 'yield' the password of the multimillion-dollar account to Le Chiffre. In a last ditch effort to extract Bond's precious secret, Le Chiffre tells Bond that he will exchange Vesper's life for the password. Although Bond seems noticeably worried (even scared) for Vesper, he manages to put on his poker face, choosing to keep secret the password that bears Vesper's name rather than give up that name in order to save the woman he loves. And yet, if Bond is bluffing and he really cares for Vesper, as much as, if not more than, his phallic duty to maintain a stiff upper lip, then his bluff is not just meant to deceive Le Chiffre but himself. Which means, in order for Bond to uphold his identity and withhold the phallus from Le Chiffre, he has to first hoodwink/convince himself that this symbolic victory in defeat means more to him than Vesper's life. And second, he must suppress and hide the effects of his bluff (the 'tell') from himself.

This masquerade is necessitated by the fact that Bond's masculine identity (that which defines Bond as 'Bond') is tied to his ability to evade emasculation by withholding Vesper's name, while its opposite (showing his vulnerability by giving up her name) signifies self-emasculation. In uttering this treacherous speech act (that is, Vesper's name), Bond would be *acting* against himself, deviating from his normative identity as a cold-blooded assassin by divulging his secret to a sworn enemy. Therefore, it is not just woman, as an object of heterosexual masculine desire, that affects how men perform their masculine identity, but the particular role in which 'woman' is cast by the hegemonic order of masculinity. Here, Vesper's name (acting as a secret password in these spy games) is the phallic marker that the two men vie for in order to substantialise the effects of the phallus. So despite Bond's feelings of righteous indignation at the conclusion of the film, in this scene, at least, it is Bond who (in staying 'true' to a certain notion of himself) betrays Vesper and his love for her by refusing to utter her name. Bluffing, then, is not just a strategic form of bravado used to produce the effects of the phallus by outmanoeuvring and outfacing external forces that threaten emasculation, but also an essential mode of self-deception and self-denial that actively guards the subject's ego ideal and the privileged role of the phallus from inward threats of emasculation by pitting the subject against himself.

In masking his feelings for Vesper, Bond denies Le Chiffre his phallic victory but he also hoodwinks himself into thinking that despite the fact that his pursuit of hegemonic masculinity will kill him (before it fulfils him) the game is still worth playing. This explains why Le Chiffre's threats of castration, 'I'll feed you what you seem not to value', are not effective and why Bond would rather eat his own penis and suffer castration than give up the phallus through symbolic emasculation. For what ultimately defines Bond's masculine identity (or gives it 'value') is not the penis but a culturally constructed notion of the phallus and those performances that retroactively produce the effects of that phallus. And yet, Le Chiffre's threat of castration also shows that, in order to hold on to this illusory notion of the phallus, one must be willing to give up or sacrifice an essential part of one's self.

In turn, it is only after his latest ordeal, where Bond nearly loses everything but the phallus, that he becomes disillusioned with his phallic pursuit and decides to stop performing/repeating the identity that, although giving him his name, strips him of his humanity. As Bond sits in his wheelchair contemplating his future, Vesper, who had earlier told Bond, 'You've got a choice, you know … just because you've done something doesn't mean you have to keep on doing it', now proposes a new direction. She tells him, 'I just want you to know that if all that was left of you was your smile and your little finger, you'd still be more of a man than anyone I've ever known'. In essence, Vesper is telling Bond that what makes him a man, in her eyes, is not the phallus but something else, an identity operating outside the jurisdiction of hegemonic masculinity; an identity far more heterogeneous, humble and benign, like a 'little finger' and a 'smile'.

Epilogue and conclusion

As the film nears its end, Vesper Lynd is forced to betray Bond, and, shamed, chooses to die rather than to allow Bond to rescue her. Soon after, we see that Bond has once again donned his armour, agreeing unequivocally with M that he really does trust no one. But we sense, too, from Bond's all-too-stoic silence in response to M's suggestions about Vesper's altruistic motives for betrayal, that 'behind the bravado', (or bluff) something is still eating away at Bond's soul – a humble recognition of emotional (rather than physical) vulnerability that completes the rite of passage into manhood (and double-0 status) that has been the agenda of *Casino Royale* from frame one.

As he prepares to interrogate/torture Mr White (Jesper Christensen), the head of the international terrorist-financing network, in the final scene of the film, Bond is presented to us from White's point of view on the ground (to which he has fallen after Bond has shot him in the leg). The camera tilts from Bond's expensive shoes and up the pin-striped trousers and jacket of his designer suit, and we finally see Bond as we have expected to see him – in complete control (not reckless), self-assured (not arrogant) and cool as hell. But has Bond achieved the self-awareness of which M spoke early in the film? Will he move into his next adventure with the lessons of his open-gender experiences intact? Or has *Casino Royale* merely been an exercise in origins, a way of explaining how the Bond we have already known came to be? Is this new Bond a work in progress or a *fait accompli*? While the answer to these questions lies in the coming Bond films – starting with *Quantum of Solace* (2008) – *Casino Royale* itself forever changes long-held gender assumptions about one of popular culture's most celebrated (and persecuted) heroes.

6

DOUBLE-0 AGENCIES: FEMININITY, POST-FEMINISM AND THE FEMALE SPY

Estella Tincknell

The reinvention of the Bond movie in 2006 with the brutally violent 'back to basics' *Casino Royale* was also interesting for its foregrounding of a female double-agent, Vesper Lynd (Eva Green), whose role in the narrative – and action – was apparently very different from that of the traditional 'Bond girl'. Lynd seemed in some ways to be a deliberately 'post-feminist' character in her social independence and her adult, knowingly mocking relationship with Bond. However, *Casino Royale*'s mobilisation of the question of the female double-agent's sexual treachery or loyalty as its central narrative enigma is itself hardly new, drawing as it does on generic conventions within the spy thriller that can be traced back through *Austin Powers: International Man of Mystery* (1997) and *North by Northwest* (1959) to World War One, and mobilising cultural anxieties about women's social and sexual freedom to 'betray' men that go back considerably further. This essay will explore the extent to which the character of Vesper Lynd in the 2006 film represents a meaningful shift in the way female agency is configured in the Bond stories and considers her importance to the 'rebirth' of Bond and the Bond franchise.

Back to Fleming: sadism and sex

The pre-release publicity for *Casino Royale* insistently trumpeted that this would be a new Bond for a new age, complete with a new actor playing the central role (Daniel Craig), a new emphasis on global realpolitik and a new set of aesthetic and narrative concerns. A stunningly visceral early sequence, set on a Madagascan building site, effectively establishes the terms for this new realism. Rejecting the use of CGI in favour of 'real' stunts performed wherever possible by the cast, including the French 'free-runner' Sébastien Foucan playing Mollaka, a bomb-maker chased by Bond across towering cranes and through a maze of apparent death traps, these scenes establish that this Bond is first and foremost an action hero, in radical contrast to the suave but somewhat wooden version offered by Craig's immediate predecessor, Pierce Brosnan. Indeed, this set-piece tour-de-force of stunts and camerawork is preceded by a very different but equally important pre-title sequence shot in black-and-white that has a further function in the transformation and 'rebirth' of the Bond films and of James Bond as a character. First, it establishes the moment – and the conditions – in which Bond secures his 'double-0' status, this time emphasising the character's ruthlessness and tendency to recklessness. Second, it repositions the Bond films in relation to a tradition of noirish British thrillers (Michael Caine in two decidedly anti-Bond texts, *The Ipcress File* (1966) and *Get Carter* (1971) spring to mind) that are overtly different to the glossy escapism of the Bond model. In these very different sequences, *Casino Royale* skilfully re-sutures the meanings of Bond in terms of the emphatic re-masculinisation of the character together with a physical and graphic realism that signals the new authenticity claimed by the producers.

Crucial to the text's articulation of this newness and rebirth is that the now immortal lines, 'the name's Bond … James Bond', together with the equally famous signature tune, are only uttered at the very end of the film as Bond cold-bloodedly wounds Mr White (Jesper Christensen), the shadowy go-between who sets the plot in motion. At this moment John Barry's musical theme swells on the soundtrack, and the point has been made: Bond has only 'become' himself now, at this moment, and as the culmination of the prior series of narrative events. This necessary rebirth is a thread that runs throughout the narrative from the very beginning. Bond's initial crudeness as a killer – his recklessness and immature impetuosity – is repeatedly signalled, most importantly through M's anger with him at the way he has endangered a larger project in order to pick off an unimportant agent. In the tradition of the masculine romance, Bond can only then gain M's full approval and 'become' the assured Secret Service agent both she and the state requires by undergoing a series of tests and endurances that will transform him. In order to do this, however, he must renounce the feminine romance offered by Vesper Lynd.

It is useful to remind ourselves at this point of two things pertinent both to *Casino Royale*'s original appearance as a novel in 1953 and to its reworking in 2006. First, Ian Fleming's contribution to the reinvention of the thriller as a popular genre in the 1950s and in the context of the Cold War not only came at a point of national crisis and decline for Great Britain, as Michael Denning (2003) has argued, it also constituted an important intervention in the way the privileges claimed by upper-class white men were being struggled over. Fleming himself was not only an ideologist of empire, he was also a direct beneficiary, who enjoyed a quasi-colonial lifestyle in what is routinely described as his 'Jamaican retreat', 'GoldenEye'. Second, Fleming himself circulated the claim that his author-ship of *Casino Royale* had been prompted by his forthcoming marriage and the prospect of renunciating the supposed 'bachelor freedoms' he enjoyed (although, since he went on to use the same mix of elements in eleven further novels featur-ing James Bond, this catharsis appears to have been less than successful). This de-liberate contribution to the emergent mythology around Bond was also an artful intervention into the postwar ideological battles over gender in which the Bond novels themselves participate. These two points are important because it was the novels' peculiar mix of cultural elitism, racism, sex and sadism which helped to configure the male spy as sexual and cultural connoisseur as well as operative, and they also re-established the centrality of female sexual treachery and instabil-ity to the ideological concerns of the genre. Fleming's novels feature a couple of female agents, of course, including Tatiana Romanova in *From Russia, With Love* (1957) as well as Vesper Lynd.

The spy story, emerging in the late nineteenth century with the growth of competing European imperial powers 'scrambling for Africa' and engaging in 'the great game' of international intrigue, was first codified in the novels of H. Rider Haggard, William Erskine Childers and John Buchan from the late 1880s through to the 1920s. Yet the mystified and profoundly threatening figure of the female double-agent is largely absent from these stories, although a kind of precursor does appear (intriguingly, in every sense) in one of the earlier Sherlock Holmes stories, 'A Scandal in Bohemia' (1891), in the form of Irene Adler, a woman whose ability to outwit Holmes is also linked to uncertainty over her sexual fidelity. Mata Hari, the Dutch 'exotic dancer' turned spy who was executed towards the end of World War One remains the template for the idea of the female spy whose sex-ual treachery is bound up with political and national betrayals, and the figure of the female double-agent has become a powerful feature of Western mythologies about spying. Such figures are frequently fascinating because of what they repre-sent rather than what they were or actually are. Mata Hari was not a particularly good secret agent and it remains doubtful that her actions made much difference to the progress of the war. She was, however, a woman who claimed a degree of social autonomy in her actions and in her sexual relations with men. Hari's reputation as a profoundly dangerous spy rested thus almost entirely on her other (sexual) reputation, or lack of it, and the threat this posed to patriarchal power.

In fictional spy narratives female agents are almost always double-agents. Their untrustworthiness for the state is, then, systematically linked to their availability to the central male character and to the threat desire poses for him. This anxiety, although represented in the terms of the genre's overt concern with protecting national (or Western) power interests, can also be understood as a symptom of the threat femininity poses to the stability of masculinity. The female double-agent's 'doubleness' is constituted in her apparent lack, her fragmented subjectivity, rather than the wholeness of masculinity. But the presence of this lack is also what threatens patriarchal certitude. The double-agent must therefore be 'called into being' – that is, deliberately inserted into the text – in order to be destroyed. The female agent, however autonomous she initially appears, then, will always be cast as a sexual lure to the central male character, the means by which he is trapped, whether it is into the arms of the villain or – at the end – into marriage, the most powerful and threatening of traps for men. Succumbing to momentary desire can thus lead to a lifetime's containment (especially in the discursive world inhabited by Fleming) unless the male agent can find ways to avoid this. In *Casino Royale* Bond has only just secured his 'double-0' status. We therefore already know marriage is unlikely to be the resolution to this particular narrative, or if it is that something will destroy either the marriage or the wife, as in *On Her Majesty's Secret Service* (1969).

In *North by Northwest*, a film evidently referenced by *Casino Royale* in its setting up of the encounter between Bond and Lynd in the dining car of a luxury train taking them both towards danger, Eve Kendall's (Eva Marie Saint) role as

Strangers on a train: Roger Thornhill (Cary Grant) and Eve Kendall (Eva Marie Saint) in *North by Northwest* (1959)

a double-agent is deliberately muddied and mystified. The audience, initially positioned with Roger Thornhill (Cary Grant), has no reason to trust her any more than he has, since we too do not know what motivates her behaviour and her willingness to help him. Her appearance in the dining car at Thornhill's table, like that of Lynd, appears to be a component of her claim to agency and to a subject position that the text itself struggles to allow her. On the one hand, Kendall is represented as a fetishised object of desire, on the other she knows too much, as Tania Modleski (1988) has argued of other Hitchcock heroines. Her smooth golden hair in particular signifies both her desirability and her potential untrustworthiness: as Thornhill moves towards a romantic embrace he cannot quite allow himself to touch it until he has regained mastery over what it is she knows. It is imperative, therefore, that she must be returned to a subordinated position which no longer threatens Thornhill, and which requires him to rescue her, before he can recognise his desire for her.

North by Northwest, as has been observed by many critics, offers a master class in the organisation of suspense in the service of generic expectation. It skilfully permits the audience a certain amount of information in order to sustain and intensify the pleasurable agony of uncertainty about the way in which the plot will unfold. Crucial to this is the figure of Kendall, whose coolness and apparent confidence not only renders her mystified but also suggests that her punishment (marriage to or murder by Vandamm (James Mason)) is somehow justified. The possibility that Vesper Lynd also cannot be fully trusted is only temporarily and contingently part of *Casino Royale*'s narrative, although it is important that we know very little about her. Since her background is only revealed through what the character herself says and not what the film shows, it is never clear to what extent her career in the British Treasury is an intrinsic part of her own contradictions and uncertainties as a woman who claims a full subject position in a social context that ultimately insists on this as an impossibility.

'Post-feminism', modernity and the 'Bond girl'

The context of new beginnings circulating around *Casino Royale* also informed the construction of new discourses around the 'Bond girl'. In place of a tradition of sexism and casual misogyny, it seemed the new Bond would be both tough and tender, the 'Bond girl' a sophisticated career woman. The character of Vesper Lynd was, then, to be a part of the revision and refreshment of the Bond franchise, integral to the modernisation process that would simultaneously retain and reinvigorate the existing audience for Bond while establishing new constituencies, especially perhaps amongst women. In the public discourse around casting for the film the idea that this new version of the 'Bond girl' would be an appropriately 'post-feminist' equal to Bond, perhaps in age as well as economic status, was clearly stated. For example, one film website quotes the Chairman (sic) of Columbia Pictures, Amy Pascal, arguing that: 'you need to have palpable sexual tension in the movie and in casting Vesper, we really needed to up the ante, *because this character is very much an equal to Bond* and central to our story' (see anon. n.d.; emphasis added). The choice of Eva Green, a French actress hitherto best known for her role in Bernardo Bertolucci's self-consciously daring homage to 1968 and to classical cinema, *The Dreamers* (2003), suggested that the role of Lynd would also carry with it a degree of quasi-art house 'seriousness' not usually expected of 'Bond girls'.

Yet the idea that a character still routinely described in terms of an infantilised relationship to the central male figure could actually occupy an equal role in the narrative is, of course, deeply problematic. Elisabeth Ladenson dismissively describes the earliest 'Bond girls' as 'nothing more than animated Barbie dolls', pointing out that Fleming himself specialised in giving these characters names that were 'onomastically determined', such as Pussy Galore and Honey Rider (2003: 188). 'Vesper Lynd' is not as suggestively sexual a moniker. It is even quite traditionally romantic – and her film character is considerably more developed – but it is still ultimately constructed around a fantasy of feminine 'otherness', as we will see. Moreover, the character's importance derives entirely from her relationship to Bond, and while the producers of the 2006 film clearly intended to present Lynd in terms of a modernised femininity, this is not the same thing as according her real equality or narrative agency. It is more akin to a politics of 'equal opportunities lite' in which women are offered the opportunity to prove themselves in the public sphere alongside men, but are not vouchsafed the same discursive space.

Indeed, given that the film's main publicly avowed intention was to sustain as much fidelity as possible to this, Fleming's very first Bond novel (1953 was a key moment for the development of postwar anti-feminism), it was never very likely that Lynd would be a genuinely feminist character. This is not the same thing as saying that she is not independently minded, 'spirited' even, in the tradition of the romantic heroine. Fleming himself emphasised these qualities – and their challenge to a stable masculinity – in the original novel:

> She put her arm through his. 'Do you mind if we go straight into dinner?' she asked. 'I want to make a grand entrance and the truth is there's a horrible secret about black velvet. It marks when you sit down. And, by the way, if you hear me scream tonight, I shall have sat on a cane chair.'
>
> Bond laughed. 'Of course, let's go straight in. We'll have a glass of vodka while we order our dinner.'
>
> She gave him an amused glance and he corrected himself: 'Or a cocktail, of course, if you prefer it. The food here's the best in Royale.'
>
> For an instant he felt nettled at the irony, the light shadow of a snub, with which she had met his decisiveness, and at the way he had risen to her quick glance. (2002: 60–1)

Chillingly, this scene artfully prefigures the sadistic torture of both Bond and Lynd that will follow the card game and Lynd's kidnap by Le Chiffre's associates (attentive readers will remember that in both the book and the film a cane chair is the site of Bond's own screams when he is genitally brutalised). But such independent characteristics in fictional females, rather than signifying sexual and social equality with men, tend to function rather as signifiers of sexual challenge to men. They are presented as symptoms of an excitingly alluring potential to resist and then succumb to the hero's sexual desire. Certainly, Lynd's character as it was written by Fleming conforms to these tendencies, with her 'independence' working to signal her availability as a sexual partner for Bond rather than anything else. Fleming's primary cultural concerns in 1953, too, were with establishing Bond's virile masculinity in the context of continuing anxieties about gender. He was certainly not a writer who endorsed (either deliberately or by default) feminist concerns. So, the proposition that the new film version can offer a Lynd sufficiently remodelled to counter the original text's underlying anti-feminism while also retaining fidelity to that text must be met with some scepticism. Instead, I would argue that the film's sadistic tendencies are indeed faithful to Fleming's original, and it is Lynd, whose challenge to Bond provokes a profoundly sadistic punishment, who is perhaps the most important carrier of this fidelity, as we will see.

At the same time it would be a mistake to assume that *Casino Royale* is the first Bond film (as opposed to book) to engage with feminist concerns, or at least to attempt to acknowledge women's changing social roles, precisely because of the necessity of securing a wide audience. From the very beginning of the Bond film franchise in 1962 with *Dr No*, the Bond films have always made space for a partial critique of the excessive masculinity Bond himself seems to embody, and it is in this that they also speak to a female audience. More often than not, Bond's absurd machismo has been subjected to an ironic critique by a female character whose relationship to Bond is a combination of affection, desire and scepticism. These concerns were originally voiced by the figure of Miss Moneypenny in the earlier Bond films. Now they are articulated by the reworked figure of M (Judi Dench), who occupies both the position of feminine scepticism and potential critique as well as the now partially feminised authority of state power. The presence of this feminine counter-discourse in the films thus rescues them from simplistic accusations of 'sexism'. They are much more complex than this.

However, the calculated absence of Moneypenny from the 2006 *Casino Royale* film (she also does not appear in the book) is intrinsically linked to the remodelling of the 'Bond girl' and to Vesper Lynd's function as sexual foil and sexual threat. Tara Brabazon has pointed out that Moneypenny's role in the Bond films was considerably transformed throughout the years of the franchise and as the actress playing her changed from Lois Maxwell (1962–87) to Samantha Bond (1987–2002). As Brabazon notes, although Maxwell was exactly the same age as Sean Connery in 1962, as the years went by the character of Moneypenny changed from youthful sparring and potential sexual partner to Bond to a disappointed, slightly camp spinster, while Bond himself (whether played by Connery, Roger Moore or Pierce Brosnan) apparently retained his virile allure (see 2003: 206). For Brabazon, 'for "equality" to be constructed, Moneypenny had to be young and beautiful. The decline of Moneypenny's role signalled a loss of the plural representation of femininity within the Bond discourse. Through the Roger Moore and Timothy Dalton years the Bond gender order became rigid and binarised' (2003: 210). By removing Moneypenny altogether, and by reassigning some of her functions to M and to the 'Bond girl', *Casino Royale* actually limits the possible agency available to women, it does not expand it. M's reconfiguration as a maternal figure with real state power behind her (not to mention the casting of Judi Dench, whose credentials as an actress who has played two Queens of England lends her additional intertextual conviction) also works to make 'the girl' more disposable.

It is also important to remember that because of the need to engage with women's changing social expectations, the 'Bond girls' from the late 1970s onwards were repeatedly represented as having superficially 'feminist' credentials, whether these involved their status as a fellow spy or as overdetermined 'career women', their initial refusal of Bond's sexual overtures or their economic independence (however weakly this was conceived). For example, Anya Amasova (Barbara Bach) in *The Spy Who Loved Me* (1977), is a Soviet agent who genuinely threatens Bond's power; Holly Goodhead (Lois Chiles) in *Moonraker* (1979) is a NASA Astrophysicist; Kara Milovy (Maryam d'Abo) in *The Living Daylights* (1987) is a professional cellist; and Dr Christmas Jones (Denise Richards) in *The World Is Not Enough* (1999) is a nuclear physicist. These impressive careers undoubtedly outstrip the achievements of 'real' women in the 'real' world, as fictional representations of women's emancipation nearly always do, and sexual equality has a long history of being represented as 'already achieved', especially in texts most anxious to defend patriarchal power. Yet each of these characters functions in the narrative primarily in the terms originally outlined by Umberto Eco (2003); and as the narrative progresses their role is exposed as that of sexual reward or victim (if they live), and their claims to any kind of meaningful equality with Bond are proved futile. They are almost universally inept, imbecilic or inadvertent when it comes to danger.

The 'Bond girl' is, then, a necessarily secondary figure, whose availability to be captured, tortured, victimised and – only then – made love to by Bond is an important component in the franchise's formula. If we subject the 2006 film of *Casino Royale* to the same kind of structural analysis Eco performed on the original novel, we may well find, then, that Lynd's function in the narrative, far from representing a radical break with convention, is entirely consonant with it and with Fleming's conceptualisation of female character and female characters as fundamentally masochistic. As Eco himself observes:

> The general scheme is (i) the girl is beautiful and good; (ii) she has been made frigid and unhappy by severe trials suffered in adolescence; (iii) this has conditioned her to the service of the Villain; (iv) through meeting Bond she appreciates her positive human chances; (v) Bond possesses her but in the end loses her. (2003: 44)

While we learn little about Lynd's early life in the film, other than through the hints offered in the sequence in which she and Bond meet, where both appear to be identified as orphaned in childhood, and while her dominance by the Villain (Le Chiffre, played by Mads Mikkelsen) is only indirectly achieved and revealed at the very end of the film, much of what Eco has to say remains valid. Lynd appears to challenge Bond, refuses his overtures, is herself sexually alluring but 'difficult', finally succumbs after she has been threatened with violence (although not by Bond, of course) and ends up dead.

As in the film, Lynd kills herself in the novel because she cannot live with the knowledge that she has betrayed Bond. The final words are Bond's – 'the bitch is dead' (Fleming 2002: 219) – and they produce a very powerful form of ideological closure: not only is no regret to be expressed for the death of a woman who has transgressed the rules of patriarchy, there is absolutely nothing more to be said about her. While the film is much more ambiguous than this, as I discuss later (Bond does use the phrase 'the bitch is dead', but this is in the penultimate scene in conversation with M, who then tells him that Lynd had been forced to betray him by Le Chiffre), the woman is still dead at the end. Indeed, if we want to test the extent to which feminism has successfully challenged these prescriptions we can examine what one of the scriptwriters for the 2006 *Casino Royale*, Paul Haggis, has said about the scriptwriting process – that it somehow seemed right that Vesper should die:

> Yeah, and the draft that was there was very faithful to the book. And there was a confession. So in the original draft the character confessed and killed herself. And then she sent Bond to chase after the villains. And Bond chased the villains into the house. And I don't know why but I thought that Vesper had to be in the sinking house and Bond has to want to kill her and then try and save her and she has to kill herself. (In Lawson 2007)

There could hardly be a better demonstration of the way in which the ideological unconscious is articulated. Assumptions about how stories 'should' work, and how feminine betrayal should be punished, are justified incoherently yet insistently. Lynd's death appears simply to be appropriate for reasons Haggis cannot discern but which chime with culturally approved ways of dealing with the threat she poses to Bond's masculine autonomy.

Tony Bennett and Janet Woollacott (2003) have identified the extent to which the Bond films in the early and mid-1960s attempted an 'ideological remodelling' of the figure of Bond himself for a popular, internationalised audience in which complex meanings around masculinity, power, nation and politics were reworked and partly democratised. Yet such remodelling did not (does not) disrupt the underlying discursive principles on which the texts are built. In the same way, the 'Bond girl' has been repeatedly remodelled and recast, but the underlying structures through which meanings about her are organised do not change. Her primary function is to stabilise what can be said about the invincibility of masculine power by being herself subject to a process of objectification, fragmentation and subjugation. So, Lynd's narrative function remains that of the conventional 'Bond girl': she is both allure and a lure; a necessary entanglement in the sense that sex plus violence are central to the meaning of the Bond films. Her 'feminism' (her refusal to be overtly subordinated by Bond) is a part of the contemporary reworking of old anxieties. On the one hand, she is represented as Bond's social equal. On the other, this autonomy is what makes her a real threat to his masculinity. At the same time, it is her cultural function as a double-agent that presents some more complex problems.

'I'm the money': power and gender

The character of Vesper Lynd only appears around halfway through the film of *Casino Royale*. By the time she makes her entrance, or rather, suddenly appears in the seat opposite Bond on the Montenegro Express, Bond has already been

Verbal sparring: James Bond (Daniel Craig) and Vesper Lynd (Eva Green) on the Montenegro Express in *Casino Royale* (2006)

seen in Madagascar, London, Miami and the Bahamas, has seduced one woman, foiled one part of the Le Chiffre plot, prevented an aeroplane from blowing up, has killed two rival agents and thoroughly riled M by despatching what appear to be some usefully disposable black Africans from an equally conveniently imaginary state, Nambutu. In other words, by the time we encounter Lynd (about whom we know nothing) we know quite a bit about this Bond and have, presumably, come to identify with him even if we do not know how much we like him. Lynd, on the other hand, enters the text in the classic manner characteristic of mainstream cinema's representation of femininity – she is presented from Bond's point of view, entering the audience's field of vision as she enters Bond's, as a mystified and potentially untrustworthy object of desire. At first, briefly, we have no idea of who she is or what she represents. Her mystery is wholly bound up with the genre's operation of mystification; if we knew her better we would not enjoy the suspense she provokes.

Her first words to Bond, 'I'm the money', are sufficiently suggestive and ambiguous as to render his approving reply entirely convincing – 'every penny of it'. Yet that phrase, 'I'm the money', while apparently a statement of economic autonomy or independence, is immediately rendered as a come-on by Bond's (our?) response, with its knowing acknowledgement of a double meaning. Far from simply being a neutral statement about Lynd's role in HM Treasury, it is a disavowal of her as an economic agent and an assertion of her status as potential sex object. Bond's response, which is to deliberately misread the meaning of the phrase from its more direct reference to the government treasury to an indirect reference to the only kind of treasure women are permitted – beauty and sexual allure – instantly sets up the tensions around their struggle for power. But it is Bond's entitlement to comment on her physical appearance, his apparent right to reposition her through his rereading of language, which also signals Lynd's culturally problematic status.

Importantly, it is this scene on the train which has been widely interpreted in reviews as the moment in which a new equality between Bond and the 'Bond girl' is fully established. Initially, this claim seems justified. For example, the two characters are seated opposite each other, but in the shot/reverse-shot sequence of their verbal exchange their eyelines are not matched. In fact, Lynd is positioned looking down disdainfully while Bond looks slightly up towards her, thus destabilising the usual male/female axis. This hostile relationship is then apparently mirrored in a verbal duel of sharply witty dialogue that, by genuinely invoking the sparring between lovers in the classical Hollywood romantic comedy, indicates that initial dislike is simply a cover for profound attraction. But this is largely because in order for Bond's eventual loss of Lynd to be convincing as a tragedy we must first be persuaded that their relationship is grounded in more than basic lust. It is an attraction of wits as well. Lynd asks, 'What … can you surmise, Mr Bond?', to which Bond replies, 'about you, Miss Lynd? Well, your beauty's a problem. You worry you won't be taken seriously.' Lynd's response is conventional enough – 'Which one can say of any attractive woman with half a brain.' But then Bond responds with a knowingly 'post-feminist' argument that appears at first to display a perceptive awareness of Lynd's position:

True. But this one overcompensates by wearing slightly masculine clothing. Being more aggressive than her female colleagues. Which gives her a somewhat 'prickly' demeanour, and ironically enough, makes it less likely for her to be accepted and promoted by her male superiors, who mistake her insecurities for arrogance.

Lynd rapidly responds to this by asserting: 'My guess is you didn't come from money, and your school friends never let you forget it. Which means that you were at that school by the grace of someone else's charity, hence that chip on your shoulder.'

Lynd's ability to engage with Bond in verbal sparring therefore seems to suggest the achievement of a genuinely 'feminist' transformation, although the references to an earlier Hollywood tradition also problematise this assumption. As played by Eva Green, Lynd certainly embodies many of the characteristics culturally coded as typically 'post-feminist' in popular representations: she is not only economically independent, she is self-assured, confident and also sexually desirable, glamorous and cosmopolitan. Yet because this exchange is staged as a 'battle of the sexes' in which both are equally adept, it also serves to recuperate the feminism it appears to foreground. Later, Lynd's own recuperation will be achieved, first as object of desire then as a figure of abjection. In the meantime, this initial encounter is followed by a further series of scenes in the Hotel Splendide in which Lynd's ability to hold her own in the verbal sparring between them is developed. She magnificently refuses to share a lift with Bond because 'there isn't room for me and your ego'.

At this point it seems that it is Lynd who holds all the aces (to use an appropriate metaphor): not only is Bond still in disgrace with M, Lynd directly controls the finances that he needs to recover his position. He is absolutely dependent on retaining her trust, if not her goodwill. At the same time, the film also cleverly establishes in the train scene that Bond's overt arrogance and sexual ruthlessness conceal his own insecurities – but these are presented as deriving from his class origins, not from his gender. However, this balance of power changes once we have moved to the casino, the heart of the narrative. Crucially, it is during the poker game itself, the central sequence of the film, that this takes place. It is signalled by the introduction of the character of the American CIA agent, Felix Leiter (Jeffrey Wright), at the casino. Once Leiter has appeared and offered his financial support to Bond, Lynd is effectively returned to her 'proper' role as 'Bond girl' – as an increasingly disempowered object of desire whose earlier confidence is systematically broken down or rendered troubling. Leiter is thus introduced in order to provide Bond with a 'real' support rather than the fake support Lynd appears to promise but cannot deliver. Lynd's resistance to this 'truth', exhibited by her misguided attempts to become the equal of Bond, is demonstrated to be futile when she is kidnapped, bound and – in a graphically terrifying scene – left lying in the middle of a mountain road as a lure to capture Bond.

Indeed, the sheer brutality of the violence Lynd is subjected to and witnesses works to emphasise her weakness. She becomes part of a terrifying game of cat and mouse in the back corridors and stairs of the casino, and is involved in a range of gruesome acts – including Bond's killing of Le Chiffre's would-be assassins – whose viscerality is utterly convincing. In these scenes her inability to act like a man, to engage in the physical violence that the film represents as both inevitable and essential to be an effective Secret Service agent, is what disqualifies her. Lynd's claim to equality, her 'feminism', must be even more thoroughly problematised and then punished because it has been so clearly staged earlier in the narrative. She becomes first a victim to be rescued and then an enemy to be defeated, not an ally in the project. And as I have said, Bond can only truly fall in love with Lynd once she has been put back in her proper place through violence.

It is only after the scenes of torture and after the casino game when the two of them are recovering at the sanatorium in Italy that we witness an apparently idyllic lovers' interlude in Venice. But this has itself only been possible because it has been made clear that, despite her efforts, Lynd is not Bond's equal in the things that matter as represented by the world of the film: the ability to claim full agency in the sense of Bond's masculinity – his right to the 'double-0' rather than the doubling or fragmentation of femininity.

Sadism, water, abjection

I want to conclude my argument by pointing to the way in which *Casino Royale* is heavily structured around a series of 'watery moments' that are both the site of the film's most violent deaths and of Bond's encounters with adversaries or with a threat of some kind, including, finally, Lynd's betrayal. As I noted earlier, the film opens with a scene that establishes Bond's own violent proclivities and hyper-masculinity: we see him savagely beating a nameless enemy in a public washroom. Bond renders his adversary utterly abject, having beaten him almost to death he sadistically forces the body face down into a running washbasin so that water pours over what is left of his head. The second of these watery moments is the gruesome death in the Bahamas of Solange (Caterina Murino), the wife of Alex Dimitrios (Simon Abkarian), which the film does not directly depict but which is indicated by the sight of her tortured body strung up in that conventional signifier of relaxation not murder, a beach hammock suspended between two trees on a shoreline rendered in startlingly lucid colours. The last (almost) watery death (or at least, that is what we are meant to suppose) is that of Mr White, shot by Bond at the villa on Lake Como in the final moments of the film in which Bond also announces his rightful claim to subjectivity and to the end of his quest: 'The name's Bond ... James Bond.'

My main focus here, however, is on the way in which these deaths, both actual and inferred, prefigure Vesper Lynd's own demise and its symbolic centrality to Bond's own rebirth. This is very different from the novel in terms of setting and the actual means of death, although in its rapid establishment of the supposed 'twist' of Lynd's betrayal it follows the original quite closely. First, towards the end of the first night's poker game, and after the encounter with Le Chiffre's Ugandan creditors on the hotel staircase, Lynd retreats distraught to her bathroom, and is later found by Bond collapsed and drenched beneath a torrential cascade of water in the shower, weeping. She is comforted by Bond, also exhausted, who climbs under the running water and puts his arms around her in a gesture of unaccustomed tenderness. It is at this moment that we are to understand that their love affair begins. But this is also a moment of abjection for Lynd, in which she is first covered in blood and then soaked in water. It is at this point that she

A warm shower: Bond (Daniel Craig) and Vesper Lynd (Eva Green) recover from a violent encounter with Le Chiffre's Ugandan creditors in *Casino Royale* (2006)

is forced to confront her femaleness – not only her inability to deal emotionally with the violence she has just witnessed but the lack that her body bestows together with its necessary purification. This moment prefigures both her torrentially watery demise and Bond's romantic (both in the sense of a quest and in the sense of romantic love) recovery of her dead body at the end of the film.

In the later scenes set in Venice, having been found out in her attempt to steal the poker winnings for Le Chiffre, Lynd is eventually cornered by Bond inside a derelict canalside warehouse near St Mark's Square and becomes trapped in the building's ancient lift system during a shoot-out between Bond and Le Chiffre's henchmen. As the building shudders and collapses under the pressure from the shots, Lynd, increasingly terrified, is suddenly propelled into the turbulent canal by the destruction of the cage's girders and she disappears from view with a scream. Having dealt with his would-be assassins, Bond decides that he does not want to kill her after all and jumps into the water desperately attempting to rescue her, but here something changes again. It is at this point that Lynd appears to embrace her impending death, refusing to be rescued or redeemed, apparently acknowledging that it is a necessary sacrifice. She stares defiantly out through the cage bars of the lift, whispers 'I'm sorry, James', kisses his hand, and is then rapidly forced back against the cage by the water's surge. Ophelia-like, she drowns – beautifully.

This combination of abjection, purification and masochism is both powerful and disturbing. It is beautifully realised aesthetically, but this is what temporarily disguises the extent to which it is viciously punitive. Bond's attempts to resuscitate her are, we know, futile, but that is not the point. It is his desire to save her that not only positions him as morally complex, it absolves him of any responsibility for her death, enabling Bond to disengage from his misplaced and tragic emotional attachment to her in order to assume a new power, while returning the blame to the woman. The scene is extraordinarily sadistic in its representational focus on the female body as the site of anxiety while simultaneously casting her as masochistically accepting a predetermined fate. In this way, not only is Lynd physically punished for her betrayal of Bond, her acceptance of that punishment is presented as poetically just, necessary even. In case we had doubts, M makes it clear that while she loved Bond she was still attached to her Algerian boyfriend and it was this which had motivated her betrayal. So, Lynd's doubleness is itself doubly emphasised. As Paul Haggis implies, it had to be.

But the abject persists, for Lynd's watery death is also a moment of birth – or rebirth – for Bond. His 'birth' is therefore dependent on Lynd's death: in order to call into being a Bond now ready to serve effectively the woman must die. It is only when he has loved and lost Lynd, and discovered that his love was betrayed, that he can finally claim his name (as the theme song tells us). The film's ending thus transform's Lynd's betrayal into sacrifice: her actions enable Bond to finally 'become himself' and to serve the state more fully, but this is achieved through her own violent self-obliteration. This is post-feminist primarily in the sense that Lynd's feminist agency is given space only to be removed from the frame altogether. It certainly returns the film to Fleming's own taxonomy of gender. Indeed, the aggressive re-masculinisation of Bond as action hero here, however pleasurable in many ways, serves to remind us that the successes of feminism remain limited and can themselves be obliterated, recuperated or romanticised – as long as they are dead.

7

MALE MASOCHISM
IN *CASINO ROYALE*

Audrey D. Johnson

In the September 2006 issue of *Esquire*, Chuck Klosterman posits the idea that there are three things that fans and non-fans know about James Bond. These are (1) 'James Bond is a terrible boyfriend'; (2) 'James Bond has only one emotion'; and (3) 'James Bond is a highly specific concept within a radically unspecific universe'. The perception of the character as misogynist, one-dimensional and in a state of arrested development was a condition that the rebooting of the franchise with *Casino Royale* (2006) offered an opportunity to change. The films themselves acknowledged the first item on Kosterman's list in *GoldenEye*, when the franchise returned to the screen in 1995 after a six-year absence, by having Judi Dench's M tell Pierce Brosnan's Bond that she thinks he is 'a sexist, misogynist dinosaur – a relic of the Cold War – whose boyish charms, though wasted on me, obviously appealed to the young lady I sent out to evaluate you'. Apparently, its association with sexist attitudes concerned the franchise itself by the mid-1990s, and this question remained as it sought to go forward with a new Bond ten years later.

Tara Brabazon argues that the 'gender order of the Bond discourse was changed radically through *GoldenEye*' because of the casting of M as a woman and the reinvigoration of the character of Moneypenny in the Brosnan era (2003: 211). While I agree with her assessment that the greater presence of female characters in the franchise and their voicing of disapproval of Bond's attitudes and behaviour are positive signs in introducing feminist discourse within the films, I view those changes as only superficial, acknowledging the issues without doing much to address them in meaningful ways. For M and Moneypenny may chastise Bond, but they do so only within the office or from a distance. Bond does not have to change and neither do the overall attitudes of the films since most of the action of each film takes place on his missions, allowing him and the films to keep his attitudes unreconstructed. *GoldenEye* may have a female M and a Moneypenny (Samantha Bond) who rebukes Bond about sexual harassment, but it still has Xenia Onatopp (Famka Janssen). The discourse surrounding Bond may have changed, but he and the tropes of the franchise do not change appreciably in these instances.

Additionally, framing feminist discourse in this way – as a matter of rebuke and chastisement – reaffirms the stereotype of the humourless feminist. Brabazon discusses the positive power of Moneypenny occupying the role of the 'bitch, a demanding woman who cannot be trusted' by the patriarchy (2003: 205). Yet only presenting feminist discourse as a matter of negation, as it is in the *GoldenEye* examples, plays into the patriarchal idea that feminist women are simply trouble-makers, there to spoil everyone's fun. In short, making M and Moneypenny into the equivalent of scolding schoolteachers makes them into figures for both Bond and the audience to escape in order to go on to what we as the audience know is the real business of the films: the glamour, wealth and adventure to be found on the missions. That introducing feminist discourse is a matter of introducing an-other female stereotype is a symptom of the thoroughness of patriarchal attitudes underlying the franchise's presentation of women. If a revision of gender politics were to take place in the next iteration of the James Bond films, more than a few lines of metacommentary would be needed.

In her essay on female characters in the Bond novels, Christine Bold argues that constructing a feminist counter-discourse is possible within the novels by reading against the grain: 'We can choose to know that (fictional) women make Bond's existence possible. We can choose to supplant him by imagining a new lineage of feminist power, escape the constraints of traditional gender categories, and refuse the objectification of "others" on which their male counterparts so precariously depend' (2003: 181). This argument applies equally to the films in the ways that we can choose to see beyond the camera's gaze in their presentation of female characters. However, the question remains of whether or not a Bond film can construct an affirmative feminist discourse and whether it can deliberately problematise the character of Bond himself. *Casino Royale*, I will argue, does so in its reboot of the franchise.

Casino Royale offered an opportunity to reimagine the Bond formula since the producers could start fresh with a new actor in the role as well as start the char-acter over from his beginnings, having secured the rights to Fleming's first Bond novel. The film's tagline emphasises this aspect when it states, 'Everyone has a past. Every legend has a beginning ... discover how James ... became Bond'. What is significant about the franchise's reboot is the way it subverts the iconic aspects of the Bond image and, in so doing, enacts a more thoroughgoing change to the franchise's gender politics by both feminising Bond's body and by constructing more fully rounded and humanised female characters who are, in some instances, more powerful and knowing than Bond. The film presents its Bond as a male masochist so that it subverts the character's privileged position as a heterosexual white male while reframing his relationships to women and to the feminine.

Critics have noted that these subversive tendencies are present in the Bond franchise before *Casino Royale*. In his essay 'James Bond's Penis', Toby Miller argues that 'Bond's gender politics are far from a functionalist world of total domination by straight, orthodox masculinity', and that from his earliest appearances Bond anticipates the commodification of the male body in subsequent decades (2003: 233). Miller's discussion notes that Bond's penis is a site of anxiety as well as authority and that Bond's body is on display in scenes associated both with sexuality and with pain (ibid.). He argues that Bond represents the 'equal legitimacy of male and female extra-marital desire', making him a particularly threatening figure to the social order when read in the context of his earliest appearances in the 1960s (see 2003: 235–7).

While I agree with Miller's point that the dynamics of gender in the Bond films are complex, sexist clichés continue to underpin the films' presentation of female characters in ways that become more and more problematic as they move further into the twenty-first century. Of the women in Fleming's novels, Bold notes, 'Whatever skills female characters demonstrate ... their one great prowess – insisted on by narrative voice and Bond's own comments – resides in their bodies' (2003: 172). *Die Another Day* (2002) may have Halle Berry as an agent with skills equal to Bond's, but her onscreen introduction objectifies her body in a sequence that visually references Ursula Andress's entrance as Honey Ryder in *Dr No* (1962). These attitudes continue into the films in the ways that women's bodies are displayed while their other talents are downplayed. As Bold notes, Ryder is 'a much less resourceful figure' on film than in the novel (2003: 178). Though Bond's own body may be commodified or displayed, he is allowed to be more than his body as he exercises his intelligence and personality while 'women's bodies are designed to pleasure others' (Bold 2003: 172). Female characters are generally denied full humanity and agency, by being presented as objects for male sexual pleasure or as obstacles to be overcome and then either turned into pleasurable objects or, failing that, destroyed. Bond's masculinity may not always be 'straight' and 'orthodox', but masculinity is still the norm against which others deviate.

Even so, one factor that somewhat mitigates the continuing sexism of the franchise is the fantastic quality that became part of the subgenre of Bond films. The broadness of characterisations, the gadgets and the villains with outlandish plots to take over the world signal that perhaps the worlds of the Bond films are not really a part of ours and exist in parallel universes where the spread of feminist consciousness moves at varying paces. The argument can be made that the women in the Bond films do not represent women in our known world as directly as they might in a more realistic setting. However, the watchword for *Casino Royale* from script to production design was 'realism'. As the documentary *Becoming*

Bond (2006) stresses, the producers aimed to remain faithful to the spirit of the action depicted in Fleming's novel, and, of the novel, director Martin Campbell remarks, 'The book is very real. You know, the book is based in ... you know, it's a much grittier kind of realistic portrait of Bond in the world. There's no sort of fantastic hollow volcanoes.' This change in aesthetic necessitates a change in the characterisation of women. Sexist stereotypes that might be excused as merely being a part of the Bond formula and its fantasy world would become noticeably out-of-date in a world closer to our own, and simply reinscribing Bond as a 'sexist, misogynist dinosaur' in that revisioned world runs the possibility of alienating new audiences who are used to seeing an array of strong female characters both on television and film.

Casino Royale signals the difference in its approach to Bond through its revisioning of the opening credits and the pre-title sequence, both of which have become trademarks of the franchise. Both of these emphasise the vulnerability of the male body and call into question masculinity as a refuge. Rather than including the nude female silhouettes that have become part of the opening credits of the previous Bond films, the opening of *Casino Royale* features fully-clothed male silhouettes fighting in a fantastic, stylised landscape of detailed playing card designs. These figures crumble into piles of hearts, clubs, spades and diamonds as they are shot, stabbed, punched or crash into the ground. These images enhance the vulnerability of the bodies even as they aestheticise the violence and as the undefined and disembodied nature of the landscape decontextualises that violence.

The pre-title sequence, though, brings violence and its consequences up close. That sequence opens with Bond about to perform his second termination, that of section chief Dryden (Malcolm Sinclair) who has been selling state secrets, when the scene flashes back to Bond's earlier termination of Dryden's contact. The two scenes contrast strongly, with Bond ultimately being in complete control of the confrontation with Dryden, whose execution he completes easily. The execution of Dryden's contact, on the other hand, is messy and brutal. While Bond is able to set the scene so that he kills Dryden with a gunshot that does not even require Bond to stand up from the chair in which he is seated, his confrontation with Dryden's contact results in a physical fight in which the two crash through partitions and break fixtures in the inelegant setting of a public restroom. Bond eventually resorts to drowning the man in a sink, with close-ups on the strain on Bond's face as he holds the contact's head down in the water. As Bond says when Dryden asks him how the contact died, 'Not well.' Dryden replies, 'Made you feel it, did he?' Indeed, Bond is dishevelled and out of breath after this exertion, forming quite a different image than his iconic one of smooth self-assurance, even in dire circumstances. Dryden starts to assure Bond that the first kill is always the most difficult while the second is easier, when he is cut off mid-sentence as Bond shoots him. Bond appears to be in control, quipping, 'Considerably', to end this scene. The implication, especially since this scene is a formative one of Bond gaining his double-0 status, is that Bond has learned physical mastery over situations and emotional mastery over himself.

Yet the images of the earlier fight serve to undercut this assurance when considered with the images of dissolving bodies from the credits. Additionally, the graphics in the credits emphasise the penetrability of the male body in one section that shows bleeding bodies impaled by diamonds from playing cards with pools of blood beside each body. Rather than the bodies disappearing bloodlessly in flurries of playing card designs, they remain in this section as reminders of lives lost and physical injury. That the bodies are specifically male indicates that masculinity offers no refuge as all are at risk – no matter how big, how tough, how hard, how masculine they are. This idea is significant in light of the casting of Daniel Craig who has a more muscular and ruggedly masculine presence than his immediate predecessor, Pierce Brosnan.

The action sequences of the film continue to emphasise physical risk and vulnerability of the male body by putting Bond's body and its wounds on display while simultaneously stripping him of the usual panoply of elaborate gadgets that have become another trademark of the franchise. The franchise's technophilia reached a zenith during Brosnan's tenure. As Martin Willis notes in 'Hard-wear: the Millennium, Technology, and Brosnan's Bond', the technology of that era represents both a throwback to the Connery years and something new with a 'fascinating reinvention of James Bond as a technological maestro who uses his virtuosic skills to alleviate increasingly hysterical millennial anxieties' (2003: 152). Willis goes on to argue that Bond's mastery of machines displays an attitude that favours humanity over technology in contrast to that of the villains of these films, all of whom become partially mechanical themselves (see 2003: 158). Additionally, Willis sees Bond's use of technology as a way to double or extend his own body (see 2003: 159).

While I agree with Willis's reading of the way that technology in the films is grafted on to Bond's body, I would also argue that the gadgets provide insulation against outside dangers at the same time as they become extensions of the body. Bond is able to accomplish feats at both a greater physical and emotional distance. The relative lack of gadgetry and the type of action in *Casino Royale*, however, close this distance by requiring that Bond's body be physically involved. The killing of Dryden's contact, as discussed above, requires Bond to use his bare hands in drowning the man, though later Bond finishes him off with a gunshot. Similarly, the first two major action sequences in the film – Bond's pursuit of the bomb-maker Mollaka (Sébastien Foucan) in Madagascar and then the pursuit of the airplane bomber at Miami International Airport – are chase scenes that take place mainly on foot.

The lower-tech aesthetic functions as part of the franchise's move towards realism in contrast to the technological excesses of previous films, which sometimes seem to have a gadget for every occasion. Part of that realism includes casting actors who at least look as though they could reasonably perform the actions on screen. Of the star, David Katz writes that although Sean Connery 'may have been vaguely menacing … Daniel Craig looks like he could actually hurt you' (2006). Mollaka in the Madagascar sequence is played by the co-founder of 'free-running', an urban sport that uses what are usually obstacles in the urban environment in order to propel oneself through the landscape as quickly and efficiently as possible. This casting and training allows the actors to be more physically present in the scenes in a more credible way, thus also drawing attention to the physical presence of the characters.

This realism extends to the consequences of such action as well. As Craig remarks on the stunts in *Becoming Bond*, 'I think the fights should make you wince a bit. It was painful. And it should look painful.' During the action scenes, Bond's body is marked by dirt and sweat, as well as blood from various cuts and scrapes, and these injuries do not disappear magically. After the Miami chase, he appears in subsequent scenes with healing scratches on his face. This continuity stands in contrast to, for example, *Die Another Day* in which Bond seems to have retained most of his physical robustness after 14 months of torture in a North Korean prison. Craig's Bond loses the Teflon quality of previous incarnations.

The contrast between the treatment of torture in *Die Another Day* and *Casino Royale* offers more insight into the differences between the latter's revisioned Bond and previous incarnations. Bond's torture at the hands of Le Chiffre (Mads Mikkelsen) in *Casino Royale* puts Bond's body and its suffering on dramatic display, but his torture in the North Korean prison takes place mostly in the background of the opening credits of *Die Another Day* while the usual nude female silhouettes cavort in the foreground. In fact, it is difficult to tell if the figure being tortured is Bond, and we have to make the supposition based on scenes where we can clearly identify Pierce Brosnan being dunked in ice water at the beginning of the sequence to the concluding scene with the chyron stating, '14 Months Later', over Brosnan sitting in a cell, now with long hair and a beard. The scene in *Casino Royale*, however, brings us up close to the torture of Craig's Bond. An establishing long shot shows a naked Bond in the bottomless chair, and, as it proceeds, the scene contains close-ups on the expressions of pain on his face throughout. Just as we see the physical presence of Bond, we hear his pain since he does not try to remain stoically silent but instead exhales and howls loudly.

This scene makes a significant connection among the ideas of physical display, pain, pleasure and the dynamics of power. Traditionally, the intellectual has been identified as the province of men and 'the masculine', while the bodily concerns have been identified with women and 'the feminine', so that the emphasis on Bond's body throughout the film subtly feminises the character not just through the body's display but also through the way this Bond is identified with and through his body. At the same time, the paradoxical presentation – that this male body is presented in the way that we expect a female one to be – opens a space that separates the biological sex of the body (male) from the way it is gendered (masculine) and reveals that the equation of sex and gender is a social condition, not a natural one. As Judith Butler argues, gender is a matter of performance, so that:

> If gender attributes and acts, the various ways in which a body shows or produces its cultural signification, are performative, then there is no preexisting identity by which an act or attribute might be measured; there would be no true or false, real or distorted acts of gender, and the postulation of a true gender identity would be revealed as a regulatory fiction. (2006: 180)

Feminising a male body enacts an even more powerful challenge of the notion of 'true gender' and the boundaries it enforces since feminised men are frequently less acceptable than masculinised women in our society. This difference in acceptable gender boundary-crossing demonstrates the way gender is tied to power: men should not be willing to give up the power of masculinity while women may go further in taking on the trappings of that power as long as they do not provide a true challenge.

Bond further crosses and confuses traditionally acceptable gendered behaviour because his reaction in this sequence resembles that of the masochist in the sense that Bond turns the torture into a means of pleasure by submitting to the pain. He laughs in Le Chiffre's face, telling him, 'I've got a little itch down there. Would you mind?' and 'No, no, no! To the right. To the right. Yes!' so that, as Bond taunts him, 'Everyone will know you died scratching my balls.' Though

Bond (Daniel Craig) grimaces in pain during the torture scene with Le Chiffre (Mads Mikkelsen) in *Casino Royale* (2006)

the insult seems to lie in a juvenile homophobia, reading the scene as an encounter between a sadist and a masochist returns us to the issue of gendered power and reveals that the more insulting implication for Le Chiffre as a sadist rests in the idea that he is giving pleasure to his victim. Le Chiffre's impulse is sadistic in that he administers pain in order to gratify his own needs, while Bond's strategy is to subvert the encounter into a masochistic one in which his needs, as the submissive partner, are being met as well.

In Gilles Deleuze's discussion of masochism, he theorises that sadists destroy the law in order to gain the pleasure from which they believe the law separates them, while masochists submit to the law in order to achieve their pleasure because they see the law as the site of the forbidden pleasure (2004: 129). Le Chiffre's status as a criminal, engaged in destroying the law, marks him as a sadist. Bond as an MI6 operative is someone who has submitted fully to the law to the point of becoming an agent of it. Yet Bond's masochistic response opens up another gendered space because masochism, as Carol Siegel notes, 'has been deemed unnatural in members of the culturally dominant group ... at the same time that it has been naturalised as essential to the character of all women, homosexual men, and male members of minority groups' (1995: 22). The regulation of behaviour again ties together gender and power since what is unacceptable in the dominant group is the submission that masochism entails.

Deleuze's reading of sadism and masochism theorises the two as incompatible rather than different sides of the same coin, so that Bond's attempt here is not to complement Le Chiffre's action but to turn their encounter into something else entirely (see Deleuze 2004: 126). His subversion invites Le Chiffre to submit to the law, but Le Chiffre refuses. Deleuze further notes that one of the defining characteristics of masochism is 'the taste for the contract' (ibid.). This contract sets out the terms of what is expected of each party, and they enter into it before proceeding with the relationship. Bond and Le Chiffre, however, have no such contract. There are no boundaries that Le Chiffre is obligated to respect in his treatment of Bond. Le Chiffre sets terms – Bond will tell him what he wants to know or he will be beaten until he is permanently disabled or dead – but only after Bond has been made an unwilling partner.

The presence of the contract is invoked in the background of this scenario because Le Chiffre's torture of Bond occurs as Bond is carrying out the contractual obligations of his job. The contract brings forward the figure of the woman and the feminine, for, as Deleuze states, 'There is no masochism without a contract with the woman' (ibid.). The masochistic contract is a means of holding masculine society up to ridicule by taking a basic element of that society – the contract – and instituting a reversal of power so that 'the contract here expresses the maternal predominance of the woman and the superiority of the maternal principle' (Deleuze 2004: 126–7). Deleuze's later work with Félix Guattari in *Anti-Oedipus* (1977) rejects the psychoanalytic model that this reading is based on by turning to a model in which societies and the bodies in those societies are made up of machines rather than structured around the Oedipal family drama. Desire flows through these machines, and desire is a positive, creative force rather than one formed out of lack. Societies create ways to regulate these machines and this desire. Thus, keeping in view the gendered language of the psychoanalytic model while reading it through Butler's performative gender model combined with Deleuze and Guattari's mechanistic one points us back to the way that so-called appropriate expressions of gender are used to regulate behaviour.

That the position of Bond's supervisor in the film is filled by a female actor serves as a visual representation of his masochism via his job that is otherwise invisible when his supervisor is male. Masochism is inherent in the nature of Bond's job because it dictates the full submission of his physical and emotional being while M as Bond's supervisor is both the representative and the conduit for the state power – the law – for which Bond carries out this function. In her function as his superior, M directs the actions of Bond's body and the way that he uses his time, similar to the way the contract allows the dominant woman to direct the submissive man and even gives her power over his life and death (see Deleuze 2004: 126). The assassination of Dryden demonstrates M's exercise of these powers. Bond is there by her order, and Dryden will die by her order. As Bond tells him, 'M doesn't mind you earning a little money on the side, Dryden. She'd just prefer it if it weren't for selling secrets.' M similarly shows this power with Bond later, after he has botched the mission in Madagascar and brought the displeasure of the fictitious country of Nambutu on the British government and MI6. She tells him to 'go and stick [his] head in the sand' until the fervour dies down 'because these bastards want your head, and I'm seriously thinking of feeding you to them'. Later, she directs that Bond be microchipped, with a device that resembles a more advanced version of those used for domestic pets. Thus, M's power can extend down to the smallest details of Bond's life.

Yet it is through this submission to the law, both Her Majesty's and M's, that Bond achieves pleasure. Beth Butterfield argues that Bond is a hedonist in order to compensate for and to escape from the threat of death that constantly hangs over him and in order to combat boredom (see 2003: 14–15). However, rather than seeing these pleasures as compensations or rewards for enduring the hardships of his job, thus implying that the punishment could be done away with, reading Bond as male masochist highlights the idea that Bond's pleasure in this circumstance is inseparable from the punishment of the job. As Deleuze, summarising Theodore Reik's theory of masochism, explains, 'masochism is not pleasure in pain, nor even in punishment; at most, the masochist gets a preliminary pleasure from punishment or discomfort; his real pleasure is obtained subsequently, in that which is made possible by the punishment' (1971: 77–8). Thus, Bond has access to some of the finest that society provides in sensual pleasures while at the same time his anti-social behaviour – his 'licence to kill' – is sanctioned by that same society. The paradox is that male masochism, usually viewed as emasculating, is the very mechanism that allows Bond to participate in hyper-masculine behaviour as part of his job.

Bond's other significant relationship with a powerful woman in the film is the one with Vesper Lynd (Eva Green), and he will use his submission to her as a means to move out of his masochistic relationship to his job. Vesper's professional role and her power are expanded in the film. In the novel, Vesper is a 'wireless expert' who 'speaks French like a native' (Fleming 2002: 30–1), but, beyond that, it is not clear exactly what her role is to be on the mission, though she describes it as a 'liaison job' (Fleming 2002: 67). The novel infantilises Vesper by describing her as a 'girl'. When she discusses having to borrow her couture clothing, she appears almost as though she is playing dress-up. This impression is further reinforced by Bond's thoughts on her kidnapping: 'Damn fool girl getting herself trussed up like a chicken, having her skirt pulled over her head as if this business was some kind of dormitory rag … Her naked legs looked so childish and defenceless' (Fleming 2002: 123–4).

In the film, however, Vesper has power over Bond. Since she monitors Bond's gambling stake, he has to perform satisfactorily in carrying out his mission or be cut off, as she eventually does when she judges he is losing too much. In addition, she saves his life twice, showing an ability to handle pressure that rivals Bond's. The first instance occurs after Bond's poisoning at the poker table. Bond gives himself an antidote but passes out before he can complete the necessary step of shocking his slowing heart with a defibrillator. Vesper finds him and revives him. The second instance occurs offscreen during Bond's torture when Vesper makes a deal to give Mr White (Jesper Christensen) the money in exchange for Bond's life. Thus, Vesper not only demonstrates competency but also shapes events in ways of which Bond is unaware.

Considering Vesper's ensuing relationship with Bond in the film further contrasts the ways in which the Vesper of the film is a more positive figure than the Vesper of the novel. Her motivation remains the same in both the novel and the film, in that she agrees to the group's demands in order to save Bond, but the film Vesper is a somewhat more innocent figure since she is not a double-agent passing along information over a long period of time, but only agreeing to commit this one act. In addition, the film Vesper uses her submissive position via her blackmailers to her advantage to strike a second deal with them in order to save Bond's life. In both the film and the novel, Vesper dies. However, in the novel she commits suicide over her extreme guilt while in the film she dies by drowning, trapped when the Venetian house in which she is meeting with Mr White collapses. Though she is destroyed in both versions, the novel has her do so by her own hand as a punishment for her sins while the film makes her death and her motivations more complicated. As M tells Bond, 'Of course, she hoped they'd let her live, but she had to know she was going to her death.' Had the collapse of the house not happened, there is a possibility that she may have survived. Still, even during the house's collapse, Bond attempts to rescue her, but, when that proves too difficult, she indicates that he should leave her to die rather than be trapped himself. While Vesper in the novel seems to have ultimately been overwhelmed by her circumstance, Vesper in the film deals with many of the same situations as Bond when she makes deals with dangerous people while keeping her troubles to herself. The exception to her self-control is her breakdown after she witnesses Bond kill the assassin who is sent after them.

In her first meeting with Bond, Vesper has a duel of psychological analysis with him, in which she shows herself able to put him under a microscope. Indeed, she tells him later, 'I sized you up the moment we first met.' This reference is literally to the dinner jacket that she has had tailored for him, which fits perfectly, and that scene further highlights Vesper's more potent role in the film. That exchange over dressing for their first public appearance at the poker table is quite significant in its subversion of expectations and its establishment of Vesper's power in the relationship. Bond enters the scene with a dress for Vesper to wear to the game because, as he tells her, 'I need you looking fabulous', and directions on what she is to do there to use her 'neckline' to distract the other players. Yet he returns to his room to find a dinner jacket laid out for him. To his protest that he already has one that is sufficient, Vesper tells him: 'There are dinner jackets and *dinner jackets*. This is the latter. And I need you looking like a man who belongs at that table.' Not only does this Vesper apparently not need to borrow fine clothing (she is getting ready when Bond enters with the dress and she appears in what is apparently one of her own later), but she brings couture to dress Bond. The scene then shows Bond admiring himself in the mirror in the new jacket with a cut to Vesper's point of view, watching him. The reverse angle then shows her laughing at his reaction. What we learn in this sequence is that, in this version of the Bond universe, it is a woman who is instrumental in providing Bond with part of his iconic image and forming his identity. This sequence recalls Deleuze's summary of Sacher-Masoch: 'It is when the senses take works of art for their objects that they become masochistic for the first time … And the masochist gives back to art all that art gives to him: it is through being painted or photographed, through catching his image in a mirror, that he experiences and comes to know himself' (2004: 126).

This scene plays against viewer expectations that Bond would be the shaper of identity rather than the one shaped. Audiences are familiar with the plot in which the plain woman undergoes a makeover that helps her discover her beauty and femininity, courtesy of her male partner, after which they then fall in love in actuality. The expectation set up when Bond enters with the dress for Vesper is that we are about to watch another such scenario unfold, especially since during their exchange on the train Bond needles her about wearing 'slightly masculine clothing and being more aggressive than her female colleagues' as ways to be taken more seriously. While Eva Green's Vesper could hardly be said to be in desperate need of a makeover, the implication is that she needs help becoming secure in her femininity and that we are about to see such a transformation. What we see instead is that it is Bond who is transformed and who sees his own beauty.

The film goes on to frustrate the expectation that remains after this scene that we will later see Vesper's triumphant entrance into the casino and that experience will then transform her. Though we get the entrance, it is comparatively low-key. There is a brief shot on her entering the doorway, but as she approaches the poker table, the camera does not linger directly on her. It goes instead to a close-up on Bond, and she is out-of-focus in the background. Though Bond's direction to her had been to enter so that his opponents could see her first and be distracted, she enters on the opposite side so that Bond sees her first. He becomes the one most distracted, under the control of his own strategy.

What is significant here is that this scene continues the trend in the film away from gratuitously displaying the female body in favour of putting the male body on display. What starts as a sequence about inviting the audience to look at Vesper becomes a sequence inviting us to look at Bond. Something similar happens earlier in the film when Bond first sees Solange (Caterina Murino) on the beach. She seems set to join the tradition of bikini-wearing 'Bond girls', yet the camera never lingers to invite us to look at her. The full-length shot of her from Bond's point of view is taken from a distance, so she is a comparatively small figure.

Bond (Daniel Craig) emerges from the water in *Casino Royale* (2006)

The figure the camera lingers on and admires in this sequence, however, is Bond. His appearance as he emerges from the water in this sequence closely recalls that of the first iconic 'Bond girl' in *Dr No*. The audience is invited to look and to take in Daniel Craig's physique, emphasised by retro swimming trunks. Craig makes this connection explicit in an interview in *Becoming Bond*: 'Yeah, I tried on quite a few pairs of swimming trunks. Ursula Andress', he says, 'that was me.'

The significance of these scenes is that displays of the male body in the film are not restricted only to those associated with pain and suffering, as with the torture. While such displays are subversive in the way that they feminise the male body, the violence nonetheless enables that body to be engaged in a still acceptably masculine activity, even allowing for the possibility of demonstrating the machismo of 'manfully' resisting. However, putting the male body on display as an object of beauty further feminises it since that is the context in which female bodies are usually displayed.

Yet Bond and Vesper eventually develop a relationship in which the power dynamic is flexible. While Vesper fulfils the expectation that the female lead in a Bond film will fall in love with him, she only confesses her feelings after his torture. She makes herself emotionally vulnerable after he has been most physically vulnerable. This type of submission has been naturalised for women, but here it serves as an opening to the contract that the two will negotiate. Vesper tells Bond, 'You can have me anywhere.' Bond offers his own submission to her and further sees that submission as a refuge, as a way to save himself from the effects of his job. He pledges himself to her after she accuses him of retreating behind his emotional defences again. He confesses, 'I have no armour left. You've stripped it from me. Whatever is left of me, whatever I am, I'm yours.' He also tells her he loves her 'enough to quit [his job] and float around the world until one of us has to get an honest job' because 'it's as you say, you do what I do for long enough, there'll be no soul left to salvage.' Bond surrenders to her even to the point of acknowledging that Vesper will probably have to be the one to support them eventually since he 'has no idea of what an honest job is.' While his masochistic relationship to his job carried with it a way to transgress society in order to play out an extreme edge of masculinity in a socially acceptable way, masochism now is the means through which Bond will opt out of that social structure.

Bond and Vesper will go on to redefine masculinity and its limits as well. As Bond is recovering from the torture, Vesper tells him, 'You know, James, I just want you to know that if all that was left of you was your smile and your little finger, you'd still be more of a man than anyone I've ever known.' This line provides an answer to Le Chiffre's threats that if Bond does not yield to the torture in time there will be little left 'to identify [him] as a man', thereby complicating the question of what identifies him as masculine. Masculinity can be redefined so that it need not express itself solely through forms of dominance. When Bond tries to lighten the seriousness of Vesper's confession by replying, 'That's because you know what I can do with my little finger', he enacts a reversal in not shoring up a conventional definition of masculinity, but rather agreeing that it can take forms other than domination. Vesper tells him she actually does not know, and Bond says, 'But you're aching to find out.' Vesper's body is not only for Bond's pleasure in this case; his is for hers. Her pleasure takes primary importance so that her pleasure becomes his pleasure. Such a relationship could be defined as masochistic, but it also could be defined as loving. As Carol Siegel, writing about female-dominant narratives, argues:

> Considered together, such narratives indicate that what is now called masochism has been represented, throughout history, even if inconsistently, as an attitude and set of behaviours that, when taught to men by women, can make possible a mutually satisfying marriage; this masochism can, in essence, transform the male body from an instrument of punishment for women into a medium through which women can generate pleasure for both themselves and their partners. (1995: 119)

Thus, James Bond has the potential to be a good boyfriend after all.

In the context of the film franchise, we could say that Bond's masochism – as a way of responding to changes in social consciousness brought about by feminism – transforms the character into a medium of pleasure for a wider array of viewers. *Casino Royale* ends with Bond standing over Mr White in an impeccably tailored pinstripe suit, casually toting the rifle with which he has just shot his quarry. James has, apparently, with this scene, become Bond. But, to draw on Christine Bold's comments, the film has shown us at least two of the women who make Bond possible – Vesper and M. We know that Bond has tracked down Mr White thanks to the information Vesper left him and suspect he has also developed a taste for better tailoring because of her. We have also seen Bond as a submissive man and a problematic figure for gender categories. These subversions make the iconic pose seem a mask. For though Bond's comment on Vesper's death is the same cold line from the novel – 'The job is over, and the bitch is dead' – we have also seen his desperate attempts to revive her, and his intense mourning. *Casino Royale* revisions Bond and his relationship not simply to women, but also to femininity, and in so doing indicates a way forward to question and revision the gender categories of the broader genre of action films to which the Bond franchise belongs.

PART 3

EMBODYING BOND

8

IMPROVISATION, ACTION AND ARCHITECTURE IN *CASINO ROYALE*

Monika Gehlawat

Barbarism? Yes, indeed. We say this in order to introduce a new, positive concept of barbarism. For what does the poverty of experience do for the barbarian? It forces him to start from scratch; to make a new start; to make a little go a long way; to begin with a little and build up further, looking neither left nor right.

– Walter Benjamin, 'Experience and Poverty'

This characterisation of the new barbarian suits the miraculous agility of Daniel Craig's James Bond in *Casino Royale* (2006), his resourcefulness in the ruins, corridors and skeletal spaces of contemporary experience. Walter Benjamin's theory of the new barbarian reflects a creative energy that is paradoxically further developed in his description of the 'destructive character', a figure who destroys the old in order to clear space for what is to come. In an unexpected but logical turn, Benjamin writes that 'the destructive character stands in the front line of traditionalists' (Benjamin 1999b: 542). Simply put, the destructive character, in clearing away all that came before, represents the advent of a new tradition. This dialectic of old and new is crystallised in the latest Bond film where Daniel Craig presumably represents 007 in his originary form and, in so doing, shows him at his most contemporary.

Indeed, the strange temporality of *Casino Royale* punctuates this confluence of the first and last, of creative and destructive energies. The story takes places at the start of Bond's career, just as he has earned his double-0 status. Yet the film is utterly up-to-date; it occurs in a post-9/11 world where Judi Dench's M expresses nostalgia for the kinds of agents who operated during the Cold War and where the fashion, technology and cultural artefacts reflect not a bygone era, but an immediate one. The audience accepts this anachronism as a necessity and yet its result is fascinating: Craig's Bond is both the inheritor of the 007 tradition and its forefather. We cannot help but compare him to those who came before and recognise his *newness* as a consequence of his contemporaneity, and yet, that newness must be understood in narrative terms as the *birth* of his character. This simultaneous and paradoxical inhabiting of the old and new, the creative and destructive impulse, is represented, I will argue, both in the way that Bond fights and the transitory spaces in which this action takes place.

This essay focuses on the contingency of action in liminal spaces depicted in *Casino Royale* in order to argue that the film deviates from standard 007 representations by stressing improvisation over forms of technological or social mastery. This emphasis reflects the Bond figure in an embryonic mode while consistently calling attention to issues of temporality, destruction and change. In order to develop this reading, I look to major action sequences: the long chase in the construction site early in the film, the short intense fights in the stairwell and bathroom, and the final action scene in the crumbling Venetian building. I decipher the particularity of these architectural sites to show how they require the human body to perform a kind of ingenuity that is equally coarse and versatile. *Casino Royale* continually sets its action sequences in shifting spaces that force the body to be both nimble, imagining new ways to use the weapons at its disposal, and tough, as it survives the destruction and crudeness of the territories it inhabits. Set design includes buildings that are either being built up or torn down; their rickety and often literal lack of foundation requires a new mode of inhabiting space in an emergency.

Counter to the visual spectacle of previous 007 action sequences, *Casino Royale* often engages the most pedestrian of liminal spaces – the bathroom or stairwell – to exhibit Bond's ability to manipulate and dominate his opponent. The film's pre-title sequence depicts Bond earning his double-0 status as the episode cuts back and forth between the agent's first two kills. This early scene initiates what will be a consistent pattern throughout the film: action sequences represent transitional narrative moments which are staged within spaces that reflect this in-between-ness in their architecture. Bond's first kill, for instance, takes place in a bathroom, the clinical glare of which is exaggerated by the grainy black-and-white film used to shoot it. Bond throws his opponent into a bathroom stall and then the camera, shooting from above, shows the men as they fight and crash through one stall to the next. The visual focus draws attention to boundaries and its effect is simultaneously claustrophobic and uncontrolled. Bond makes use of found objects (the urinal in the first kill and the double-agent's gun in the second) to master the situation and thus establishes a certain pattern of appropriation that is highlighted by the mostly impoverished spaces of the film's action sequences.

These spatial contexts reflect the uncut and formative quality of Bond at the start of his career while drawing a stark contrast with the more traditional 007 weapons that Craig regularly abandons in the film. Indeed, when he uses any 007 'toys' at all, he finds them either insufficient or else employs them in spontaneous, unconventional ways. Craig's Bond prefers to use others' technological gadgets rather than seeking his own, and his guerrilla methods, even at their most destructive, always author a kind of creative wedge, a way where none existed before. What is immediately distinctive about these scenes and often discussed by the film's critics is Daniel Craig's physicality and brute force as compared to previous 007s. However, I want to go beyond a discussion of Craig's body by considering it in terms of and within a spatial dialectic that highlights the relationship between the action and context. The primitive quality of Craig's performance, its lack of polish and hence, peculiar incompatibility with the Bond tradition, emerges through his relationship in space. Indeed, my focus is less on the brute force of Craig's 007 and more on the unstructured and tactical integration of body in space that he makes possible.

I want to begin with the two major action sequences at the beginning and end of the film that occur in the construction site in Madagascar and the building under renovation in Venice. As narrative bookends and equally lengthy action scenes, these two episodes help to establish a dynamic dialogue between architecture and action in *Casino Royale*. They are also decidedly unique to this film in that, unlike the major action sequences of previous 007 projects, these scenes commit to a distressed or decaying aesthetic. I believe that Craig's Bond is deliberately placed in such spaces in order to accentuate his own attempts to emerge from underdevelopment. The set locations for both fights share a particular malleability; despite the fact that they are formally fixed structures (as opposed to cars, planes or other moving objects), these buildings are in flux. Initially depicted as buildings undergoing (re)construction, when Bond arrives on the scene, they rapidly transform and ultimately disintegrate. They are literally moving spaces and, as such, are also liminal. Neither skyscraper nor house nor ruin, these sets straddle multiple categories while presently lacking any particular function. Thus, they allow for and in many ways demand Bond's improvisation while highlighting his destructive capacity. The contingency of action, risk and reward depends as much on Bond's violent ingenuity as the buildings' speedy demise. The scenes, then, reference an architecture that is fragile and decrepit, an aesthetic of rubble that is rare in the sophisticated set design of previous Bond films.

In the first scene, Bond chases after Mollaka, a bomb-maker played by *parkour* artist Sébastien Foucan. *Parkour* was started in the early 1990s by Foucan and David Belle in Paris and has been described as 'free-running', or the practice of 'throwing yourself over impossible gaps and using urban surroundings as your canvas'. Key to *parkour* is the idea of moving around obstacles or else using them creatively as a means to an end. This flexibility then lends itself to a fluid, dance-like aesthetic that explains why those who practice *parkour* consider it an artform. Although at first it appears as though Craig performs *parkour* as he chases Foucan, careful viewing reveals that the latter's movements are more artful and less violent than Craig's. Mollaka glides through open windows, curves around corners and leaps from platform to platform while Bond breaks through walls and destroys obstacles using sheer force of momentum. His movements are damaging and lack finesse; the jolt of their impact regularly eradicates what it encounters.

Perhaps the most obvious example of this contrast occurs when Mollaka first enters the construction site. He thinks he has lost Bond; the action soundtrack grows quiet and the scene appears suddenly quotidian and uneventful. Suddenly a huge digger bursts through a small building and then a chain link fence, toppling piles of equipment and scattering workers in all directions. As Bond accelerates towards Mollaka, altering neither direction nor target, the bomb-maker leaps from one object to another until he is a couple of storeys off the ground on a platform of the building. Bond drives the digger straight into the building, destroying its platform, foundation and threatening the stability of the entire edifice. Here Mollaka's feline flexibility is contrasted with the blunt aggression of Bond. The camera films Craig's face as expressionless, while shots from his perspective reveal an accelerating and unwavering vision, headed straight for the bomb-maker and the building. The crudeness of Bond's act is equalled by the rudimentary machine he uses to perform it. This will be one of many times in *Casino Royale* when Bond uses a found object to improvise, often inflicting rough damage, in order to dominate his opponent. The speed with which Craig's Bond moves and the camera's multiple, jarring angles result more often in the eradication of obstacles rather than a reformulation of them. Bond's impulse to destroy obstacles in order to achieve his ends occurs numerous times in this scene and recalls Benjamin's description of the destructive character as one who 'sees nothing permanent. But for this very reason he sees ways everywhere. Where others encounter walls or mountains, there too, he sees a way. But because he sees a way everywhere, he has to clear things from it everywhere' (1999b: 542). What I want to emphasise in Benjamin's portrayal of the destructive character is the relationship between an utterly modern perspective and the impulse to clear things away. Indeed, I read Bond's method of action in the film as indicative of the originary status of his character.

We continue see the pattern of tactical destruction in the chase scene between Foucan and Craig as it takes on a specifically **vertical** dimension. The two figures fantastically scurry all the way up the construction site and then back down, even as the building itself is highly unstable and shifting, mostly due to Bond's devastating actions. Their path of descent must alter in part because so much of

As the destructive character, Bond (Daniel Craig) uses his body as a primitive but effective tool in *Casino Royale*

the building has been demolished by the time they get to the cranes that hover isolated above the ground. In order to get up to the cranes, we find Craig taking a significantly different route from Foucan who dances up various ladders and levels to reach the cranes, a defiance of gravity that also characterises his light movements. Craig's Bond on the other hand disengages the cord of a heavy load and uses the impact of its fall to achieve the height of the crane. The camera captures this opposing dynamism as the shot is filmed from above. The viewer watches Bond zoom up the site's steel skeleton as below tons of metal pipes fall crashing into the building, destroying its frame at each impact. Craig's Bond demonstrates speed, expediency and recklessness in contrast with the svelte manoeuvrings of Foucan and yet he rivals the free-runner in his ability to 'see ways everywhere'. The action sequence on the cranes emphasises mobility in particular, perhaps because the slightest movement appears extreme when performed hundreds of feet up in the air. The combatants' mobility is matched by the motion of the cranes which shift slowly like the hands of a large clock as Bond and Mollaka themselves engage in hand-to-hand combat. Camerawork again intensifies the spatial effect of the sequence. Just as the earlier part of the chase is shot from above and below to emphasise the verticality of movement, the scene on the cranes is filmed from a helicopter that circles around the actors. The revolutions of the camera overlap with the slowly shifting cranes while the men move back and forth in a struggle for control. The multiple planes of movement create a shifting terrain in the sky and reference the shaky planar architecture of the damaged construction site below.

Indeed, a kind of precariousness characterises the entirety of this early action sequence. Despite the pace and intensity of the chase, its sense of impermanence anticipates the aesthetics and sensibility of the film as a whole. From the moment Craig begins to chase Foucan, the scene's quick-cut editing heightens the sense of shifting experience. The two men run through crowded, ramshackle spaces: a chaotic, roofless marketplace shot from above, the shell of an abandoned car, the strange middling zone of tropical forest and urban ghetto. Film theorist Susan Hayward writes that in Bond films, audiences are invited to sit back and admire the spectacle 'based on lavish plenitude' (2006: 6). My focus on the set design and architecture of *Casino Royale* attempts to show how this film deviates from the 'lavish plenitude' of the previous Bond films with its emphasis on the gritty decomposition of space over notions of fantasy and futuristic design. *New York Times* reviewer Manohla Dargis compares the action in *Casino Royale* to that of the Jason Bourne films (*The Bourne Identity* (2002), *The Bourne Supremacy* (2004), *The Bourne Ultimatum* (2007)), citing in particular the way in which 'the whole thing moves far lower to the ground than any of the newer Bond flicks' (2006). By 'lower to the ground', Dargis means to draw attention to the immediate intensity of combative action and the way in which the film stages these moments to create a sense of jarring proximity. Set design in the film, then, is intended to magnify the edginess of Bond's formative self by creating spaces that are less spectacular than they are porous, decrepit or cold.

The aesthetics of demolition particularly characterise the last long action sequence in the film which takes place in an old Venetian building. Whereas the chase scene in Madagascar is characterised by a kind of airy, upwardly-mobile speed, this scene is dominated by darkness, claustrophobia and action that, despite its best efforts, lurches inevitably downwards. From the outside the building appears to be a rather unimpressive, decaying old home but it quickly becomes as much a player in the scene as any individual character. At least half of the shots filmed in this sequence are of the exterior or interior of the building under collapse while images of Bond and his assailants emerge unevenly amidst this shifting landscape. The building (like the site in Madagascar) is under construction; in this case, it is buoyed up by enormous balloons that keep it from collapsing into the canal while it is being rebuilt. Before Bond even crosses the threshold, he dooms the structure by puncturing the balloons and therefore collapsing the building's temporary foundation. This architecture contrasts sharply with the conventional ending of most 007 films in which Bond is captured inside the villain's massive, technologically-enhanced hideout and must escape before the structure explodes. Instead, Craig's Bond reverses the process. He initiates the destruction of the building and then *enters* in order to pursue his enemies. The agenda is dictated by a self-destructive rather than a self-preserving impulse. It is possible that this impulse reflects Bond's emotional free-fall upon learning of Vesper's (Eva Green) betrayal, but it is also characteristic of his improvisational mode. Time and again in *Casino Royale*, we find Bond destroying first and acting later. He seems to trust in his ability to find a way where others may not, even as his vision (accessed when the camera films from his perspective) is often marginal and his body often curtailed or damaged by the very catastrophes he creates.

As in the earlier scene in Madagascar, here Bond pursues his enemies while the space through which he moves is itself in motion. Stairwells and landings crumble and drop into the floors below and, eventually, into the canal. Light fixtures, balustrades and random objects (as well as people) seem to detach from their context and slide helplessly downward. The cage elevator in which Vesper is trapped operates especially in this capacity; its usual up and down function is painfully exaggerated as it clangs and drops on a diagonal that seems at one moment in harmony with the rest of the building's demolition and at the next juxtaposed in weird cross-cutting angles. All the while, the atmosphere of the scene is dark, confused and foreboding. The scene's liminal quality manifests not only because it occurs in a space that is neither building nor rubble, but also because of the watery world that soon consumes it. Bond goes from running one moment to diving and swimming the next; his tenacity ensures that he will survive the tumult he set into motion while his enemies and the woman he loves will die. The fate of the Venetian building demonstrates the effect of being inhabited by Craig's Bond. An old space in the process of being brought 'up-to-date', it is, instead, demolished. Thus the destructive character stands 'in the front line of the traditionalists', just as Bond's perseverance in the face of constant impermanence and emergency inscribes him as a kind of new barbarian.

The capacity for maintaining equilibrium amidst danger and chaos has always defined James Bond, but Craig's 007 is unique in his contradictory impulse to create, and not simply survive, anarchic situations. Being in control, or the quality of having a situation in hand, is literalised in the card game that serves as a focal point of the film. The action sequences of the film's middle section echo the jarring immediacy of the previous two scenes while simultaneously complicating them with the gambling narrative. Before discussing the short violent action sequence in the stairwell of the hotel between Craig and Steven Obanno (Isaach De Bankolé), the African guerrilla fighter, I want to attend to the gambling scenes it interrupts in order to understand what the larger narrative framework signifies.

The almost mundane civility of the high-stakes poker game that Bond plays against the villainous banker Le Chiffre (Mads Mikkelsen) nevertheless compares to the intensity of the action sequences because it sustains a sense of Bond's recklessness. Indeed, the film deviates from Fleming's novel by presenting Craig's Bond as a gifted but brash card player. In the book, Fleming depicts Bond as extremely calculating and dispassionate, traits that the film's Bond aims for but often overshoots. At various moments in the film, Craig plays Bond with a kind of abrupt physicality, suddenly bursting through a door or charging towards a target, as when he impulsively grabs a dinner knife in order to assassinate Le Chiffre after losing a crucial hand. The kind of unrehearsed audacity Bond demonstrates in the film marks him as a destructive and incalculable force as well as a seeming deviation from both his cinematic predecessors and the character of Bond in Fleming's novel.

Walter Benjamin's remarks on the gambler as type might help us to overcome this apparent opposition between the cinematic and novelistic Bond. Benjamin describes the gambler as a man who believes he chooses his own fate by employing various strategies of tactical deliberation but who, ultimately, is at the mercy of the hand he is dealt. He writes in *The Arcades Project* that 'gambling is hand-to-hand encounter with Fate ... The stake is money – in other words, immediate, infinite possibilities' (1999a: 498). This description encapsulates the central conflict in *Casino Royale*: Le Chiffre must win the money that will return to him 'immediate, infinite possibilities' and Bond must prevent this from happening. Bond's objective is to foreclose on Le Chiffre's capacity to act, to limit his options so that he must turn to the British government for sanctuary. Therefore, Bond's role is to be a destructive force, less interested in achieving 'immediate, infinite possibilities' for himself but in destroying them for another. In fact, Bond has zero investment in any material gain from winning; he agrees to pass over Le Chiffre to the CIA agent played by Jeffrey Wright and promptly returns the winnings (or thinks he has) to the British government. Therefore, his motivation as a player is completely without self-interest, even as his focus is precise and predatory. Bond is, as he quips earlier to M, 'part-monk, part-hitman'. The reckless impulse we perceive in his style of play, in Benjaminian terms, merely reveals the central truth of gambling as such.

In Fleming's novel, Bond compares luck in gambling to women. His rational approach to controlling both is, of course, shattered by Vesper's betrayal. However, early in the book, he emphasises abstract calculation, ritual and steady nerves as the components to a winning hand. In gambling, Fleming writes, above all, Bond 'liked it that everything was one's own fault. There was only oneself to praise or blame' (2002: 49). Rather than interpreting this passage to mean that one can control a *particular* outcome of the gamble through strategy or performance, I want to suggest that the possibility of control occurs through one's willingness to accept *whatever* outcome may occur. The very conditions of gambling require that in 'hand-to-hand combat with Fate' one never knows what will happen. The fatalism that demands this ever-ready response is the secret to Bond's destructive character, his daring and intensity. The film's particular use of architecture highlights the contingency of fate and the unknowability that both plagues Craig's Bond and focuses him to perform at his most creative capacity. When, in the novel, M instructs Bond to 'view the situation dispassionately', he actually articulates the very quality of 'abstract passion' that characterises his actions (2002: 73).

The crucial drama of the card game at the Casino Royale is interrupted by the intensely violent encounter between Le Chiffre and Steven Obanno, and then between Obanno and Bond. In the latter, we find Bond once again in a liminal space; this time the action occurs in a stairwell with doors that do not open, thus forcing, yet again, an aesthetic of vertical movement. Bond's hand-to-hand combat with Fate persists, although this time Fate takes the form of the sword-wielding Obanno. The utterly stark and unyielding space of the stairwell drastically contrasts with the crowded set design of previous action sequences. In this episode, there are neither tools to appropriate nor a structure to destroy. The paradoxical simplicity and brutality of the scene structurally resemble the standoff in the casino between Le Chiffre and Bond, just as the action going up and down the staircase recalls the pendulum of luck that vacillates between the two gamblers. Meanwhile, as Obanno and Bond cascade down the stairwell, Vesper runs ahead, both a spectator and potential casualty of their encounter. Her uncertain movement and awkward position supplies the necessary factor of contingency seen previously in the shifting rafters and stair-wells of collapsing buildings. This scene, like the sequence on the cranes earlier in the film, is shot with cameras circling around the action, intensifying the spatiality of the spiral and giving movement a three-dimensional quality.

The architectural liminality of the stair-well as site (marginal to both horizontal and vertical frames of the building) metonymically references the narrative space it holds as an interruption to the film's central drama. This type of parallel between

The stairwell action scene in *Casino Royale* is liminal in both an architectural and a narrative capacity

space and narrative also occurs later in the film when Bond follows Vesper to the doomed Venetian house. He has just discovered her betrayal but has not yet confronted her or his enemies. As he follows her down narrow Venetian passageways shifting in shadows and sunlight, the viewer catches glimpses of her red dress, almost as after-images (or memories), cross-cut by other pedestrians, disappearing down a set of stairs or suddenly lost around a corner. Her enigmatic figure recedes from Bond even as he gains proximity to her, both visually and in terms of real understanding.

To further emphasise the process of alienation between Bond and Vesper, the camera films her from behind or above, but always at a distance so that the viewer can never make out the features or expressions on her face, but only her movements and the brilliant colour of her dress. At one point, she stops just under an archway, between a dark and light space, and turns back to see if she is being followed. The pause is almost imperceptible, but for a moment she appears as if in a still life painting, then she keeps walking and Bond steps out of the shadows. Just as the stairwell fight occurs in a liminal space that also serves as a narrative link between the first and second halves of the card game, so the extended scene of Bond following Vesper through corridors and alleyways serves to connect the two sides – false and true – of his romantic relationship. By filming action sequences in shifting, marginal spaces, the film is able to narrate Bond's transformation as constant and instinctive, evolving while in flux rather than in reflection.

Benjamin writes: 'the destructive character has the consciousness of historical man, whose deepest emotion is an insuperable mistrust of the course of things and a readiness at all times to recognise that everything can go wrong. Therefore, the destructive character is reliability itself' (1999b: 542). Here Benjamin aligns the historical consciousness with the capacity for a larger, if more sceptical, visionary position. Interestingly, Craig's Bond appears to be destructive largely because he is reckless and inexperienced, but also because his outlook matches the tough, ironic stand of Fleming's Bond in the novel. Towards the end of the film, M says to Bond, 'You don't trust anyone, do you James?' 'No', he answers. 'Then you've learned your lesson.' Again the film calls attention to Bond as he seems to evolve from ur-form, while corresponding to Benjamin's destructive character 'whose deepest emotion is an insuperable mistrust'. The seriousness of the role reflects Benjamin's 'historical man' because his depth is associated with a kind of steady unflinching doubt. In Bond's case, this condition leads to the readiness to 'recognise that everything can go wrong'; as we have seen, it is often Craig's Bond who induces the catastrophic event. His reliability in the face of disaster depends itself upon a certain improvisational skill and an ability to work with the tools that are at hand. Even when he discovers that Vesper has betrayed him, he takes action almost immediately. It is in moments of joy or tenderness that he seems tentative whereas his reliability in the face of danger or threat is unshakable.

A key distinction that marks Bond's particular adaptability in *Casino Royale* is his relative unwillingness to use traditional 007 toys. Although he rarely shows an outward disdain for these tools, he almost always fails to use them or else employs them in an unconventional way. This playful economy deviates from the standard 007 film formula where the audience is introduced to the latest in technological gadgetry just as Bond himself is educated by Q. Typically, as the film progresses, the audience receives satisfaction by watching these tools put to use as they miraculously (but predictably) get Bond out of a jam. In *Casino Royale*, Q is significantly absent and Bond seems to triumph due to his wits, resilience, or even the grace of Fate, rather than technological equipment. About the earlier Bond incarnations, Patrick O'Donnell writes:

> Bond must be both full of surprises – gadgetary and phallic – and able to meet a sudden turn of events with unflappable calm and technical precision; at the same time, he is repetitively machinic, not just in his sexual conquests, but in all of his performances: recall again the technology of the Aston Martin of *Goldfinger*, each gadget (and all of them) deployed in a precise fashion, the chaos and sudden turns of the car chase punctuated by Bond's robotic engagement with the car's prosthetic attachments. (2005: 64)

Here O'Donnell seems to reference the readiness that I recognise in Craig's Bond, but in the earlier 007s this quality depends in large part on the gadgetry that defines him as 'repetitively machinic'. Being given handy tools and weapons, the earlier Bond obediently and skilfully uses them, thus performing with the kind of 'unflappable calm and technical precision' we associate with his character. In *Casino Royale*, however, this reliability is based on the destructive impulse rather than a dependence on technology.

Take, for instance, the film's variation on the standard 007 trope: the Aston Martin. Although the car figures in *Casino Royale*, its functional presence is short and relatively unsuccessful. After he is poisoned, Bond goes to the car where he attempts to use a device to restart his heart. This is the first 'gadget' that we have seen him use and his failure to employ it successfully is exaggerated by the relative ease with which he has survived previous brushes with death. He desperately punches the button that is meant to start his heart but because the device is not plugged in properly, we witness his pathetic collapse. It is only after Vesper arrives on the scene and intuits how to fix the machine that she is able to punch the button and save Bond. This moment reverses Martin Willis's theory of the traditional relationship between Bond and technology. He writes that 'for each of the five actors who have played James Bond there has always been a clear connection between technology and masculinity/sexuality' (2003: 156). Instead of technical mastery, Craig's Bond seems to assert his power of masculinity through more primitive virtues of stoicism and endurance. When he wakes up in the car and sees Vesper, he asks, 'Are you all right?', thus automatically reinstating his readiness to stand in the role of the protective figure. Meanwhile, the scene seems to highlight technology's unreliability rather than its precision. Indeed, Craig's Bond seems to disregard the car for the most part. The next time he uses the Aston Martin, he chases after Vesper, and promptly crashes the car, destroying it completely. That is all we see of the Bondmobile, much less any secret compartments of gadgetry it might have held.

Indeed, when Bond does employ technology to achieve his ends, he has usually appropriated it from someone else in a manner that recalls guerrilla tactics rather than the calculation of a secret agent. If Craig's Bond has his own computer, phone or gun, we rarely see him use it because he prefers tools, cars and women that belong to others. Early in the film he steals into M's apartment to use her computer and later uses her secure password to access files and information. He uses Mollaka's mobile phone after he kills him and later the phone of Alex Dimitrios (Simon Abkarian), the Greek gambler who collaborates with Le Chiffre. In fact, he not only co-opts Dimitrios's wife, Solange (Caterina Murino), phone and car, but ultimately uses the latter's knife to kill him. Later, he destroys a second bomb-maker at Miami International Airport using the man's own bomb, consequently foiling Le Chiffre's plot by, once again, working within the other's tactical design. In nearly every situation, Bond triumphs without a technological advantage. Even in the stairwell scene when Obanno wields a huge sword, Bond fights him in hand-to-hand combat, using his dinner jacket as a shield. Although he often carries a gun, Bond rarely uses it. In nearly every action sequence, the gun is kicked out of the way in the initial moments of the fight and Bond ends up tackling his opponent or using unusual devices that appear at hand. In the final action sequence in the Venetian building, there is a moment when Bond tracks his opponent by watching the man's reflection in a piece of broken glass and then at the right moment lunges at him with a broken wooden beam. The man's machine gun goes sputtering down the corridor and falls away. This scene is typical both of Bond's crude tools and his natural ingenuity in finding them. Even the film's central drama – the card game against Le Chiffre – shows Bond once again imposing his will on another's game. It is Le Chiffre who has set the rules. His many attempts to sabotage Bond fail even as the latter improvises to come out the winner.

If we are to understand Craig's Bond as a kind of new barbarian or destructive character, then it is important to consider why this formulation is a contemporary one. As with all Bond films (and despite the anachronism of the formative storyline), *Casino Royale* seems to reflect a familiar cultural and political context. Here, the villain is not trying to take over the world, he merely wants to profit from it. Diabolical motives are replaced by a kind of blank amorality. Le Chiffre seems not to care one way or another about the African guerrilla groups whose money he invests, the Sky Fleet that he tries to destroy, various bomb-makers or even Bond in particular. He is driven purely by the logic of capitalism and seems to be more archetypal than human, the accountant with a gift for gambling, a purely rational type. Craig's Bond faces a villain and a central conflict, then, that lack the kind of social or symbolic framework that previous Bonds relied upon in their adventures. The Cold War is over, and unlike the world of the Brosnan Bond films, there is no emphasis on technology or cybernetics as either a means or an end to the villain's agenda. Instead, Le Chiffre's plan is abstract, and when it fails, his strategy for survival represents just another, perhaps more orthodox, form of gambling. The narrative of *Casino Royale* thus demands that Bond be primitive, direct and anarchic. This characterisation determines through his actions and tactical decisions, as well as the confining and immediate situations he finds himself in throughout the film.

It is only at the end of the film, after learning of Vesper's betrayal and losing her in Venice, that Craig's Bond assumes the pose and armour of Bond as we have known him in previous films. In Umberto Eco's essay on James Bond, he cites Fleming's *Casino Royale* in order to illustrate how, at the end of the novel, Bond evolves from man to machine. Eco writes: 'Bond is to abandon the treacherous life of moral meditation and of psychological anger, with all the neurotic dangers that they entail'; all this in order to be 'a magnificent machine, as the author and the public ... wish' (2003: 35). Indeed, the rationality and detachment of the machine model sets the tone for the end of *Casino Royale*. Everything about the final scene differs from the other action sequences in the film. The set design is vast, stable and opulent. The dark, liminal spaces of earlier scenes are gone, as is the violent proximity and quick-cut editing we have seen throughout the film. Instead, the scene is set at a serene and luxurious lakeside villa. Mr White (Jesper Christensen) steps out of his car and walks to the edge of the driveway, gazing at the water and the hilly landscape that surrounds it. He is still and the scene is lit with sun and space. His mobile phone rings and before we see Bond, we hear his voice on the phone, followed by a shot that has been fired at Mr White from a distance. This act introduces for the first time a formal detachment (via audio and visual technology) that Craig's Bond, for all his seriousness, has previously failed to access. It is only after Mr White has dropped to the gravel, writhing in pain, that we see the looming figure of James Bond. Dressed in a natty polished suit, carrying an enormous automatic weapon in one hand and a mobile phone in the other, he says: 'The name is Bond. James Bond.' The slight smirk that appears on Craig's face as he delivers the formulaic line reveals a perverse self-consciousness caught in the mould of a familiar performance. It is at this moment that we perceive the birth of the individual as type, or perhaps more accurately, the fossilisation of the individual.

9

'GALLIVANTING ROUND THE WORLD': BOND, THE GAZE AND MOBILITY

Brian Baker

A helicopter shot circles a crowd in a small arena. From a low angle, we see the crowd, predominantly African faces. A title indicates that we are in Madagascar. This is a snake pit, the crowd betting on snake or mongoose. A man, a black African, is picked out in the crowd: betting, drinking from a bottle of beer, viewing a text on a mobile phone. A cut to a medium shot of this man is disrupted by a white male face entering in the foreground from the right side, saying 'Looks like our man.' A whip pan reveals Bond standing high above the snake pit, arms folded, half-turned away from the action, leaning against a half-built wall. The film cuts again to snake and mongoose, to the African man on the phone. The white

Bond in stasis vs. Bond in motion: *Casino Royale*
(2006)

man in the foreground, who we learn is called Carter and is an associate of Bond, touches his ear, and the man on the phone recognises the gesture: he is fiddling with an earpiece. He runs. Bond is still, watching the scene, as Carter falls into the snake pit, his handgun accidentally going off. The crowd flees, in a sequence of rapid edits, handheld camera dominant, transmitting the energy of the dispersing crowd. The man with the phone (we now see he also has a small rucksack on his back) runs up some steps, and the camera tilts up to find Bond still standing in the same pose. Then Bond runs.

This short scene begins one of the most exhilarating chase sequences in contemporary cinema, and certainly the most kinetic in the Bond film canon: the foot race between Bond (Daniel Craig) and the bomb-maker, Mollaka (Sébastien Foucan), in *Casino Royale*. This chapter will analyse the sequence is some detail later, but I begin this chapter here to emphasise the contrast between stasis and mobility that is central to the film's visual economy and to its politics of representation. Bond *stands* aloof, watching the snake pit; Bond *runs*. This chapter will take its critical cue from recent work done in the field of 'mobilities', particularly that of Tim Cresswell and John Urry, to investigate what I propose is *Casino Royale*'s aesthetic of total mobilisation in terms of spectatorial gaze and free-running bodies in motion. This, I will argue, signals a rupture in the visual regime of the Bond series, embracing contemporary globalised capital's emphasis upon free movement: of information, of resources and of the gaze, and at the same time the necessity to police this movement and maintain borders or erect barriers to restrict this fluidity.

I will also compare *Casino Royale* to *A View To A Kill* (1985), which engages a modern spectatorial sensibility through the visual insistence upon panoramas seen from great height (the top of the Eiffel Tower, the top of the Golden Gate bridge) and tourist spectacles. At this stage in the Bond production cycle, the tourist-location *mise-en-scène* which increasingly comes to characterise the films turns self-conscious: in *A View To A Kill*, at the bottom of the Eiffel Tower, in another chase sequence (markedly less kinetic than the one in *Casino Royale*) in which Bond engages his antagonist on foot, Bond knocks over stalls displaying the bric-a-brac of tourist consumption before stealing a Parisian taxi and launching it onto the roof of the 'Paris-Istanbul' coach, itself a relic from the 1920s. Abandoning the car, he dives off a bridge over the Seine and plunges through the glass roof of a large river-cruiser containing a wedding party. Tourism and consumption become part of the very fabric of the world of *A View To A Kill*. Its very title indicates its emphasis on seeing and spectatorship. I will return to this sequence later in this chapter.

First, however, I would like to outline the conceptual framework that I will use in the first half of this essay with regard to movement and vision. Tim Cresswell, in *On the Move: Mobility in the Modern Western World* (2006), revisits the way in which movement has been thought in Western culture, suggesting that 'mobility' enters the English language in the seventeenth century 'when it was applied to persons, their bodies, limbs and organs' (2006: 20). In the eighteenth century, the Latin term *mobile vulgus* is used to characterise the 'moveable and excitable crowd' (ibid.), the Latin later shortened and anglicised to the 'mob'. 'Mobility', as distinct from 'movement', is 'thoroughly socialised and often threatening' (ibid.). However, it is modernity that is Cresswell's true focus, a modernity that is fissured by mobility:

Modernity has been marked by time-space compression and staggering developments in communications and transportation. At the same time, it has seen the rise of moral panics ranging from the refugee to the global terrorist. The celebrated technologies of mobility simultaneously open up the possibility of an increasingly transgressive world marked by people out of place at all scales. (2006: 20–1)

I will return to the threatening figure of the global terrorist as a spectre that haunts mobile modernity in relation to *Casino Royale* later in this chapter. Cresswell's critical intervention in the field of mobilities is organised in *On the Move* around two opposing principles that he sees as underpinning much social theory of movement and human geography: a *sedentarist metaphysics* is opposed to a *nomadic metaphysics*. Cresswell appropriates the term 'sedentarist metaphysics' from the anthropologist Liisa Malkki, and by this Cresswell means 'ways of thinking about mobility in the Western world [that] see it as a threat, a disorder in the system, a thing to control' (2006: 26). A sedentarist metaphysics privileges rootedness or locatedness, 'the moral and logical primacy of fixity in space and place' (ibid.). This metaphysics 'reaffirm[s] and enable[s] the commonsense segmentation of the world into things like nations, states, countries, and places' (2006: 28). There is a tension between mobility and place in modernity, argues Cresswell, but it is not that between an inauthentic spatial flux and an authentic sense of locatedness. Rather, modernity produces an irreducible tension between free flows of capital, labour, information and populations, and the need to restrict or control this mobility, as it may destabilise the geopolitical and economic structures than enable these flows. I will turn to the economic and political implications of this tension towards the end of this essay, but here I would like to address what Cresswell places in opposition to the 'sedentarist metaphysics': the 'nomadic metaphysics'.

As Cresswell points out, in contemporary social theory, 'words associated with mobility are unremittingly positive' (2006: 25). Flux, fluidity, dynamic, mobile: all words that seem to offer the possibility of disrupting the ideological landscape, to resist or destabilise hegemonic forms of subjectivity, cultural representation or everyday life. 'Mobility has become the ironic foundation for anti-essentialism, antifoundationalism and antirepresentationalism' (2006: 46), he writes. The figure of mobility as resistance can be found in the work of Michel de Certeau, Guy Debord and contemporary psychogeographers, or the 'nomadology' of Félix Guattari and Gilles Deleuze and others. Cresswell is suspicious of 'nomad thought'. In appropriating the figure of the 'nomad', such thought falls prey to 'androcentric tendencies' and ethnocentrism, if not a repeating of 'centuries of Western romanticisation of the non-Western other … Insofar as nomadology looks to the representations of colonial anthropology for its conception of the nomad, it is a thoroughly Orientalist discourse' (2006: 54). It is no coincidence that the free-running footrace in *Casino Royale* takes place in Madagascar, just as it is no coincidence that the dangerous 'terrorist' figure is represented as a black African (although he is played by Sébastien Foucan, the French exponent of *parkour*). The connection between the nomad, the mobile subject and the colonial subject is all too evident in *Casino Royale*.

Although the binary Cresswell deploys between a *sedentarist* and *nomadic* metaphysics may, like all binaries, appear problematic, it does provide a framework for thinking through mobility and representation that does not fall into the trap of a crude moral or ideological coding: mobility good, fixity bad. In fact, in my understanding of Cresswell's argument, modernity is characterised by an irreducible tension between mobility and fixity that insists upon their mutual implication rather than placing a final value upon one or the other. Where Cresswell attempts to deconstruct the informing premises of Western thinking about mobility, there is a long history of thought that connects mobility to vision and spectacle, and it is to this that I wish to now turn. Cresswell's proposal of opposing metaphysics provides the overarching conceptual framework for this essay, but it is crucial to historicise and (irony notwithstanding) *locate* my discussion of mobility, the gaze and modernity in specific historical and cultural contexts and the history of theorisation of these concepts.

My argument in this chapter rests upon evidence that the nineteenth century experienced the development of a particular kind of visual culture which placed the consumption of spectacle at the centre of the experience of everyday (urban) life. Gillen D'Arcy Wood, in his book *The Shock of the Real: Romanticism and Visual Culture 1760–1860* (2001) locates the rise of the 'society of the spectacle' not in the Second Empire Paris of the 1860s, but in London at the turn of the nineteenth century. Wood suggests that a growing economy of spectacular consumption, an identifiably modern visual culture, is a major motivating force behind the rise of Romanticism and its critique of industrial modernity. Wood notes that Wordsworth, in *The Prelude*, includes a section in which he visits a 'panorama' in London (a kind of large, artificial, painted vista, usually of a cityscape such as London or Paris) and then contrasts this to the real or unmediated experience of nature available to those who seek it out – in the Lakes, for instance. In the Preface to the second edition of the *Lyrical Ballads*, Wordsworth contrasts a modern 'degrading thirst after outrageous stimulation' (1970: 161), which would include panoramas, the theatre and other elements of visual spectacle, with 'organic sensibility' and poetry as the 'spontaneous overflow of powerful feelings' (1970: 160). Panoramas and spectacle paintings were very much in vogue in the early nineteenth century, particularly in Europe but also, in the paintings of Frederick Edwin Church, in the United States. Church's *Niagara* of 1857 was a huge success when exhibited, almost as huge as the canvas itself. Church frames the water thundering over the Falls as an awe-inspiring spectacle, devoid of human life and framing a moment of direct communion between spectator and Nature in its most powerful guise. The spectacle of Nature, the falls themselves, become in Church's hands, a spectacle painting, complete unto itself as a kind of marvel or 'event'. There is no Wordsworthian anxiety here.

I am not the first to note a connection between the rise of a nineteenth-century culture of spectacle and the forms of spectacular cinema at work in contemporary culture. Scott Bukatman, in 'The Artificial Infinite', writes:

> The paintings of Frederick Church are particularly appropriately considered alongside [Douglas] Trumbull's [special] effects [in the sequence that ends *2001: A Space Odyssey*]. The astonishing, bold colour experiments (special effects) that Church unleashed in depicting his twilight skies and volcanic eruptions were the result of new technologies in cadmium-based pigment production. These effects were placed at the service of atmospheric and cosmological phenomena: not just the sky, but the sun and the moon, a meteor, and the aurora borealis ... Through slitscan technologies, Trumbull created a set of images that were little more than organised patterns of light – the very stuff of cinema. Light, with its implications of revelation and blinding power, is also the very stuff of the sublime. (1999: 263–4)

In slightly different terms, Gillen D'Arcy Wood also offers a connection between early nineteenth-century forms of spectacle and the cinema when he suggests that 'the panorama anticipated the early twentieth-century newsreel. In commercial terms it operated more like the contemporary movie industry than the traditional art market' (2001: 101).

Although these continuities are important, I would like to suggest a complication here in the spectacular forms of modernity that I have outlined above. The panorama, the exhibition, the arcade, are mobile forms of the gaze that rest upon static displays. The forms of contemporary cinematic spectacle conform more to what Anne Friedberg suggests is a 'virtual mobile gaze'. In *Window Shopping: Cinema and the Postmodern*, Friedberg proposes not a rupture between a modern and a postmodern visuality, but instead an 'epistemological tear along the fabric of modernity, a change produced by the increasing cultural centrality of an integral feature of both cinematic and televisual apparatuses: a *mobilised "virtual" gaze*' (1993: 2; emphasis in original). The distinction Friedberg makes between the *mobilised gaze* and the *mobilised 'virtual' gaze* is organised around the central term of cinema. The *mobilised gaze* is produced by 'cultural activities that involve walking and travel' (ibid.), such as *flânerie*; tourism; mobility created by trains, bicycles, steamships, elevators, automobiles, airplanes; and cultural sites such as exhibition halls, winter gardens, arcades, department stores and museums. The gaze is mobilised because the spectating subject circulates around a fixed display of objects that are actually present (museum exhibits, tourist attractions). The gaze becomes 'virtual' when this experience is 'but a *received* perception mediated through representation' (ibid.; emphasis in original). Like Wood, Friedberg connects the panorama with cinema, suggesting that the panorama was a kind of 'building machine ... designed to *transport* ... the spectator-subject' (1993: 20; emphasis in original) through the presentation of a vast cityscape that imitated (or perhaps 'virtualised') the experience of taking the whole of London or Paris from a great height. The cinema audience do not move themselves; their gaze is mobilised 'virtually' through what is shot and then presented on the cinema screen. The gaze is then dislocated from the actual movement of bodies in space. As a cinematic spectator, we occupy a de-realised subject position that presents us with the illusion of corporeality through point of view and the kind of immersive experience (and suppression of spectatorial self-consciousness) presented to us by the Hollywood continuity system.

The movement of bodies in space is crucial to what John Urry, in *The Tourist Gaze*, argues to be a particular form of visuality produced by tourism and travel, the tourist gaze of his title. In fact, Urry's tourist gaze is analogous to what Friedberg calls the *mobilised gaze*, in that it is a *corporeal* mobility. Urry makes a distinction between the '"static" forms of the tourist gaze, such as that from a balcony vantage point' (2002: 153), which he associates with still photography, and a 'mobility of vision' where 'there are swiftly passing panorama, a sense of multi-dimensional rush and the fluid interconnections of places, peoples and possibilities' (ibid.), which is connected to the development of the railway and then the automobile. A kind of whirling, kaleidoscopic visuality implied by Urry's second category has clear affinities with *flânerie*, the urban sensorium of shocks and energies analysed by Walter Benjamin. The 'tourist gaze' is still a *mobilised gaze*, however. Virtuality has yet to enter the field.

The centrality of tourism and travel to Bond texts (Ian Fleming's and the films) needs little further emphasis from me, though it is important to note how Michael Denning's analysis of Bond's 'heroic consumption' of the tourist spectacle is echoed so strongly by Urry. Denning writes, after quoting from a scene in Fleming's *From Russia, With Love*:

> Here we find the epitome of the tourist experience: the moment of relaxed visual contemplation from above, leaning on the balustrade; the aesthetic reduction of a social entity, the city, to a natural object, coterminous with the waves of the sea; the calculations of the tourist's economy, exchanging physical discomfort for a more 'authentic' view; and the satisfaction of having made the 'right' exchange, having 'got' the experience, possessed the 'view'. (1987: 104)

It is no coincidence, argues Denning, that the Bond narratives find their location in the Mediterranean, the Caribbean, or certain parts of East Asia: these constitute the 'pleasure periphery', 'the tourist belt surrounding the industrialised world'

(1987: 105). I should here like to emphasise the centrality of the tourist destination to the visual economy of the Bond films as well as the Fleming novels. In the novels and in the majority of the Bond film series, mobility is *horizontal*, ordered through the tourist-destination locations made available through jet-era travel infrastructures, the age of mass mobility. These locations, like the huge Ken Adam sets that dominate the *mise-en-scène* in the final sequences of all the earlier Bond films, signify the centrality of the *mobilised gaze* rather than the *mobilised 'virtual' gaze* (even though, as films, there is obviously a degree of virtuality at work here).

I would like to suggest that the *mise-en-scène* of the Bond films up to *Casino Royale* in 2006 is carefully orchestrated to avoid the vertiginousness and dislocation inherent in mobility, the 'shock' of visual modernity. I will take for my example Roger Moore's final film as Bond, *A View To A Kill*, whose very title indicates the centrality of looking, spectatorship and the gaze to its thematic and visual structure. The narrative of this film is a pale echo of *Goldfinger* (1964): Max Zorin (Christopher Walken), an ex-KGB agent now turned businessman and race-horse owner, plans to open up the San Andreas fault in California and flood Silicon Valley, thereby ensuring his own monopoly of the global trade in silicon chips. The main locations of the film are Paris and the West Coast of the United States, with the final confrontation between Zorin and Bond taking place atop the Golden Gate Bridge which spans the San Francisco Bay. After the pre-title and title sequences of *A View To A Kill*, Bond is informed of the problems surrounding the Zorin Corporation and then told by the Minister (Geoffrey Keen) and the Admiral (Robert Brown) in charge of this operation that he has 'half an hour to dress'. The scene switches to Ascot, where the morning-suited Bond and the Admiral watch not Zorin's horse win a prize race, but Zorin and his lover/accomplice Mayday (Grace Jones) celebrating in the stands.

The shot that begins the next sequence is the Eiffel Tower, as seen from the Trocadero, and then the film cuts inside an Art Nouveau restaurant where Bond is lunching with one Aubergine (Jean Rougerie), a detective who has been investigating Zorin's horse-racing activities. The name of this character is itself enough to indicate the level of banality and levity generally at work in *A View To A Kill*, but when Bond displays his customary knowledge of wine vintages, Aubergine says: 'I see you are a connoisseur'. Connoisseurship is an index of Bond's difference as a tourist/traveller: he is possessed of knowledge that allows him to assume a cultural locatedness that makes him seem somehow 'at home' in a diversity of cultures and places. It is also a marker of the sophistication of Bond's consumption, its superiority over that of the masses. In the scene in the Eiffel Tower restaurant, whose 'magic butterfly' act is at once high kitsch and an index of an 'authentic' Parisian locale, Aubergine is attacked by a disguised Mayday, who then escapes, chased by Bond. She first knocks out the operator of the long boom (like a fishing rod) that is integral to the illusion of the 'magic butterfly' act, then takes over, 'hooking' Aubergine through the cheek with what we must assume is a poisoned fly. It is worth taking a moment to consider Mayday's costume. The original operator is dressed entirely in black to make him or her fade into the dimness of the restaurant's periphery. Mayday's costume repeats this, but with the addition

of a seemingly superfluous cape. As Mayday runs from Bond, up the Eiffel Tower's iron steps, the cape flows out behind her, and Paris is laid out as a panorama beyond. The visual reference here is, I think, to the early twentieth-century French film serial *Fantomas*, whose costume Mayday's head-to-toe black recalls. As Mayday runs up the steps, the film intercuts shots of her

Mayday (Grace Jones) prepares to parachute from the Eiffel Tower in *A View To A Kill* (1985)

running with Bond, static, firing up at the fleeing figure (and towards the raised camera). There is a significant visual coding between mobility and immobility at this point, accentuated by the then sexagenarian Roger Moore as the less-than-athletic Bond. Mayday takes off the cape, leaps upon the handrail of the stairwell, and dives off: the cape has concealed a parachute, and the suicide dive is transformed into a base jump.

Bond, of course, does not follow suit. He waits for the down elevator, jumps onto its roof and travels downwards *statically*, Bond posed/poised in tuxedo against the Paris cityscape as the elevator moves downward through the shot. At the bottom of the Tower, Bond knocks over some tourist stalls, then steals a Parisian taxi in which he pursues Mayday to a bridge crossing the Seine, as she has landed on a large tourist cruiser. Bond jumps, to fall through the glass roof and spoil a wedding party, whereupon he is bundled away by some irate cleaver-wielding chefs. This crucial sequence in *A View To A Kill* has a multiple significance with regard to the film's organisation of spectatorship. As I have already suggested, the tourist experience of Paris (the Eiffel Tower, the Trocadero, a river launch) is already encoded into the film's *mise-en-scène* to locate the film's own audience, the 'virtual' nature of this experience insistently lensed through the more static spectacles of the 'tourist gaze' or the *mobilised gaze*.

As Friedberg herself notes, the Eiffel Tower and 1889 Paris Exposition were fundamentally implicated in the nineteenth-century's cultures of spectacle and visual modernity:

> it offered its visitors a spectacular new vista of urban space. The elevator ascension of the tower was one of the exposition's main attractions; the gaze was mobilised to a new vantage. The aerial view of Paris from the Tour d'Eiffel was previously available only to balloonists. From this lofty *passerelle*, all of Paris unfolded like a grand magasin. (1993: 84)

The last sentence also helps make sense of the puzzling centrality of a modern airship to Zorin's mobility (and the final sequence on the Golden Gate bridge) in *A View To A Kill*: the film self-consciously deploys an insistent perspective of height in its narrative and *mise-en-scène*, looking down from the Eiffel Tower, airship or bridge to produce the panorama. It also seeks to limit the possible de-corporealisation and vertiginousness of the *mobilised 'virtual' gaze* by offering overt, and culturally-sanctioned, vantage points from which to see. To this end, *falling* is a crucial visual motif in the film, from Mayday's base jump, to the disposal of a businessman from the airship after he refuses to join in Zorin's plan for domination, to Zorin's own death, plunging from the top of the bridge into the Bay. But the film consistently displaces away from Bond himself the possibility of falling, such as in his elevator ride down the Eiffel Tower, or his absurdly long clinging to the guy-rope of Zorin's airship. To sum up, I would suggest that the film offers an insistent corporealisation of the gaze, connected to Moore's fairly obvious age-related immobility as an actor (an immobility only pointed up, not masked as intended, by the casting of the even more superannuated and immobile Patrick Macnee as his 'sidekick'). In *A View To A Kill*, mobility is certainly a problem for Bond. In *Casino Royale*, by contrast, it is *immobility* that is problematic.

Here, then, we move from the category of Friedberg's *mobilised gaze* – which I have argued is coterminous with Urry's 'tourist gaze' – to the *mobilised 'virtual' gaze*, where movement is virtualised and mediated. Friedberg's contention is that the latter term is produced by photography, and cinema in particular. She is careful to bracket off periodisation (this is not modernity opposed to postmodernity), using the metaphor of an 'epistemological tear' rather than the more conclusive 'rupture'. In terms of a shift between *A View To A Kill* in 1985 to *Casino Royale* in 2006, I am also willing to avoid over-emphasising some kind of determining historical or cultural shift/rupture to locate the different visual strategies of the two films. It is not that *A View To A Kill* is a 'modern' film; it is that the film uses the mobilised gaze, and the spectatorial strategies of tourism, travel and the panorama to limit the disruptive effects of the cinematic spectacle. Certainly, between 1985 and 2006 the geopolitical environment has altered considerably, from the anxieties (yet securities) of the Cold War to the current post-9/11 world of 'the war on terror', the spectre of neo-imperialism and the growth of alternate poles of geopolitical power in China and India; and also a change with regard to financial, informational and population flows. There has also been a change within the dominant forms of popular cinema, and this is where I would like to begin.

Geoff King, in his chapter on 'Spectacle and Narrative in the Contemporary Blockbuster' in *Contemporary American Cinema*, proposes a transformation in the kinds of spectacle that characterise Hollywood cinema in the 1990s and early 2000s. He writes:

Spectacle in contemporary Hollywood is not just a matter of lofty vistas ... This is spectacle that can be understood as offering a vicarious assault on the position of the viewer through strategies such as rapid editing, unstable camerawork and, in some cases, the propulsion of objects out towards the screen. The large-scale vista is often viewed from on high, either statically, or, more characteristically in contemporary Hollywood, via expansive wheeling, arcing or panning motions of the camera. (2006: 340)

King calls this 'impact aesthetic' 'Impressive spectacular realism' (2006: 338), which offers a tension between the immersive pleasures of a world created through 'the apparently "seamless" manner with which digital artefacts are employed, either alone or in combination with "real" live-action characters and settings' (ibid.), and the 'wow-factor' of spectacle sequences which draw attention to themselves as spectacles. In the quotation above, King moves from an idea of spectacle as 'vista' (the localisation/corporealisation of the mobile gaze through the construction of a 'static' place from which to view) to one of spectacle as total mobility (the decorporealisation of the gaze through camera movement and editing to radically destabilise 'the position of the viewer'). The aesthetic of the contemporary blockbuster, of which *Casino Royale* is surely a part, then corresponds to an extreme version of Friedberg's *mobilised 'virtual' gaze*, where the virtual element causes a radical de-location of the spectator-subject. This 'wheeling, arcing or panning' can be seen to greatest effect in *Casino Royale* in the free-running sequence.

In stark contrast to Roger Moore's immobility in *A View To A Kill*, Daniel Craig's Bond is characterised by aggressive movement. Throughout the film, Bond struts – with Craig's shoulders twitching back and forward with the intensity of his walk – or he runs, in a manner not seen even in the Sean Connery or Timothy Dalton incarnations. In the sequence in which he pursues the bomb-maker in Madagascar, Bond's mobility is in fact placed in contradistinction to that of his quarry. The bomb-maker is played by Sébastien Foucan, one of the originators and a leading exponent of *parkour*, the anglicised name of which is 'free-running'. *Parkour* is a kind of pedestrian urban mobility which originated in the alienating concrete landscaping of the Parisian *banlieues*, the ring of suburbs constructed to house the dispersed inhabitants of Paris's inner-city deprived areas, many of them of North African or West African descent. The *banlieues* themselves became centres of alienated youth, racial tension and violence, unemployment and deprivation, and they found their highest popular profile in Matthieu Kassowitz's fiction film *La Haine* (1995). *Parkour* could be seen as an embodied resistance to the planned and controlled urban environments of the *banlieues*, a physical version of Michel de Certeau's formulation of the 'practices' of walking, the 'tactics' which in a micro-political way disrupt the determining fabric of the space of power and the 'strategies' of the state and ideological forces. Where the conforming urban walker will keep to the walkways, paths and streets, the exponent of *parkour* will jump, hurdle, run or vault, turning the urban environment into a kind of giant gymnasium in which the resisting body of the *parkour*-ist is located in space in a manner different from, and alternate to, that coded by the planners of the *banlieue*.

It was only a matter of time, however, before Hollywood filmmakers understood the visual and spectacular possibilities of *parkour* within the 'impact aesthetic' of contemporary cinema to turn resisting behaviours into a cinematic spectacle. The body in motion of the *parkour* exponent offers a kind of corporeal mobility that fully displays the imperatives of 'Impressive spectacular realism': without CGI, the body seems to perform 'impossible' acrobatic and gymnastic movements in space, creating the spectatorial 'wow' while emphasising at the same time the *reality* of what is being filmed. It is a special effect not created by special effect technologies; however, unlike former Hollywood genres that focused upon the body in motion (the musical in particular, which favoured the long take in order to give full expression to the dancers' performances), Foucan's free-running is at the service of exactly the kind of 'wheeling, arcing and panning' camera and rapid editing that Geoff King identifies as central to the formal properties of the contemporary blockbuster. This does not restrain or undermine the spectacular nature of Foucan's stunts, however. The camera, which, as the sequence in *Casino Royale* progresses, becomes increasingly de-corporealised in the terms I discussed above (dis-located from a static point of view from which to see), performs or inhabits the same kind of mobility in space as the free-runner. Camerawork and filmed body are of a piece. In fact, the camera itself could be seen to engage in a kind of visual *parkour*, a radical destabilisation of the codes of representation offered by the *mobilised gaze*.

The bomb-maker (Foucan) runs from Bond and the snake-pit to a construction site. Vaulting over the wire-mesh fence, he zig-zags across the site, up a building and then on to the gridded space of the steel-frame skeleton of an under-construction curtain-wall skyscraper, of course the signature building of a certain form of urban modernity. Bond pursues: on foot, at the wheel of an earthmover (smashing one of the buildings), and then follows the bomb-maker by ascending vertically on a crane pulley. (Bond smashes off the load to do so, which then plunges onto the workers below.) After ascending the building, the bomb-maker jumps onto a crane, followed by Bond on the pulley, where he is finally able to force a physical confrontation with his antagonist. Up to this point the film heightens the kineticism of the action by rapid editing, shots lasting a second or less, intercutting between the fleeing Foucan and the pursuing Craig. On the crane, however, helicopter shots predominate, the camera swirling and wheeling around the figures on the huge industrial structure. This sequence emphasises a fantastical, almost dream-like bodily mobility, where 'real' human beings launch themselves (seemingly impossibly) across vertiginous spaces, from building to crane, from crane to building. In keeping with this fantastical mobility, the camera of director Martin Campbell and director of photography Paul Meheux is always on the move, 'tracking' almost impossibly several hundred feet in the air, circling around the protagonists, who are themselves always in energetic motion. The film does not allow

Parkour co-founder Sébastien Foucan free-running as Mollaka in *Casino Royale* (2006)

the spectator a fixed point from which to view, but fully emphasises the vertiginous, decorporealised effect of the *mobile 'virtual' gaze*.

That the free-running sequence takes place largely on a building site, in Madagascar, is an index of the change in the geopolitical landscape that informs *Casino Royale* in contradistinction to some of its forerunners. Rather than being in the 'pleasure periphery', this sequence takes place in a developing-world locale in which the imperatives of contemporary capital are beginning to be inscribed, in terms of a 'Western' (or developed world) architecture, upon the topography of the country. The brilliant blue sea that forms the backdrop to Bond and the bomb-maker on the crane also signifies that this development is connected (still) to the postcard-panorama aesthetics of tourism.

Further, *Casino Royale* can be seen not only as a post-9/11 Bond film, but also as the first truly post-Bretton Woods Bond film. The Bretton Woods system is described by Robert Wade as an 'international financial system [in which] the world economy operated with fixed exchange rates; an international medium of exchange and store of value – the US dollar – backed by gold; and restrictions on capital movements' (2006: 116). Its collapse in 1973 introduced a financial world of flexible exchange rates and free capital movements, the basis for rapid credit expansion which led to a 'surge' in 'world liquidity' (ibid.). Wade argues that this financial mobility, coupled with national policies of deregulation, was the motor of global economic expansion, but at the same time 'the surge of liquidity since the end of Bretton Woods and the resulting financialisation of the economy have created an inherent source of instability in the world economy' (2006: 118). That the casino is the crucial space of (political) conflict in this narrative is indicative of *Casino Royale*'s place in what John Urry, quoting Zygmunt Bauman, calls 'liquid modernity' and its globalised system of 'free' capital flows. There is no 'super-villain' plotting world domination as there is in *A View To A Kill*. Here, Bond's ultimate antagonist is a financier, a card-player and a facilitator of the globalised 'free flow' of capital that finds its physical analogue in the free-running bomb-maker, or terrorist. When M (Judi Dench) tells Bond, after he has killed the bomb-maker, that he needs to think of the bigger picture rather than being satisfied with having one less bomb-maker alive, it masks the truth that it is the very financial system that Bond represents and protects that is the ultimate enabler of global terrorism, rather than the bomb-maker, or even the villainous banker Le Chiffre (Mads Mikkelsen).

There is evidence, in *Casino Royale*, of the irreducible tension in contemporary capital between the imperative towards the reduction or removal of barriers to the 'free flow' of capital, and the imperative of developed nations to restrict this flow (certainly in terms of population flows, particularly immigration) or transform this population liquidity into a legitimated form: migrant workers who perform the labour roles that indigenous populations do not want to do, or into tourists. Ginette Verstraete proposes a 'contradictory logic' at the heart of the EU's 'geopolitics of mobility' that can stand as a diagnostic case for the kind of economic world represented in *Casino Royale* (2001: 27). Verstraete argues that since the Schengen agreement of 1985 (curiously, the same year as *A View To A Kill*) the EU:

has implemented the gradual abolition of national border controls (which became common frontiers), and replaced them with limited passport and other document checks ... The Schengen agreement was meant to: minimise delays caused by traffic congestion and identity checks; stimulate the free and competitive flow of goods, money and people; create a common European market at a scale that would improve productivity, distribution, and consumption; attract large foreign investments; and enable Europe to compete with the USA and East Asia. (2001: 28–9)

The contradictory logic that Verstraete diagnoses can be seen in this abolition of *internal* barriers that found its correlative in 'the introduction of firm external frontiers to keep illegal immigrants, terrorists and drug-dealers out, and guarantee internal security and stability' (2001: 29). Most importantly in the context of this chapter, 'the freedom of mobility for some (citizens, tourists, business people) could only be made possible through the organised exclusion of others forced to move around as illegal "aliens", migrants, or refugees' (ibid.). Very largely, Verstraete argues, this distinction is racialised: white Europeans are placed in the former category, non-white Europeans and others in the latter.

This casts the free-running sequence in *Casino Royale* in a particular, if not peculiar, light, for the difference between the free-running bomb-maker and the chasing Secret Service agent is also played out as a racial or ethnic difference. Craig's aggressive, almost angular physicality is at odds with Foucan's physical agility and fluidity. Where Foucan slides feet-first through a narrow head-height window, Craig bursts straight through the plasterboard wall. *Casino Royale*'s geopolitical space is an extension of Schengen space: for Bond, mobility is unrestricted (despite the fact that M is in high dudgeon and sends him to the periphery), whereas for the non-white bomb-maker, his free-running emphasises danger, and the need to impose restrictions upon his movement. (For Bond, even the violation of diplomatic protocol by invading the embassy of another country in pursuit of the bomb-maker has no real consequences for him, even if the 'political' realities of such an act are stressed by the film.) As I noted above in relation to Bond's 'heroic tourism', Bond is 'at home' anywhere, a condition often validated by his connoisseurship. But as Vivian Halloran notes in 'Tropical Bond', the issue of 'passing' for local recurs in Bond texts which consistently, she argues, 'complicate Bond's whiteness' (2005: 165). Following Edward Said's argument about Kipling's Kim in *Culture and Imperialism* (2002), I would like to stress here that Bond can 'pass', even as a non-white other (see the film of *You Only Live Twice* (1967) for a concrete, if risible, example); but the non-white other (the free-running bomb-maker) most assuredly cannot. In *Casino Royale*, the bomb-maker's proficiency in *parkour* is, ideologically, another sign of his dangerous and uncontrolled mobility.

Casino Royale is deeply embedded in a system of representation in which can be traced the foundational tension between mobility and immobility in contemporary culture. Mobile phones and laptop computers are ubiquitous in *Casino Royale*, as are laptop computers connected to the Internet; the narratively central card-game standoff between Bond and Le Chiffre emphasises financial mobility and liquidity; Le Chiffre is a kind of financier, offering banking facilities to 'freedom fighters' (who require 'access around the world' to their deposited monies). Bond himself is a figure of almost fantasy mobility, as I have indicated above, both in terms of bodily movement and in geopolitical space. His journey around the Mediterranean on the yacht with Vesper Lynd (Eva Green) towards the end of the film also signifies a fantasy of tourist mobility, an endlessly-financed Grand Tour ending in that most liquid of cities, Venice.

In fact, it is *immobility* that is most dangerous to Bond. When captured by Le Chiffre, Bond is strapped naked to a cane chair and his genitals beaten; recovering in a wheelchair, he reveals both the password to his bank account and his love for Vesper Lynd, the loss of his secret agent 'armour'. The tension between mobility and territorialisation that characterises the unstable geopolitics of the 'financialised', post-Bretton Woods economic world can also be found in Hollywood cinema itself, and according to Geoff King, is integral to Hollywood's productive imperatives in the age of contemporary spectacle. 'In the contemporary global-scale moving-picture economy', he writes, 'Hollywood creates a territory on which it, alone, can compete ... Spectacle *as* spectacle is, thus, a matter of strongly market-driven aesthetics' (2006: 339; emphasis in original). The decorporealisation of the *mobilised 'virtual' gaze* is thereby put into the service of a further territorialisation. I need not elaborate on the politics of copyright, the region-coding of DVDs, or the campaigns by the film industry against pirated, downloaded copies of movies to emphasise the tension between a global market (facilitated by the Internet) and the desire for restrictions on the 'free flow' of capital or trade, nor the attendant ironies of this tension. As I hope to have outlined here, the Bond films are deeply implicated in systems of cultural representation which negotiate the place of the mobile subject and the mobile gaze in an increasingly, if not disturbingly, mobilised world. While some forms of mobility – economic, visual, informational, physical – are legitimated, others are shown to be radically destabilising and dangerous to the anxious nation-states of the 'developed world'. The *mobile gaze* of the tourist is now haunted by the spectre of the gaze of the other, the one who sees and visits 'us': the terrorist.

10

BOND, BENJAMIN, BALLS: TECHNOLOGISED MASCULINITY IN *CASINO ROYALE*

Keren Omry

The 2006 release of Daniel Craig's James Bond in the long awaited *Casino Royale* sparked a flurry of debates, with topics ranging from the relevance and nature of Bond's prominent mythology within popular culture, to the merits and implications of a blond Bond, in terms of aesthetics and sexual politics, as well as in relation to the Bond legacy. So many of these debates pivot on the ways in which the latest film plays with narrative and stylistic chronology; it both reproduces and rewrites those recognisable and definitive Bond features which set it apart from other contemporary texts of parallel genres. It is precisely this historical process of repetition that is opened by the narrative juncture of the film in question, that becomes key to resolving so many of these debates. Centrally, the production of *Casino Royale* raises the question: how can a twenty-first-century adaptation remain true to the *beginningness* of a novel which spawned one of the most successful series in popular culture, while meeting the demands and expectations of an audience trained on nearly half a century of Bond; all the while creating an autonomous and new work of art?

Drawing from the terminological framework set out by Walter Benjamin as he describes the 'formulation of revolutionary demands in the politics of art' in the age of mechanical reproduction (1970: 219), this essay will explore the renovated relationship of 'technology' and 'authenticity' in the twenty-first century. Specifically, I will examine the ways in which the 2006 film, *Casino Royale*, bridges the gap between the two terms identified by Benjamin, by means of a dramatic return to the body. Much has been written about the relationship between the body of the state and the bodies in the Bond series (see Black 2001; Lindner 2003a; Jenkins 2005), but it is only with the 2006 adaptation of the novel that the conflation of the two with both the technological body and the gendered body creates so potent a matter.

Where Benjamin identifies the radical rupture of the work of art from ritual and from fundamental dependence on originariness, which resulted from the technology of reproduction, I would like to suggest that *Casino Royale* marks a clear revision of the impact of technology. Here, it is precisely in the late creation of an antecedent original, both stemming from existing patterns and needing to stand before them, that the film revises Benjamin's paradigmatic chronology. As we are brought back to the newly created moment of origin, that historical *here-and-now*-ness absent from the work of art becomes relocated onto Bond's body. The audience becomes witness to the scar of technology as it is inscribed on – and inserted into – his flesh.

Crucially, this flesh is first and foremost a gendered body. We move from the positively *inauthentic* dehistoricised body to a grounded, hypermasculinised, performative body. Considering Judith Butler's notions of sight, site and citation, the new integration of body and technology in the film can be seen to function as a primary mechanism of knowledge. Finally, it is the return to the knowable body as it responds to that of another (e.g. the eroticism of torture and the materiality of Craig's physique) that paradoxically revitalises that mystical *aura* which Benjamin pronounced obsolete.

In the sections that follow, I will begin by examining the key terms which guide Benjamin's analysis through a close reading of elements of the earlier films. Locating these terms within Benjamin's own politics and central argument I seek to recontextualise them within the landscape of Bond culture in general and *Casino Royale* in particular. Throughout this explication, close attention will be paid to the ways in which the body of technology and the *body politic* as Benjamin constructs them implicate our understanding of the physical and personal masculine body in Bond.

Authenticity

The 1983 film *Octopussy* opens in East Germany with a dramatic chase of a wounded man dressed as a clown by identical twin knife-throwing brothers. As the chase reaches its climax, one of the knives hits its mark, the clown is stabbed in the back, and he ultimately falls crashing through the glass door to the house of the British Ambassador. As the clown falls lifeless to the carpet, a precious Fabergé egg rolls out of his hand. This scene fades into a London landscape, zooming into M's headquarters where the audience learns that in fact this clown was himself a double-0 agent. Agent 009 was murdered in the attempt to prevent his disclosing the fact that the priceless treasure was, in fact, a fake. It is this information that sets the action of the film in motion: our hero, 007, is summoned to investigate the history of this forgery and to learn why this should have fatal consequences. This opening scene is crucial for my purposes here as it demonstrates in rather extreme form the critical implications of the notion of *authenticity*.

The egg becomes literally transformed both in its own right and in our understanding of it as the film progresses and as each layer of understanding is undermined. To begin with, even if the audience is initially ignorant of the intrinsic value of the egg, this becomes immediately established as it exacts the price of a man's life. And yet it is this exorbitant and inestimable cost which effectively eliminates the very possibility of a quantifiable value, elevating the egg to a priceless treasure. The discovery that the treasure is a forgery undercuts not only the idea of an inherent value of the egg, evident purely by its own precious beauty, but of the concomitant agent's life as well. The economy of his life thus becomes immediately destabilised, reducing the currency of state affairs and of the deadly game played by the double-0 agents to that of an inflated and ultimately worthless coin.

And yet, at the precise instant at which this knowledge eradicates the value of the shimmering object, a new object is effectively created and realised that possesses all the significance and value stripped of the former: the absent original of which this is the imitation. It is the very fact of the fake and the falsehood it manifests which establishes both the *authenticity* and the value of the original. The value of the agent's life, then, and by extension that of Bond's (Roger Moore) as well, becomes removed from but hinted at by the forgery, and estimable by that of the original, authentic treasure. This established distance between original and its reproduction, as measured by authenticity, becomes, for Benjamin, dramatically disrupted with the technology of reproduction. This post-classical moment demanded that the social function of art be critically re-evaluated. The shift carried profound political and social implications as it effectively removes *meaning* in art from its political manipulations and places its production firmly on the shoulders of the viewing public.

The fake Fabergé egg in *Octopussy* (1983)

Octopussy's Fabergé egg illustrates this political history which a classic work of art possesses, and which Benjamin identifies as eliminated through post-classical modern technology. Not only does the egg literally signify the vanquished Russian decadent Tsardom, but, in the film, it is acquired and forged to raise funds for the maniacal plans of world destruction concocted by the renegade Soviet General Orlov (Steven Berkoff). The dangerous possibilities of political manipulation, as per Benjamin (who warned in his article against fascist aestheticisation of politics), thus become absolutely clear. Not only is the life of British agent 009 paradoxically both reduced to nought through its equivalence with the forgery and simultaneously displaced to the absent original, but the original itself is destroyed by Orlov as its beauty becomes subject to his plans: 'This fake has caused enough trouble', he says, before shattering the misidentified egg. The value of the object becomes removed from any purely aesthetic realm and is subject to the cynical use made by those in power.

While I will be discussing the gender implications of this model at further length below, it is particularly significant that the value ascribed to the artefact in the auction is that of 'Property of a Lady'. This is first and foremost historical, as the Fabergé Coronation egg was made as a gift to the Tsaritsa Empress Alexandra Fyodorovna, by the Tsar Nicholas II, in commemoration of his 1894 coronation. Thus Bond's mission and his life become symbolically equated with a lost imperial political order, implicitly paralleling his own. Moreover, the *property of a lady* further denotes a characteristic that defines her as such. Bond, then, through his relation to the egg, becomes explicitly aligned with a gendered identity. The object possessed by the lady is also that which defines her, and simultaneously identifies Bond, in personal, gendered and political terms. Bond, a lady's man and a British Secret Service agent, is put into motion (in every sense) by the authority of authenticity of the Fabergé egg.

In contrast to the egg, which demonstrates the classic function of art, as per Benjamin, the film itself exemplifies his understanding of the change this function underwent. The thirteenth film in the series, *Octopussy* moves away from the classical counterpoint depicting a distant authentic point of origin (i.e. *Casino Royale*) with a present but flawed reproduction. This film, as with the others in the first twenty of the series, does not attempt to refer back to a single historical original moment; one, it must be remembered, that does not actually exist in 1983. Rather, the film actively inserts itself into a well-established process of narration, one which emphasises reiteration and replication over venerating simulation.

This move from ritual to repetition will be discussed at further length in the following section. By acknowledging and reproducing certain staple elements of the Bond franchise, each of the films effectively resists the very notion of an original. Instead, these features are importantly recontextualised for shifting contemporary audiences in ways that procure contemporary validity for each. A prevalent if somewhat frivolous illustration of this pattern are the seemingly endless and generally heated disputes as to which of the Bond actors constitutes the *real* Bond. The changes each actor brings to the character ensure that the figure's role is updated and thus maintains his hold on popular imagination. Classical authenticity is replaced by a politics of reproduction, a politics which, as Benjamin proscribed in reference to art, has allowed the Bond franchise to exist critically within a contemporary context.

While the very fact of standard and definitive Bond features (technology, women, espionage, and so forth) does anchor the films in a narrative tradition, the ways in which these have been renovated constantly moves it forward and effectively dehistoricises this tradition. In the shift from Ursula Andress's Honey Rider in *Dr No* (1962) to Carey Lowell's portrayal of the female CIA agent in *Licence to Kill* (1989), or the gradual move from the Cold War politics of, for example, *From Russia With Love* (1963), to the anxieties of the Age of Information, as in *Tomorrow Never Dies* (1997), we can see how the Bond series constantly updates its key elements to reflect and comment on existing patterns of society and government. Thus, through subtle shifts, the films defy the notion of an originary moment that ensures the authenticity of each, and instead they successfully reiterate the social functions of the character.

With the 2006 release of the film *Casino Royale* we see an altogether new relationship of an original with the reproduction. Here, the filmmakers have taken an existing pattern of reproduction and through that have recreated the heretofore absent original. The film *Casino Royale* is based on the 1953 novel of the same title, the novel which launched the legendary series. There are important allusions to, as well as differences from, the novel. While the film remains remarkably loyal to the text's plot, its numerous references to external genres, traditions and politics – as with the film noir opening, the use of technology, and casting decisions (notably, extending the remarkable choice of Judi Dench as M), for example – marks the film as succinctly different from its initial beginnings. Thus reinstating the original has important dramatic and political effects. The reverse chronology relocates this originary moment. In place of a celebrated retrospective and inexorably lost *first*, the original is rehistoricised: it is literally manifested in the new film. Instead of structurally moving *away* from origination, maturing in relation to an increasingly distant infancy, the decades-old series creates this metaphoric childhood from the height of its maturity.

Instead of the ritual of forgery-versus-original (as with the Fabergé egg), with *Casino Royale* we have a *new* original. This is done firstly by moving away from existing genres of detection, shifting the focus of authority. The effect of this change is manifold. It is with the well-known licence to kill in mind that we watch Bond assassinate his first two victims in the opening sequence of the film, acts which then award him this very licence. *Casino Royale* seeks to demonstrate the making of the Bond we know. The film noir style of the opening sequence, intercut with flashbacks to a gritty and startlingly violent first kill, offer two alternate versions of Bond, each weighted with possibilities. The black-and-white opening, depicting long shadows, sharp angles and veiled faces directly alludes to the genre of hard-boiled crime and detective films of the 1940s and 1950s. This genre tends to evoke an eroticism as well as a moral ambiguity in the crime scene as the distinction between the detective and the criminal is obscured (an obfuscation manifest not least in the play of light and dark). Moreover, in these films, typically, the very process of detection is explicitly intertwined with analytical introspection through the frequent first-person voice-over narration, so that solving the complexities of a crime becomes inseparable from resolving the complexities of the psyche.

The second possibility open to Bond, offered by the opening sequence, lies in the gritty realism of the flashbacks to his first kill. These are characterised by sharp cinematic cuts to a starkly-lit men's room where we watch Bond violently choking a man to death. The jagged violence, the visually skewed angles across blank and bloodied tiles, cutting into a close-up of the dying man's face or Bond's hands around his neck, point to a stark and uncompromisingly vivid violence. Cumulatively, the intertwined scenes offer two possibilities with which Bond can manage the violence he is destined to enact. A no-holds-barred morality which emphasises the raw physicality of evil in a hands-on kill, virtually unprecedented (certainly in its stark presentation) in the Bond series, is sharply contrasted with the more elegant and introspective second assassination; blinding neon versus cutting shadows. As the film progresses, Bond ultimately rejects both of these as exclusive patterns of action, opting instead for that hybrid blunt-suaveness seasoned fans have learned to expect. If this ethical paradigm has gone unquestioned throughout the series, the new film introduces these genres precisely to establish why Bond must reject the classic versions of enforcing social and ethical codes of behaviour. Killing a man cannot be contained or ethically comprehended either by psychological reasoning or by stark violence.

Casino Royale thus does something very different from the previous films. It simultaneously moves away from the celebration of an original and the fated failure of reproduction of the classical model, and from the mechanically flawless reproduction that rejects and annuls the very notion of an original, as in the Benjaminian model. Here the film carves a new space for authenticity, a space that is not located in a distant and irrecoverable past. Rather, through a self-aware manipulation of these forms, the role of the original becomes reconfigured: the history of the original is embedded in the very physicality of Bond's presence. In the 2006 *Casino Royale* we thus see an example of where art recognises new possibilities of *authenticity*, now stemming from the body.

Ritual

Authenticity is not only revised and recontextualised, re-sited onto the physical body, but the very mechanisms by which it is established and preserved are revisited in *Casino Royale*. As Benjamin describes, for classic art, the original artwork is established and celebrated as authentic through a ritualised process of veneration. The veneration perpetually reaffirms the centrality of the original, ascertains its authenticity, and preserves that mystical element – that inherent ungraspability – which defines the classic work of art as such. The gradual secularisation of societies marked a move away from the abstract, societies now vying for much more tangible and material bases for reality. One of the defining changes wrought by the technology of reproduction then is the dissolution of rituals of veneration and mystical faith as such, offering instead secularised repetition. Abstract rituals become replaced by repeated gestures, and meaning moves from moments of creation to contexts of reception. According to Benjamin, it is this perpetual recontextualisation which gives film its critical dimension; and, more to our purposes here, it casts new light on the function and success of the 007 series.

The series is predicated on the fundamental tale of espionage. It relies on knowledge and obfuscation of knowledge; nothing is what it seems and yet for the films to function, literality is crucial. And so, what we get is a doubling of meaning. The numerous Q quips and Bond one-liners, indeed the tongue-in-cheek humour of the women's names, all depend precisely on this. Honey Rider, Pussy Galore, Plenty O'Toole, Holly Goodhead, Xenia Onatopp are effective because of the immediacy of the double entendre. The ability to receive these names in all their irony reflects a world wherein the means of criticism, of meaning and aesthetic and social truth value, are based on repetition and reproduction.

A more serious and problematic example of the possibilities of repetition is when Sean Connery's Bond must disguise himself as Japanese in *You Only Live Twice* (1967). In a notoriously simplistic grasp of Japanese culture and ethnicity, an appalling wig, some hot wax, a fake wedding and two minutes of screen time, Bond is magically and absurdly transformed. However, Bond is endowed with the ability to simultaneously signify both all that he stands for (British, Alpha-male, hero) and that which he does not, evidenced not least by Tiger Tanaka's (Tetsurô Tanba) delight with the success of the disguise. The empty ethnic gestures are arguably redeemed by the very fabric of Bond's ethnic, ethical and individual make-up: these render him capable of containing two poles of activity, poles which allow him to perform his duty and ultimately avert disaster, and to restore balance in the world. The simultaneity of meaning demands of the audience a double-vision, not simply to enjoy the humour evinced, but to recognise the double role of Bond himself, and the critical conflict that stands at the heart of his existence. Put simply: in order to restore order Bond must eschew order, breaking civil, ethical, social and, as Q reminds us, traffic rules so that these rules may be maintained and our existence continue unshaken.

In his landmark structuralist reading of the literary series, Umberto Eco (2003) identifies a Manichean formula which guides the logic of the novels. Clearly setting out good versus evil, Bond versus villain, Free World versus Soviet Union, and so on, along unwavering moral and aesthetic structures, Eco argues that Fleming was thus able to contend with the vagaries of the Cold War world. The films similarly rely on formulaic structures by which all of them can effectively be stripped down to a single simple plot schematic (one ornamented by similarly formulaic technical devices such as music, opening gambit, weapon, drink, as well as a cast of M, Q, deformed or maniacal villain, and at least one alluring damsel with varying degrees of self-sufficiency and evil intent, but inevitably seduced by Bond's charm and ultimately in need of saving by his skills). The structural reading is problematic, not least in that it does not satisfactorily solve the important similarities between the polar entities. (A most straightforward example of this is established explicitly in *Dr No* where the character of Bond (Sean Connery) is first introduced to cinematic audiences with a close-up shot of his hands, an image later directly echoed in the prosthetic hands of the first arch-villain Doctor No (Joseph Wiseman). Where the hands of the one will always save him – particularly in the early films of the series where Bond is more the hero of action than that of mind or technology – those of the others lead to his downfall.) This qualification notwithstanding, Eco's analysis suggests key insights into how the technique of reproduction enables the audience to move away from empty ritual. As discussed, it is precisely the complexities of the dichotomy and the vital and active engagement which move the audience out of the complacency of blank repetition to the empowering resistance of reproduction.

The formulaic structure of the series methodically teaches its audience what to expect from the films. The repeated pleasure of recognition creates an intimate response to the action on the screen as the viewers actively seek that which they know and are personally rewarded for their attentive investment. Desmond Llewellyn's recurring appearance as Q, for example, himself growing older from film to film while he repeatedly echoes the reprimand, Bond 'just grow up', suggests a continuity not only for the character but for the viewers themselves. However, this is not simple replication. Instead, we have precisely this repeated character which powerfully brings each film up-to-date through the technology he introduces.

Where the villains venerate the technology they have created or harnessed, celebrating its powers, building veritable altars for it (as can be seen in the extravagant sets of evil created in the films which emphasise the near-Divine greatness of the technology – from the volcano rocket-launch in *You Only Live Twice*, to the astonishing ice-palace in *Die Another Day* (2002)) – for Bond, technology remains an (external) object tool which serves to enhance his own powers as 007. Whether this technology is a magnetic tracing device hidden in the shoe, a pen that emits nerve gas at the whistle of 'Oh Britannia', or a car that can be driven by remote control or made invisible at the press of a button, it is, importantly, precisely the technology which plays a critical role in subtly moving the film out of static (and thus increasingly irrelevant) iteration and into a constantly adjusted vision of a nearly-possible futuristic here-and-now. This here-and-nowness actively signals to viewers both their own position vis-à-vis this technological history and reminds us of the very process of viewing whereby the envisioned present is willingly accepted as it carefully extends the boundaries of what we hold true.

It is, moreover, in the technology that the similarities between Bond and Q, and Bond and the villain, can most strikingly be seen; and where the distinction between them is most clearly established. In his 'Hard-wear: the Millennium, Technology, and Brosnan's Bond', Martin Willis (2003) insightfully examines the role of technology and expertise in the Bond series. Where the seriousness of Q's role in the beginning of the series relies on his expertise in the laboratory and in his tutelage of Bond ('I never joke about my work', he declaims repeatedly), by the time of Pierce Brosnan this expertise is transferred to Bond himself. Q's assertions become instead moments of self-acknowledged comic relief. In *GoldenEye* (1995), Q has been showing Bond the latest equipment as Bond warily picks up what looks like a harmless sandwich. Q: 'Don't touch that! That's my lunch'. Q's quasi-serious quip makes it clear that by now his central function is to signal that repeatedly reproduced moment demanded by the Bond series, but herein ends his task. It is Bond himself who now has the capability of harnessing technological innovations and putting them in the service of Queen and country. The villains too are notoriously masters of the forces of nature and technology whether they disguise their lair in the belly of a volcano, have learned the mystery of alchemy or control the source of information capital via satellite. Yet they are inevitably consumed and destroyed by precisely that technology which they sought to control.

Casino Royale offers a next step in this move away from authenticity predicated on ritual. Bond's ability to read his surroundings, and our concomitant ability to read him, has shifted from the double entendre to a penetrative directness. Temporarily paralysed by the *ellipsis*, the encrypted password to disaster in the first half of the film, Bond's powers of analysis enable him to grasp this intentional omission which serves to activate, or avert, the destruction of the new airplane. We do not have here the present two-meanings of the earlier films but, in a pattern reminiscent of the signifying symbol of a Benjaminian classic era, we have a gap in knowledge and the means to bridge this gap. Tellingly, the aesthetic sensibility that serves as the context to the scene leading to Bond's understanding is defined by Gunther von Hagens's *Body Worlds* exhibition, which serves as the backdrop to an earlier scene. This is a genuine art show, first exhibited in Tokyo in 1995, that displays preserved human bodies and organs, revealing inner anatomical structures, where the figures are put on display in a series of both classical and everyday poses. With this backdrop in mind, we can see how the move from veneration to repetition here is transformed into *penetration*: the physical body establishes new sites of knowledge and thus begins to re-enact that mystery eradicated in the age of reproduction.

Aura

To recap, then, it is my argument that – until *Casino Royale* – the Benjaminian ritual whereby an absent original is venerated through traditions of aesthetic or divine rites is displaced by a pattern of repetition that makes the notion of an original redundant, in favour of the immediacy of each new iteration. With the new film, the mystique of veneration is reinstated and what Benjamin terms the *aura* of authenticity is restored. Crucially, as already intimated, this is enacted through bodies, in general and, particularly, through the body of Bond. Indeed, a key component of Daniel Craig's Bond is the utter physicality of his screen presence.

There is a distinct shift here. Certainly film audiences from the beginning of the series were awarded the view of many-a-shirtless Bond, with Connery even donning the infamous short towel suit in *Goldfinger* (1964). However, unlike these glimpses, Craig's physique is made into a spectacle as it is explicitly put on display. Standing in the stead of the memorable Ursula Andress and her more recent counterpart Halle Berry, in *Casino Royale* it is Craig who emerges from the water and stands sparkling in the sun. The narrative seems to pause as Craig stops onscreen to allow us to gaze at him, and it is he who becomes the image of Botticelli's Venus emerging from the water. Thus oddly reflecting love, beauty and fertility, Craig's Bond begins to rewrite the possibilities and the strictures of masculinity through an erotics of body.

Both Andress's Honey Rider and Berry's Jinx are fixed and framed by Bond's gaze. The women are, as far as they know, alone, while the viewer is aligned with the voyeuristic Bond who then immediately proceeds to seduce Honey and Jinx, respectively. In *Casino Royale*, on the other hand, the camera begins by directing the viewer's attention to the object of Bond's gaze: the woman, Solange Dimitrios (Caterina Murino). Only then are we allowed to see Bond; he all-the-while fixes his gaze on her, thus moving the focal point of the scene from his own body to that of the woman who is fixed by the surrounding eyes of the staring children, those of the glistening Bond and of her sinister husband. She, in turn, moves her eyes to Bond, before returning home. So, where in the early films we have a narrative break that focuses on the body of the woman, here we have a system of gazes and objects creating a moving centre of attention.

Rather than capturing its object, this moving gaze identifies Bond both as man and as subject, and concentrates on the erotic mystique of his body. Recalling Judith Butler's (2006) description of gender as based on performative *citation*, Bond's manliness is as such because he both articulates and repeats structures of masculinity and embodies them. Citation is crucial not only in that it affirms normative categories but in that it inescapably attests to the variability of these categories. They are not static nor are they ever whole: as the categories of sex and gender must be endlessly verbalised and embodied it is then an articulated, penetrable (that is, not whole) body that becomes definitive, not an impossible object totality of earlier models.

This dynamic, open system of observation, the penetrative focus, and the penetrated body move the locus of knowledge and meaning and thus shift the social and political function of technologies of scrutiny and surveillance. As Martin Willis powerfully argues, as we trace the technological advancements throughout the 007 series, we can see it gradually becoming more and more intimate and personalised. However, until *Casino Royale*, the technology always remains external to Bond himself. This is precisely what distinguishes him from the villains, in fact, as they are often grotesquely penetrated by the evil technology they have propagated. Bond, on the other hand, resists this penetration and turns instead and inevitably to a more reassuring sexual penetration (reassuring in that it is both more natural, the boundaries of his body have not been violated and – importantly – because it reasserts precisely that heteronormative masculinity which had been implicitly or explicitly threatened by the grotesquely unnatural villain). With *Casino Royale*, however, we have a rather different use of technology.

After spectacularly shooting up an embassy under the watching eyes of worldwide television, Craig's Bond manipulates the technological expertise of Brosnan to gain access into M's home and hard drive. He uses technology in order to transform the public into the private, to blur the boundaries between job and home. This is a boundary that arguably has not been clear-cut throughout the series, as we have seen that the very possibility of 007's success relies on the complete immersion of his own life into the priorities of Queen and country (with the important exception of *Licence to Kill* when he temporarily turns renegade). However, in *Casino Royale*, Bond steals into the very home of M, he gains knowledge of her name and access to her files. This perpetration temporarily destabilises the mystery of her authority (knowledge as power), an authority immediately reclaimed as she both silences him and instructs him.

The hierarchy of power – its manifestation as knowledge, body and technology – is made explicit a few scenes later when M has a tracking device inserted into Bond's arm. This signals a new era when the technology no longer remains external to Bond's body but penetrates him. We must remember that this is a Bond who is still purportedly coming into himself. He still wavers and falters between the 'half-monk half-hitman' binary which M sets out for him. Technology thus becomes a physical object that grounds him – it is through this that he cannot disappear, he is under constant supervision. As in the exposed and aestheticised innards of the *Body Worlds* exhibit, the very matter of his body then becomes the basis and the location of knowledge. The link of technology to knowledge and life is such that even upon being poisoned he is able – through remote control readings of his vital signs transmitted through a needle inserted into his vein – to survive an attack which should have killed him. The technologically penetrated body becomes more than human; and yet, importantly, it is only with the aid of another, the well-timed arrival of Vesper Lynd (Eva Green), that he is able to survive.

This link to an *other* (a gendered *other*) is thematically developed through the exaggerated scenes of romance on the one hand, and through erotics on the other – principally, the erotics of torture. For each, the power of the relation to another is established on the mystery of the unknowable: the erotic preserves a mysticism, a space for lack of knowledge which is based on the body, and romance preserves a mysticism, a space for the unknown that is based on the heart. Thus the body is both knowable and unknowable, material and mysterious. Its ultimate truths, however, become manifest in its response to the *other*.

Erotica is fundamentally based on desire: a recognition of absence and a thirsting impulse to fill this absence. In the notorious torture scene, the spectacle of Bond's body is enhanced by the explicit threat to his masculinity, and his nearly inhuman ability to withstand the pain. Le Chiffre (Mads Mikkelsen) explains the effectiveness of his torture technique as 'it's not only the immediate agony, but the knowledge that if you do not yield soon enough, there will be little left to identify you as a man. The only question remains: Will you yield in time?' Stripped

The spectacle of Bond's (Daniel Craig) tortured body in *Casino Royale* (2006)

naked, what we expect will expose his vulnerability in fact enhances his strength. In an unambiguously erotic scene, Le Chiffre begins by tantalisingly slinging the flaccid rope-whip over Bond's shoulder as he admires his physique and whispers in his ear. It is Le Chiffre, sweating under the strain of whipping Bond's bare genitals, whose calm begins to crumble as he tries unsuccessfully to penetrate Bond's resolve. Presumably having taken complete possession of Bond, reducing him dramatically to a knowable body through the sadism which relies precisely on the narrative of power and submission, Le Chiffre is frustrated as the knowledge evades him.

Tellingly, his own name translates from French as 'the figure', 'the cypher' or 'the number': he is a stand-in variable, a system of encoding that signifies meaning, but meaning that remains absent and undecipherable. Unlike the materiality of Bond that surpasses human limitations, and one that has become penetrable but only within bounds and under control, with Le Chiffre we have an open body, a body whose limits are vague and undetermined: as when blood wells from his eye or when he requires an inhaler to assist his breathing. Significantly, the historical model for Fleming's villain was Aleister Crowley. A figure of late-nineteenth- and early-twentieth-century Britain, Crowley was a notorious and successful occultist, apparently bisexual, racist and misogynist, and infamously dubbed 'The Wickedest Man In the World' (see Levanda 2002: 248–50; Sutin 2002: 388–9).

Fleming's decision to base Bond's first arch-villain on Crowley serves to re-flect on Bond himself. Le Chiffre, both in the novel and in the film, is a slippery character that moves away from precisely that kind of restorative physicality of Bond's body and the empowering mystery it entails. The erotics of the torture scene mirrors in important ways the implications of the heightened romantic elements of *Casino Royale*. The film offers us an unprecedented glimpse into the heart of our hero, complete with extended scenes of romantic clichés. The very use of formulaic structures (as in the lovemaking scene in the clinic, the intimate conversation on the beach, or the Venetian gondola) is telling of the filmmakers' own nod to the possibilities but also the weight of tradition. They are signalling to their viewers, if rather heavy-handedly, that this love is the love of fairy tales and ideals. A love we then begin to suspect cannot be possible.

Thus, crucially, the return to the body is simultaneously complicated as the film also begins to re-establish the possibilities of the body's mystery. This mystery can be seen in terms of Benjamin's *aura*. For Benjamin, the aura is the rem-nant of mystical inspiration which signals and contains both the originary event of creativity and its manifestation in art. In *Casino Royale*, the mystery of the body is preserved through the romantic – and, as seen above, the tortuous – link with an *other*. The reconciliation between the tangible (the body) and the intangible (the erotic and romantic mystery) is caught up in the matrix of gender relations which, Judith Butler tells us is 'prior to the emergence of the human. This process humanises the subject' (2006: 7). In other words, Butler proposes a revised 'return to the notion of matter, not as site or surface', as indeed we have seen Bond's body now has depth as it too is penetrated, 'but as *a process of ma-terialisation that stabilises over time to produce the effect of boundary, fixity, and surface we call matter*' (2006: 9; emphasis in original). Judith Butler's proposal, then, combined with the terms set out by Walter Benjamin, urges a dramatic reformulation of the nature of the body's boundaries. It is not a classical, revered and static, impenetrable whole. Nor does its authority any longer stem from the post-classical formula of repetition. Rather, we have arrived at a new configura-tion of aura and authenticity that is based on the body as language and process, as well as matter.

However, despite the temptation to do so we cannot leave it there, for the film ends with a fierce rejection of this conclusion: Bond is betrayed, his tracking device is extracted, and he ultimately rejects romance, stoically concluding: 'The bitch is dead.' He has been penetrated twice: once by the government, through technology and M, and a second time by Vesper, through love – this latter was so strong as to sway him to abandon his life as 007 and seek an altogether new life. What he perceives as Vesper's betrayal of him teaches him his final lesson, for his bonds with her, unlike the tracking chip in his arm, make him lose control, not gain control – indeed making him dangerously close to losing himself altogether. In returning to the site of origin, the filmmakers have sought not simply to relate the history of Bond's love life but to depict how he has become himself, that same self that retrospectively enacts the Bond exploits of all the preceding films.

Finally relieving the tension subtly building through the film via the music, narrative, character and even film style, the conclusion brings us precisely to the opening of *Dr No*. And yet, coming back to it from the new original moment of *Casino Royale* we arrive newly different. *Casino Royale* carves out a new role for the aura, enacted on and within the spectacular body of Bond, opening possibilities of masculinity and technology, history and art, that are critical for a twenty-first-century reception of Bond, James Bond.

Bibliography

Anon. (n. d.) *MI6*. http://www.mi6.co.uk/sections/articles/bond_21_cast_confirmed. php3 (accessed 9 September 2009).

____ (2006) *Movie/TV News Studio Briefing* (2006) 17 February. http://www.imdb. com/news/sb/2006-02-17 (accessed 10 February 2008).

____ (2007) *Daniel Craig Is Not Bond*, 22 Oct. http://www.danielcraigisnotbond.com (accessed 17 December 2007).

Armes, R. (1978) *A Critical History of British Cinema*. New York: Oxford University Press.

Arp, R. and K. S. Decker (2006) '"That Fatal Kiss": Bond, Ethics, and the Objectification of Women', in J. B. South and J. M. Held (eds) *James Bond and Philosophy: Questions Are Forever*. Chicago: Open Court, 201–13.

Associated Press (2003) 'Mr. Moneymaker Nets $2.5m Poker Prize', *CNN.Com*, 24 May. http://www.cnn.com/2003/US/West/05/24/offbeat.poker.win.ap/ (accessed 10 January 2008).

Banner, D. (2002) 'Why Don't They Just Shoot Him? The Bond Villains and Cold War Heroism', in S. Gillis and P. Gates (eds) *The Devil Himself: Villainy in Detective Fiction and Film*. Westport, CT: Greenwood, 121–34.

Barthes, R. (1982 [1966]) 'Introduction to the Structural Analysis of Narrative', in *Barthes: Selected Writings*. Oxford: Oxford University Press, 251–95.

Bederman, G. (1996) *Manliness and Civilisation: A Cultural History of Gender and Race in the United States, 1880–1917*. Chicago: University of Chicago Press.

Benjamin, W. (1970 [1935]) 'The Work of Art in the Age of Mechanical Reproduction', in *Illuminations*. Trans. Harry Zohn. London: Jonathan Cape, 219–53.

____ (1992 [1939]) 'On Some Motifs of Baudelaire', in *Illuminations*. Trans. Harry Zohn. London: Fontana, 152–96.

_____ (1999a) _The Arcades Project_. Ed. R. Tiedemann. Trans. H. Eiland and K. McLaughlin. Cambridge, MA: Belknap Press.

_____ (1999b) 'The Destructive Character', in M. W. Jennings, H. Eiland and G. Smith (eds) _Walter Benjamin: Selected Writings of Walter Benjamin, Vol. Two 1927–1934_. Trans R. Livingstone _et al._ Cambridge, MA: Belknap Press, 541–2.

_____ (1999c) 'Experience and Poverty', in M. W. Jennings, H. Eiland and G. Smith (eds) _Walter Benjamin: Selected Writings, Vol. Two 1927–1934_. Trans. R. Livingstone _et al._ Cambridge, MA: Belknap Press, 731–5.

_____ (2005) 'In Parallel With My Actual Diary', in M. W. Jennings, H. Eiland and G. Smith (eds) _Walter Benjamin: Selected Writings, Vol. Two, Part Two 1931–1934_. Trans R. Livingstone _et al._ Cambridge, MA: Belknap Press, 413–14.

Bennett, T. and J. Woollacott (1987) _Bond and Beyond: The Political Career of a Popular Hero_. Houndmills: Macmillan Education.

_____ (2003) 'The Moments of Bond', in C. Lindner (ed.) _The James Bond Phenomenon: A Critical Reader_. Manchester: Manchester University Press, 13–34.

Black, J. (2001) _The Politics of James Bond: From Fleming's Novels to the Big Screen_. Westport, CT: Praeger.

Boehm, E. (1999) 'Inside Moves: McClory in Bond Pic Talks', _Variety_, 2 June. http://www.variety.com/article/VR1117502662.html (accessed 14 June 2007).

Boehm, E. and P. Karon (1998) 'McClory Makes Official Claims to Bond Rights', _Variety_, 14 July. http://www.variety.com/article/VR1117478405.html (accessed 14 June 2007).

Bold, C. (2003) '"Under the Very Skirts of Britannica": Re-Reading Women in the James Bond Novels', in C. Lindner (ed.) _The James Bond Phenomenon: A Critical Reader_. Manchester: Manchester University Press, 169–83.

Bogue, R. (1989) _Deleuze and Guattari_. New York: Routledge.

Brabazon, T. (2003) 'Britain's Last Line of Defence: Miss Moneypenny and the Desperations of Filmic Feminism', in C. Lindner (ed.) _The James Bond Phenomenon: A Critical Reader_. Manchester: Manchester University Press, 202–14.

Bukatman, S. (1999) 'The Artificial Infinite', in A. Kuhn (ed.) _Alien Zone II: The Spaces of Science Fiction Cinema_. London: Verso, 249–76.

Butler, J. (1993) _Bodies That Matter: On the Discursive Limits of 'Sex'._ London: Routledge.

_____ (2006) _Gender Trouble: Feminism and the Subversion of Identity_. New York: Routledge.

Butterfield, B. (2003) 'Being-Towards-Death and Taking Pleasure in Beauty: James Bond and Existentialism', in J. B. South and J. M. Held (eds) _James Bond and Philosophy: Questions Are Forever_. Chicago: Open Court, 3–15.

Carpenter, R. (2002) 'Male Failure and Male Fantasy: British Masculine Mythologies of the 1950s, or Jimmy, Jim, and Bond, James Bond', _Minnesota Review_, 55–7, 187–201.

Chancellor, H. (2005) *James Bond: The Man and his World: The Official Companion to Ian Fleming's Creation*. London: John Murray.

Chapman, J. (2003) 'A Licence to Thrill', in C. Lindner (ed.) *The James Bond Phenomenon: A Critical Reader*. Manchester: Manchester University Press, 91–8.

_____ (2007) *Licence to Thrill: A Cultural History of the James Bond Films*. London: I. B. Tauris.

Clark, R. (2005) 'The Phallic', *The Literary Encyclopedia*, 1 Nov. http://www.litencyc. com/php/stopics.php?rec=true&UID=857 (accessed 8 February 2008).

Clausewitz, C. von (1976) *On War*. Ed. and trans. M. Howard and P. Paret. Princeton: Princeton University Press.

Clinton, H. (2004) *Living History*. London: Headline Book Publishing.

Cole, E. (2002–07) 'Luck be a lady … A short history of Baccarat', *SportsCrew*. http:// www.sportscrew.com/casinos/casino_sectionstory.php?sectionid=94 (accessed 12 January 2008).

Comentale, E., S. Watt and S. Willman (eds) (2005) *Ian Fleming & James Bond: The Cultural Politics of 007*. Bloomington: Indiana University Press.

Connell, R. W. (2005) *Masculinities*. Berkeley: University of California Press.

Cork, J. and B. Scivally (2002) *James Bond: The Legacy*. New York: Harry N. Abrams.

Cresswell, T. (2006) *On The Move: Mobility in the Modern Western World*. London: Routledge.

Dargis, M. (2006) '*Casino Royale*: Renewing a Licence to Kill and a Huge Movie Franchise', *New York Times*, 17 November. http://movies.nytimes.com/2006/11/17/ movies/17roya.html (accessed 14 September 2009).

de Goede, M. (2005) *Virtue, Fortune, and Faith: A Genealogy of Finance*. Minneapolis: University of Minnesota Press.

Deleuze, G. (1971) *Masochism: An Interpretation of Coldness and Cruelty*. New York: George Braziller.

_____ (2004) 'From Sacher-Masoch to Masochism', trans. C. Kerslake, *Angelaki: Journal of the Theoretical Humanities*, 9, 125–33.

Deleuze, G. and F. Guattari (1977) *Anti-Oedipus*. Trans. R. Hurley, M. Seem and H. R. Lane. Minneapolis: University of Minnesota Press.

Dempsey, R. (2006) 'What is the Best Bond Movie? Bonding … by the Numbers', in G. Yeffeth (ed.) *James Bond in the 21st Century: Why We Still Need 007*. Dallas: BenBella Books, 49–72.

Denning, M. (1987) *Cover Stories: Narrative and Ideology in the British Spy Thriller*. London and New York: Routledge and Kegan Paul.

_____ (2003) 'Licenced to Look: James Bond and the Heroism of Consumption', in C. Lindner (ed.) *The James Bond Phenomenon: A Critical Reader*. Manchester: Manchester University Press, 56–75.

Doyle, A. C. (1988) 'A Scandal in Bohemia', in *The Adventures of Sherlock Holmes*. Harmondsworth: Penguin, 1–22.

Dyer, R. (1987) *Heavenly Bodies: Film Stars and Society*. London: Macmillan.

Eco, U. (2003) 'Narrative Structures in Fleming', in C. Lindner (ed.) *The James Bond Phenomenon: A Critical Reader*. Manchester: Manchester University Press, 34–55.

Elsaesser, T. (2007) 'Contingency and Agency: Cinema After the Image', in I. Becker, M. Cuntz and A. Kusser (eds) *Unmenge - Wie verteilt sich Handlungsmacht?* Paderborn: Fink, 159–92.

Fleming, I. (1967) *The Spy Who Loved Me*. London: Pan.

____ (2002) *Casino Royale*. London: Penguin.

Friedberg, A. (1993) *Window Shopping: Cinema and the Postmodern*. Berkeley: University of California Press.

Fritz, B. and M. Learmonth (2004) 'Sony Ponies Up for Lion', *Variety*, 13 September. http://www.variety.com/article/VR1117910349.html (accessed 14 June 2007).

Geraghty, C. (2000) *British Cinema in the Fifties: Gender, Genre and the 'New Look'*. London: Routledge.

Giddens, A. (2006) 'Fate, Risk and Security', in J. Cosgrave (ed.) *The Sociology of Risk and Gambling Reader*. New York: Routledge, 29–61.

Grusin, R. (2004) 'Premediation', *Criticism*, 46, 17–39.

Halloran, V. (2005) 'Tropical Bond', in E. Comentale, S. Watt and S. Willman (eds) *Ian Fleming and James Bond: The Cultural Politics of 007*. Bloomington: Indiana University Press, 158–77.

Hayward, S. (2006) *Cinema Studies*. London: Routledge.

Hern, A. and J. McLusky (2005) *Casino Royale*. London: Titan Books.

Jenkins, T. (2005) 'James Bond's "Pussy" and Anglo-American Cold War Sexuality', *Journal of American Culture*, 28, 309–17.

Karon, P. (1998) 'Studio Report Card: MGM', *Variety*, 9 January. http://www.variety.com/article/VR1117434943.html (accessed 14 June 2007).

Katz, D. (2006) 'Bond is Dead', *Esquire*, September. http://www.esquire.com/features/movies/ESQ0906CRAIG_200_1 (accessed 31 January 2008).

Kindleberger, C. P. and R. Aliber (2005) *Manias, Panics, and Crashes: A History of Financial Crises*. New Jersey: John Wiley.

King, G. (2006) 'Spectacle and Narrative in the Contemporary Blockbuster', in L. R. Williams and M. Hammond (eds) *Contemporary American Cinema*. New York: Open University Press/McGraw-Hill, 334–55.

Klein, N. (2007) *The Shock Doctrine: The Rise of Disaster Capitalism*. London: Penguin.

Klosterman, C. (2006) 'Three Things You Already Knew About James Bond', *Esquire*, September, 2006. http://www.esquire.com/features/movies/ESQ0906CRAIG_200_2 (accessed 31 January 2008).

Kristeva, J. (1982) *Powers of Horror: An Essay On Abjection*. New York: Columbia University Press.

Ladenson, E. (2003) 'Pussy Galore', in C. Lindner (ed.) *The James Bond Phenomenon: A Critical Reader*. Manchester: Manchester University Press, 184–201.

Lane, A. and P. Simpson (2002) *The Bond Files: An Unofficial Guide to the World's Greatest Secret Agent*. London: Virgin.

LaSalle, M. (2006) 'Meet the New Bond. Not Quite the Same As the Old Bond', *San Francisco Chronicle*, 17 November, E1.

Lawson, M. (2007) 'Paul Haggis', *Guardian*, 4 December. http://film.guardian.co.uk/interview/interviewpages/0,,2223256,00.html (accessed 7 December 2007).

Leach, J. (2003) '"The World Has Changed": Bond in the 1990s – and Beyond?', in C. Lindner (ed.) *The James Bond Phenomenon: A Critical Reader*. Manchester: Manchester University Press, 248–58.

Levanda, P. (2002) *Unholy Alliance: A History of the Nazi Involvement With the Occult*. London: Continuum.

Lindner, C. (2003a) 'Criminal Vision and the Ideology of Detection in Fleming's 007 Series', in C. Lindner (ed.) *The James Bond Phenomenon: A Critical Reader*. Manchester: Manchester University Press, 76–88.

____ (ed.) (2003b) *The James Bond Phenomenon: A Critical Reader*. Manchester: Manchester University Press.

____ (2005) 'Why Size Matters', in E. Comentale, S. Watt and S. Willman (eds) *Ian Fleming & James Bond: The Cultural Politics of 007*. Bloomington: Indiana University Press, 223–37.

Lycett, A. (1995) *Ian Fleming: The Man Behind James Bond*. Atlanta: Turner.

McCarthy, T. (1997) *Howard Hawks: The Grey Fox of Hollywood*. New York: Grove Press.

McNary, D. (2006) '"Casino" Sets Worldwide Bond Record', *Variety*, 24 December. http://www.variety.com/article/VR1117956300.html?categoryid=13&cs=1 (accessed 14 June 2007).

McInerney, J., N. Foulkes, N. Norman and N. Sullivan (1996) *Dressed to Kill: James Bond, the Suited Hero*. New York: Flammarion.

Miller, T. (2003) 'James Bond's Penis', in C. Lindner (ed.) *The James Bond Phenomenon: A Critical Reader*. Manchester: Manchester University Press, 232–47.

Modleski, T. (1988) *The Women Who Knew Too Much*. New York: Methuen.

Mulvey, L. (1988 [1975]) 'Visual Pleasure and Narrative Cinema', in C. Penley (ed.) *Feminism and Film Theory*. New York: Routledge, 57–68.

Norman, N. (1996) 'The Return of the Suited Hero', in J. McInerney, N. Foulkes, N. Norman and N. Sullivan *Dressed to Kill: James Bond, the Suited Hero*. New York: Flammarion, 93–126.

O'Donnell, P. (2005) 'James Bond, Cyborg-Aristocrat', in E. Comentale, S. Watt and S. Willman (eds) *Ian Fleming and James Bond: The Cultural Politics of 007*. Bloomington: Indiana University Press, 55–70.

Parlett, D. (1991) *A History of Card Games*. Oxford: Oxford University Press.

Pfeiffer, L. (2006) 'Bland ... James Bland', in G. Yeffeth (ed.) *James Bond in the 21st Century: Why We Still Need 007*. Dallas: BenBella Books, 23–32.

Reith, G. (1999) *The Age of Chance: Gambling in Western Culture*. London: Routledge.

Rosenberg, B. and A. H. Stewart (1989) *Ian Fleming*. Boston: Twayne Press.

Said, E. W. (2002) *Culture and Imperialism*. London: Chatto and Windus.

Schwartz, D. G. (2006) *Roll the Bones: The History of Gambling*. New York: Gotham.

Shprintz, J. (2000) 'Court: License to Nil', *Variety*, 31 March. http://www.variety.com/article/VR1117780103.html?categoryid=18&cs=1 (accessed 14 June 2007).

Siegel, Carol (1995) *Male Masochism: Modern Revisions of the Story of Love*. Bloomington: Indiana University Press.

Smith, J. (2003) 'Creating a Bond Market: Selling John Barry's Soundtracks and Theme Songs', in C. Lindner (ed.) *The James Bond Phenomenon: A Critical Reader*. Manchester: Manchester University Press, 118–34.

South, J. B. and J. M. Held (eds) (2006) *James Bond and Philosophy: Questions are Forever*. Chicago: Open Court.

Strange, S. (1986) *Casino Capitalism*. Oxford: Blackwell.

Sutin, L. (2002) *Do What Thou Wilt: A Life of Aleister Crowley*. New York: St. Martin's Press.

Taylor, C. (2007) 'The James Bond Title Sequences', *Salon.com*, 29 July. http://dir.salon.com/story/ent/masterpiece/2002/07/29/bond_titles/index.html (accessed 15 December 2007).

Taylor, M. C. (2004) *Confidence Games: Money and Markets in a World Without Redemption*. Chicago: University of Chicago Press.

Urry, J. (2002) *The Tourist Gaze*. London: Sage.

Verstraete, G. (2001) 'Technological Frontiers and the Production of Mobilities', *New Formations: A Journal of Culture/Theory/Politics*, 43, 26–43.

Wade, R. (2006) 'Choking the South', *New Left Review*, 38, 115–27.

Watt, S. (2005) '007 and 9/11, Specters and Structures of Feeling', in E. Comentale, S. Watt and S. Willman (eds) *Ian Fleming and James Bond: The Cultural Politics of 007*. Bloomington: Indiana University Press, 238–59.

Willis, M. (2003) 'Hard-wear: the Millennium, Technology, and Brosnan's Bond', in C. Lindner (ed.) *The James Bond Phenomenon: A Critical Reader*. Manchester: Manchester University Press, 151–65.

Winder, S. (2006) *The Man Who Saved Britain: A Personal Journey Into the Disturbing World of James Bond*. New York: Farrar, Straus and Giroux.

Wood, G. D. (2001) *The Shock of the Real: Romanticism and Visual Culture, 1760–1860*. London: Palgrave.

Wordsworth, W. (1970) *The Prelude*. London: Oxford University Press.

Yardley, H. O. (1957) *The Education of a Poker Player Including Where and How One Learns to Win*. New York: Simon and Schuster.

Yeffeth, G. (ed.) (2006) *James Bond in the 21st Century: Why We Still Need 007*. Dallas: BenBella Books.

Žižek, S. (2002) 'Welcome to the Desert of the Real', *South Atlantic Quarterly*, 100, 385–9.

Index

Guy Named Joe, A 19

Hagen, Gunther von 167
Haggard, H. Rider 101
Haggis, Paul 29, 68, 107, 112
Hall, Stanley G. 84
Halloran, Vivian 157
Hammer horror 15
Hawks, Howard 13
Hayward, Susan 135
Hegel, Georg Wilhelm Friedrich 77
hegemony/hegemonic 4, 82–4, 86–90, 94, 97–8, 146
Hern, Anthony 22–3
hero 11, 15–16, 20, 22–4, 31, 33–4, 37, 40–3, 49, 67, 73, 95, 98, 100, 104, 113, 149, 157, 160, 165–6, 171
high-stakes 2, 4, 16, 38, 69, 72, 87, 92, 137
Higson, Charlie 14
Hill, George Roy 88
Hitchcock, Alfred 4, 15, 18, 58, 88, 102
Holden, William 25
Horak, Yaroslav 22
House of Games 88
Huston, John 24–5
hyper-masculine/hyper-masculinity 82, 86–7, 89, 111, 122

icon 5, 32, 44, 49, 53, 65, 82, 86, 115, 117, 124–5, 127
ideal/idealised 43, 49, 51, 82–4, 86, 97, 171
identity 2, 4, 6, 12, 32, 40, 58, 87–91, 93–4, 96–8, 120, 124, 156, 162
ideology/ideological 3, 11, 17, 20, 22, 26, 29, 37, 76, 83–4, 100–1, 107, 146–7, 154, 157
immobility 151–3, 157
imperial/imperialism/imperialist 3, 12, 16–18, 83, 101, 152, 162
improvisation/improvisational 5, 131–43
individualist 22, 63
industrialisation 83, 149
insecurity/insecurities 38, 85, 87–9, 91, 95, 109–10
international terrorism 31, 67, 88, 98
Ipcress File, The 100

Jeffries, Jim 86
Johnny English 49
Johnson, Jack 84, 86
Jones, Grace 150–1

Kassowitz, Matthieu 153
Katz, David 119
Kerr, Deborah 25
KGB 46, 150
Kindleberger, Charles 76
King, Geoff 152, 154, 157
Kiss Me Deadly 21
Klein, Naomi 75–7
Klosterman, Chuck 114
Kubrick, Stanley 19

La Haine 153
Ladenson, Elisabeth 103
Lang, Fritz 19
LaSalle, Mick 85
Lawrence, Jim 22
Layer Cake 28, 52
Lazenby, George 13, 44–5, 54–5
Leach, Jim 29, 60–1, 64
Lee, Bernard 28, 37
Licence to Kill 13, 55, 163, 169
Licence to Thrill 6
liminality/liminal 5, 74, 82, 132–3, 137–9, 143
Lindner, Christoph 17–18, 68
Live and Let Die 26–7, 40, 44, 47
Living Daylights, The 13, 35, 37, 40, 44, 55, 106
Llewellyn, Desmond 166
Long Goodbye, The 19
Lorre, Peter 19, 56
Lowell, Carey 163
Lundigan, William 19

machine/machinic 39, 44, 72, 118, 121, 134, 140–3, 149
MacMillan 12
Macrae, Duncan 24
male/maleness 5, 18, 21, 28, 32, 36, 38, 41, 82, 84–5, 87–9, 91, 101–3, 109, 114–27, 144, 165
Malkki, Liisa 146
Maltese Falcon, The 19
Mamet, David 88
manhood 18, 43, 68, 82–3, 87, 92, 98
market/market economy 12, 14, 26, 30, 47, 64, 68–9, 71–4, 76–8, 135, 148, 156, 158
Markham, Robert 14
Mascott, R. D. 14